SEXUAL POWER

SEXUAL POWER

What is it? Who's got it? And how to use it to succeed in love and life!

Sandra Sedgbeer

Thorsons

An Imprint of HarperCollins*Publishers*

Thorsons
An Imprint of Grafton Books
A Division of HarperCollins*Publishers*
77-85 Fulham Palace Road,
Hammersmith, London W6 8JB

Published by Thorsons 1991

1   3   5   7   9   10   8   6   4   2

Sandra Sedgbeer asserts the moral right to
be identified as the author of this work.

British Library Cataloguing in Publication Data

Sedgbeer, Sandra
Sexual power.
1. Sex roles
I. Title
305.3

ISBN 0 7225 2142 1

Typeset by Harper Phototypesetters Ltd,
Northampton, England
Printed in Great Britain by
Mackays of Chatham, Kent

Dedication

For Dave – he knows why

Contents

Acknowledgements

I would like to express my appreciation and deep gratitude to all the psychologists, psychotherapists and other professional people who have spent their entire lives studying, compiling research and data and then making their work available to people such as myself. Without their hard work and their generosity in sharing the results of their efforts, *Sexual Power* could not have been written.

I would particularly like to express my gratitude to Leslie Cameron-Bandler who has, through her written work, provided me with inspiration and knowledge that I have long been seeking.

I would also like to thank David Craddock of Bodywise Limited – for giving me his time, his knowledge, his research material and, of course, his sample sprays of pheromones for my own little experiments; NLP therapist, Stephan Schorr-Kon – for his ear, his assistance and for leading me to Leslie Cameron-Bandler's work, and psychotherapist Robert M. Young, Ph.D., for his helpful comments.

Chapter 1

What is Sexual Power?

I once knew a girl called Sue. There was nothing spectacular about the way Sue looked. She certainly wasn't beautiful. She was a big girl, both in height and in her generously proportioned body which, even her best friends had to acknowledge, erred more on the side of 'sumptuous' than slender.

Intellectually, Sue would hardly have won any prizes. To be fair, she was bright enough when it came to running her own business as a beautician but, beyond that subject, Sue's conversational abilities could, at best, only be described as limited. What her profession did give her, though, was a knowledge of how to make the very best of what nature had endowed her with.

Sue's hair was long, bottle-streaked blonde, and flowed in the Farrah Fawcett style so popular in the early '80s. Her choice in clothes was limited (or maybe even dictated) by her curvaceous body and whenever I joined her for nights out on the town she would invariably be overdressed in skin-tight, strapless, ruched Marilyn Monroe numbers that accentuated every ample curve and bulge of flesh in a way that would have horrified many other women if that abundant flesh had been their own.

On the very first occasion that I accompanied her to a disco at our local Country Club, I arrived at Sue's house (confident that I'd achieved the best I could with what nature had given *me*) in black velvet jeans, red silk shirt and cowboy boots (remember, this *was* 1981!). Sue invited me to chat to her while she showered and dressed and, as most women are apt to do when the opportunity arises, I critically appraised her body (and rapidly dismissed it as not being one I would envy) while she struggled and wiggled her way into one of the said Monroe numbers, trying, without much success, to prevent the strapless top from surrendering the fight to keep her monumental bosom covered.

After several frustrating and abortive attempts to prevent the top of her strapless bra and bodice from parting company, Sue announced, on arrival at the club, her intention of removing the offending object. Curious to see the results of such a manoeuvre, I followed her into the ladies' room and watched with admiration as she pushed the top of her dress down and whipped off the bra, totally oblivious to the gawps and stares of all the other women gathered there.

'Here, Sandie,' Sue said, 'slip this into your handbag for me will you?' Because, of course, Sue never carried anything other than the teeniest purse that was incapable of concealing much more than a lipstick and a little cash – not much, because Sue never seemed to need that particular commodity.

As I gazed in awe at the enormous confection of frothy lace, bones and wires that would have taxed even Howard Hughes' engineering ingenuity, the only response I could think of was:

'Slip it into my handbag? Good grief, Sue, I could use it as a shopping bag!'

And then a strange – and, to me, very remarkable and totally fascinating – thing happened.

As we left the ladies' room and crossed the dance floor to the bar, every single man in the crowded disco acted as one. Heads swivelled, glasses suspended halfway to mouths, eyes popped out and within twenty seconds flat Sue had more offers of drinks, dances and dates than she could possibly ever cope with!

Now, my own looks, while hardly rating much more than an unremarkable 'average' had, nevertheless, stood me in good stead throughout my adult life – enabling me to score at least as many 'hits' as 'misses' – so, until then, I certainly didn't have a problem with confidence. However, on this occasion, as I was passed over, pushed out and virtually trampled in the rush of 'bees around the honeypot', my confidence experienced a massive crisis.

Apart from the very obvious differences, what was it Sue had that I didn't?

I could have better understood her appeal if Sue had fitted into the archetypal, knock 'em dead, brainless bimbo mould, but she wasn't young enough, slim enough or beautiful enough to fit into that particular category – and besides, if that was all it truly took to set these guys champing at the bit, there were plenty of other better qualified candidates in the club that night.

Could it be the spectacular outfit? It might have been, but it wasn't.

For as it soon began to dawn on me (and was subsequently confirmed by the many other situations I observed when she was dressed more conservatively and far less spectacularly), Sue had that incredible, indefinable something that everyone covets and very few of us ordinary mortals appear to possess.

Sue had SEXUAL POWER!

If she'd been twenty pounds heavier, ten inches shorter and with mousey brown hair instead of that blonde mane, *Sue would still have had SEXUAL POWER!*

Every single one of us has met or seen, knows (or knows someone who knows) someone like Sue, or her male equivalent. Such people are the stuff of which fantasies are made.

They could be politicians, movie stars, performers, housewives or building-site workers. They may possess the intellect of an Einstein or a pea. Some are beautiful, many are plain and – in some cases – downright ugly! But these people have something special. They have the ability to attract other people; the ability to fascinate, to inspire intense devotion and to fuel incredible envy. Some have even had the ability to alter the course of history and change the world.

Sexual power defies precise description. Some people call it charisma, though I doubt that it is; after all, Hitler possessed a cold, compelling, charismatic quality, but he certainly never had what I prefer to call sexual power. Though, in truth, as we shall find out as we attempt to probe its source in this book, the quality very often has little to do with sex itself.

The pages of the world's history books are filled with famous people who, by the sheer force – and manipulation – of their own special brand of sexual power, carved out a niche for themselves that ensured their names will be remembered for ever. From powerful leaders such as Julius Caesar and the legendary Cleopatra right through to John Kennedy and even – according to some – Margaret Thatcher herself; from Casanova and Rudolph Valentino to Clark Gable, James Dean, Jean Harlow, Marilyn Monroe, Elvis Presley, Brigitte Bardot and Sophia Loren; throughout time and history, certain people have emerged to take centre stage and inspire fanatical devotion, lust, envy, fascination, emulation and adoration in the masses.

And then there are people like Sue. People who may never know fame outside their own social circles but who nevertheless inspire the same emotions – albeit on a smaller scale – in significant numbers of people with whom they come into contact.

Some of those who are fortunate enough to have sexual power, aren't even fully aware that they have it – though they often become adept at using it. Some use it to get ahead in their careers; most will exploit it to succeed with the opposite sex but none, if asked, could tell you precisely what it is.

It's not charisma. It's not merely having an abundance of charm. It's not necessarily even down to sexual chemistry. Sexual power is a quality that may contain some of these elements – or none of them.

So what is sexual power? And where does it come from?

Few of us can define it in words, but we all instinctively recognize it when we see it. If you have it, the world can undoubtedly become your oyster, as history has proved. And if you haven't, the big question is, how can you get it?

Sexual power can mean different things to different people. For some it's a certain indefinable something in the eyes, for others it's in the shape of a body, the tilt of a chin, the caress of a lingering glance.

But is there some magical ingredient that can be identified in ourselves? And once identified, can it be developed?

The answer is an unqualified *YES*! Because I've learnt that every single one of us *can* increase our own sexual power quotient.

Sexual power is a subject that has fascinated me ever since that fateful night when I first saw for myself the incredible power that those who have it can wield over those who don't.

In the intervening years I've met scores of other men and women – both professionally and socially – who have it too. And on every occasion I've watched, spellbound, as they have consciously or unconsciously used it to get everything they desire. I've read psychology textbooks and learned papers; I've talked to psychologists and psychotherapists; I've quizzed strangers and friends alike and I've conducted my own little experiments, interviews and surveys in an attempt to discover wherein its roots lie.

Why? For the simple reason (and to be totally frank), I'd like some of that for myself – and I bet you would, too!

What I've discovered, and what I now want to share with you, is the knowledge that every single one of us has the potential to have – and use – an enormous amount of sexual power.

I'm not talking about the ability to lure the opposite sex into our beds, though I don't doubt that many will find their abilities in this direction amazingly increased. I'm not talking about having the power to bend others, against their will, to yours.

What I am talking about – and intend to prove to you – is that through my research I have discovered that it *is* possible to increase your powers of attraction with *both* sexes; to alter the way people view you, both professionally and personally; to increase and enhance your own sense of self-confidence and to eradicate permanently any notion that the Sues and the Superstars of this world have something we don't.

First, we'll take a look at *What It Is*. Then we'll discuss *Who's Got It*. And, finally, I'll show you *How to Use It to Succeed in Love and Life*!

When you reach the end of this book, you will be armed with all the information you could ever want – or need – to enable you to use *your own sexual power* to shine every bit as brightly as Sue or any other Superstar you've ever admired or envied.

I can't promise you fame but I can guarantee you recognition. You may not shine in the same firmament as your heroes or heroines – but then you probably won't want to, because you'll be shining in the *real* world, which is your own.

Maslow's hierarchy of needs

Have you ever wondered (as I did with Sue) why some women seem to be able to attract any man they want? How many times have you said to yourself, 'Just what is it he's got that makes him irresistible to women?' Why should a colleague with, perhaps, less experience or inferior abilities get all the recognition or the promotion that you feel is yours?

Why, indeed, should it even matter so much to us?

In order to understand why we aspire to be successful in our careers or to be able to attract other people, we first have to examine why acceptance, recognition, affection, admiration and, ultimately, love are so vital to us.

Many scientists are of the opinion that we enter the world pre-programmed with a compelling need to give and to receive love. Psychologist Abraham Maslow seems to disagree. Instead, he suggests that human beings have a hierarchy of needs which are built on five levels. The first two levels are concerned solely with the fundamentals of ensuring survival (e.g. food, drink, protection from extremes of heat and cold, etc.) and safety; the next level is a social need, involving interreaction and integration with other human beings – the need to feel that we belong and are loved, accepted and valued by people. The fourth level has to do with the self, or ego – self-esteem, ability and our perceptions of our own status in relation to others. Finally, there is the level of self-actualization – a need that very few of us are able to satisfy, although most of us unconsciously strive to achieve it.

Maslow argues that the very fact that this is a hierarchy means we are unable to progress from one level to the next until we are totally satisfied that the prior set of needs has been satisfied. Conversely, having progressed to the fourth level – that of ego – should the slightest threat surface to jeopardize our survival, there isn't one of us who would not abandon all regard for status and self-esteem and revert to being exclusively (and, as one would expect, selfishly) concerned with protecting our survival.

And, of course, Maslow is quite right. After all, would anyone really give a fig about the relatively inconsequential concerns of appearance, self-esteem and status when faced with the prospect of literal starvation or other fundamentally life-threatening events?

However, as most people in the Western world are unlikely to encounter real starvation and are, for the most part, assured of a certain standard and quality of life, the first two levels of Maslow's hierarchy of needs are immediately leapfrogged by us, hence our preoccupation with the level of 'belonging, being loved and accepted'.

Furthermore, this level is where a large number of people are doomed to remain; which is a shame, because if we could get beyond the fourth level of being preoccupied with status, self-esteem and a desire for prestige, we would then reach what Maslow terms the 'self-actualization' level at which, having satisfied all the former (lower order) motives, we begin to experience the higher order motives of wishing to 'know', to 'understand' and, ultimately, to develop and construct a more worthwhile system of values.

Love makes the world go round

Freudian psychoanalyists, such as Melanie Klein, are, however, convinced that 'love' is a human being's driving force, that without it we cannot possibly acquire an identity and, taking it one step further, without love it is even possible for us to become ill or insane.

Love, which is the highest form of acceptance and approval we can ever hope for, is what we all crave. Love enables us to fix our identities in our own minds and helps us accept, and come to terms with, our own shortcomings or failings.

Beneath love, there is liking. If we are liked by our friends, colleagues, bosses and acquaintances, we are reassured because this liking helps us to feel that we belong, that we fit in and are, basically, okay people.

Without love, liking, affection or any form of acceptance or approval, our own self-image can suffer the most enormous, irreparable damage. If our self-esteem becomes damaged then we lose all confidence, becoming dissatisfied with ourselves, our lives, our achievements and the world around us.

Confidence is an interesting thing. We all grow up believing that everyone else has far more confidence than ourselves. It can take years of repeated experience of approval and praise for our confidence to grow, and yet, certain areas of it can be shattered in a second by one single thoughtless word.

Psychologists know that if a child receives love and approval in abundance from the moment it is born, and then goes on to receive praise from his teachers and acceptance by his school-mates, he will perform better in class, mix socially with greater ease, have a wider circle of friends and, very often, a relatively smooth transition through adolescence to adulthood with a positive outlook on life. As Maxwell Maltz, writer of the successful book *Psycho-Cybernetics*, says, 'Confidence is built upon an experience of success.'

Conversely, the child who is constantly criticized and made to feel that he is not 'good enough' will inevitably grow up with a low sense of self-esteem that will often stay with him for life.

How others see us undoubtedly affects how we see ourselves and though we might realize that the two conceptions do not match, we will invariably take others' views to be more accurate or valid than our own. Thus, if we are popular, our positive feelings about ourselves are affirmed but when we are not, all our negative attitudes towards ourselves are reinforced.

People need people

A fundamental fact of life is that *we all need other people*. There are many different kinds of relationships that we form throughout our lives and we are emotionally and materially dependent on some more than others, the degree of this dependency being directly attributable to how much of our lives these people share.

In his book *Relationships*, Dr Tony Lake describes how each person is the central pivot of a set, or system, of relationships which include every other single person that we know. Likewise, everyone else we know is also at the centre of another set of relationships that contain all the people *they* know ... but every single different set is specifically designed in an attempt to meet every particular need of the individual at the centre.[1]

Our material needs are served by our employers and colleagues because it is with their co-operation that we are able to support our standards of living. Our emotional needs are served by our families, loved ones, close friends and social circles, and *through them* we are able to support our standard of life. From time to time the two may overlap, such as when an employer or colleague becomes a close friend, thus adding to our network of emotional support, or when a parent or close friend provides us with financial assistance when we might be experiencing difficulties.

If our needs in any of these areas are not being met we can suffer acute feelings of loneliness, isolation, depression, or actual illness (whether physical or mental) and our quality of life diminishes to the point where we begin to undervalue our self-worth. Forming relationships then becomes even more difficult because we lose the confidence and the ability to make the effort.

Heroes or villains?

We all envy people who seem to have more – and better – relationships than we do, and we particularly admire and envy those people who seem to have it all, though it's often difficult to work out *why* they have it all.

If we personally *know* the people we admire and envy we may be able to attribute their popularity or success to certain factors, such as charisma, charm – or sexual power. If we don't know them, as in the case of politicians, film stars, great writers or other unattainable 'heroes', then we are apt to endow them with all the qualities we most admire and (probably) most lack in ourselves.

We imagine that our heroes or heroines are somehow 'special'; that they lead charmed lives, are successful, powerful, adored or admired by the whole world, and never, ever make the mistakes that we do.

The more inaccessible our idols are, the more inhuman qualities we endow them with. We might admire a prominent politician, but we know they're human because everything they say or do is captured on TV or repeated in the press and every mistake or error of judgement is made known to us. The greatest – and most admired – idols, therefore, have to be inaccessible because the less we *know* about them, the more freedom our imaginations have to *invent* what we *want* to believe they are.

Rudolph Valentino and Clark Gable are probably two of the most fantasized-about men this century has known. Virtually every woman in the '20s swooned over Valentino's portrayals of the archetypal 'strong, silent lover', and since its release in the '40s, hardly any woman has failed to fantasize about the devilish charms of *Gone With the Wind*'s Rhett Butler in the shape of Clark Gable.

While it's debatable whether many men deliberately tried to cultivate Valentino's charm, there is no doubt that millions, throughout the world, strived to emulate Gable's macho screen approach.

None of Gable's female fans would have wanted to hear the gossip about his reputed halitosis and, likewise, none of his male fans would have even dared to imagine that Gable could have had his fair share of rejections. It's inconceivable to us that our heroes or heart-throbs could possibly suffer from shyness, acne, boils on the backside or the odd bout of premature ejaculation or orgasmic dysfunction!

No, our heroes are immortals! They certainly don't have neuroses and hang-ups like us; they always say the right thing, wear the right clothes, maintain the perfect weight, and never, ever do anything that might suggest 'ordinariness'. Good heavens, they don't even have to live with embarrassing, bodily functions!

That's why we adore them; why we strive so hard to emulate them and why we aspire to be like them. We copy their clothes, adopt their posture and speech, style our hair the same as theirs, mirror their expressions and spend our lives and hard-earned money in a futile attempt to attract some of their magic to ourselves. Because they have sexual power – and we don't. Right?

Wrong! We *all* have sexual power – it's just that we either aren't aware of its existence within us or the extent to which it can be developed. We know it exists in our heroes (that's why they've become our heroes), and we may even be aware of it in certain people that we personally know or meet. But how many of us have the confidence to believe that we might have it, too? Particularly when we're not even sure what it is.

That's where our journey begins.

What is sexual power?

One of the first people I posed this question to was a personal friend who also happens to be Media Director in a major UK advertising agency.

In planning clients' campaigns, John, who's now 46, often comes into contact with some of the most famous names in modelling and show business, so it seemed logical to me that a man who had not only met, but seen and talked with a fair number of the very people most likely to possess this quality, might have some insight to offer:

> 'I've met pin-up models who have what I call the "Cor! factor", the ones the media describe as "sexually appealing" because they've got great bodies, or enormous boobs, and I've also met fashion and photographic models who have perfect bone structure and are quite technically beautiful to look at. I've met actors and actresses who have enormous fan clubs and get mobbed wherever they go. But none of them, to my mind, possessed what I think you're referring to.
>
> 'The person who might have sexual power for me might not necessarily have it for anyone else at all, so it must have a lot to do with one's own perceptions. On one level it doesn't have anything at all to do with sex appeal; on another, if someone had sexual power for me, then I reckon that would also *give* them sex appeal too.
>
> 'It's a very difficult question to answer, and it's one that I don't think I'm capable of answering. However, what I *can* tell you is this: to have someone interested in *me*, to have someone valuing what *I* have to offer, or what *I* have to say; or to have someone that I personally admire or like or want to spend time with, giving *me* all of *their* attention – well, now, *that* has to be one of the greatest ego-boosts of all time.
>
> 'Now, that's what *I*, personally, find incredibly attractive in people of both sexes and, possibly, even sexually powerful in the opposite sex.'

One man's opinion, perhaps, but it was an opinion that many men I subsequently spoke to seemed to echo. But why should having our ego boosted cause us to feel so responsive towards the person who does the boosting?

The reason we respond so positively to people who show interest in *us* is because, in doing so, they are displaying clear evidence that they *accept* us and, more than that, that we are *worthy* of their acceptance.

In seeking acceptance we are not, as so many of us feel, alone. Strange as it may seem, even those whom many of us admire and perceive as 'having it all' crave acceptance, too.

Take Tom Cruise, for example, who, despite being the heart-throb of millions of young (and not-so-young) women and the role-model of just as many young men on both sides of the Atlantic, has freely admitted that he went through a period when he was growing up of, 'wanting to be accepted, wanting love and attention from people; but I never fitted in'. Marriage to the actress, Mimi Rogers, gave Tom Cruise the insight and courage to state publicly: 'All the success in the world means nothing if I'm alone', although, sadly, that marriage was not to last.

Tom Cruise, a brilliant and very handsome young actor who is admired, envied, emulated and beloved by millions, may appear to have everything any young man could ever want, but the fact is that statements like those quoted above prove that, at heart, Tom's just like the rest of us: he's only human and he, too, suffers at times from a personal lack of confidence and self-doubt.

So, once we recognize and accept that fame, success or money do not automatically protect a person from romantic failure, rejection, lack of personal confidence and heartache, it becomes easier to accept that beneath the outer image and under the skin all human beings need acceptance, approval, affection and love, too.

It also becomes blindingly obvious that all our preconceptions of sexual power could be totally adrift inasmuch as sexual power might not necessarily have *anything* to do with looks, professional success, image, appearance, glamour or sex appeal at all.

In the following chapters we will take a detailed look at each one of these elements in order to discover how much your image and appearance have to do with attracting the opposite sex. Similarly, we will investigate charisma, glamour, sex appeal and power to see where they fit in. And what about chemistry? Now, there's a topic shrouded in mystery! Does it really exist, as some say, or is it simply a myth?

With *Sexual Power* (the book) you can discover:

● How to tune in to what other people *really* want and need.

● How to tap into your *own* hidden reserves of power and use the tools you *already* possess.

- How to have as much success with the opposite sex as *you* desire as well as how to reach the ultimate heights in your career.

- How to identify your strengths, how to minimize your weak-nesses and how to maximize your *potential*.

- How to tap into your *own* hidden reserves of power as well as how to recognize and *use* the tools and powerpoints you *already* possess.

And once you have understood the secret of sexual power, you'll never need to envy anyone else or question another's success again.

Chapter 2

Image and Appearance

As we have already seen, sexual power means different things to different people and while certain key words kept cropping up when I asked people to attempt to define it, no one, as yet, seems to have hit on the ultimate definition.

So let's go back and examine what those guys responded to so strongly when they first caught sight of Sue: her image, appearance and, perhaps, her aura of availability.

Well, just how much do image and appearance affect the way we see other people and, more importantly, the way they see – and relate to – us?

The successful businessman, who wields his mighty power over legions of employees and makes multi-million dollar decisions with as much ease as if he was ordering up his lunch, may appear to us to represent the pinnacle of success. We note his air of authority, his undoubted business acumen and his supreme confidence in himself and are in awe of him.

But we never give a moment's thought to the fact that, despite all of his achievements, that person may go home at night to an empty house without a loving partner to support him in his endeavours or even a close friend – apart from his business associates – to whom he can confide his deeply personal feelings of self-doubt and, yes, even loneliness. In observing him in the environment in which he shines, we buy the image of everything that he represents and it never occurs to us to question it, or look beneath it at the man himself.

Buying images is a conditioned process that we are all subjected to throughout our formative years and, without even realizing it, we become deeply (and subconsciously) influenced by our conditioning.

First impressions matter

When we first meet people, we might fool ourselves into believing that we are making sound, logical judgements about their character, status and personality based on what we perceive, but we are wrong.

Because we live in fairly tightly-packed, urban communities we naturally come into contact with literally thousands of people. The human brain just isn't capable of individualizing every person we meet; therefore, we have had to find a way of using mental shorthand to identify people.

Psychologists say that there are a number of principal techniques that we use to form impressions of strangers and the first of these is *stereotyping*. Stereotyping is something we all do when we meet people in order to fit them mentally into pigeonholes or categories that we can easily recognize and, therefore, speedily deal with.

The second method is the use of *implicit personality theories*. What happens here is that we make assumptions about people based on certain personality traits that we have been conditioned to believe go together. For example, we all have a tendency to make generalizations; believing that certain national characteristics go hand in hand, such as French girls are sexy, Latins are hot-tempered, the British are uptight, the Scots tend to be mean, and so on.

So, when we meet people for the first time who appear to fit into one of these categories, we adopt certain attitudes towards them and make assumptions based on what we have been conditioned to believe. And it doesn't only occur with nationalities, because we all tend to develop implicit personality theories about certain professions (example: all accountants are dull, penny-pinching people), ethnic groups (example: all Asians excel in business) and even about members of the same family (example: every member of the Olivier, Barrymore or Redgrave families will automatically have a talent for acting).

Implicit personality theories are, in a sense, a form of labelling. Unfortunately, because labels are inseparable from the assumptions associated with them, life for the person who has been labelled can prove trying, as we learn from the popular lament of many sons and daughters of famous parents who have had to fight for recognition in their own right!

The other difficulty that arises from our tendency to indulge in this practice is that if enough people share the assumptions that go with the label, it becomes extremely difficult for the labelled person to behave in any way other than the prescribed fashion.

This was borne out by an American survey[2] which found that male medical students mostly share a common assumption that nurses are promiscuous, and although with some the assumption partly stemmed from first-hand experience, with others there seemed to be no logical basis for the supposition other than the idea that because nurses have an intimate acquaintance with the male body (both intellectually and in practice through contact with patients) they must, therefore, have a different attitude to sex.

Consequently, the female nurses surveyed reported that it proved very difficult *not* to behave in a more promiscuous manner with male members of their profession because when they refused the men's advances, they often didn't get asked out again!

In fact, this is one survey result that I can attest to from personal experience – and it seems to be fairly prevalent amongst a large number of men regardless of their profession. A close friend of mine is a nurse. When we used to go out together, we both became very aware of (and exasperated at) the sudden spark of interest and excitement in men's eyes whenever she mentioned her profession which definitely was not echoed by the men we met on the occasions when she would tell a lie about her job. Now that she's working in the States, she has reported to me that the same attitude does persist on both sides of the Atlantic.

The third method consists of our own *personal personality theories*; those that we have adopted through our *own* previous personal experiences. For instance, if we've had a bad experience with, say, someone who had red hair, then it's possible we could develop an intense subconscious dislike or wariness of all red-haired people. Likewise, if we have had warm or rewarding experiences with blondes or brunettes, we are more likely to be attracted to those who fit into that category.

Some years ago I went out with a guy who was around 6ft 3 ins (1.9m) tall. I was attracted to him because of his sense of humour and dry wit and I know that he had been attracted to me for the same reason. The fact that we made an odd couple was not lost on either of us (I am under five feet (1.5m) tall!) and, despite the obvious reasons for our mutual attraction, I often pondered on the basis of his initial attraction towards me, prior to the discovery that we had wit and a sense of humour in common.

When I finally posed the question, 'Why?' he merely shrugged and said, 'because I prefer petite women'. His answer didn't satisfy me so I had to delve deeper because, even then, I was fascinated to know more about what attracted people to each other.

Eventually, after much probing, he admitted that he had originally only ever gone out with tall, well-built girls but, following one rather traumatic personal experience, he had suddenly found himself totally turned off that particular type and from that moment on had developed a penchant for petite women.

What had happened with Steve, I surmised, was that bigger women had become indelibly linked in his mind with that one (and, to him, horrific) experience that he never wished to repeat. He must then have subconsciously reasoned that by changing his women he could, somehow, change his experiences. A false assumption, to be sure, but evidence that our own personal personality theories do affect and shape our tastes.

The fourth method consists of the way we immediately interpret a *single incident or piece of behaviour*; for example, if a person seems relaxed and smiling when they meet us, we generally assume that he or she is an open, honest, friendly person. If, for whatever reason, they appear harassed, inattentive or are scowling, we immediately conclude that they are bad-tempered and unfriendly.

The final method of mental shorthand we use is our own *assumptions of similarity* and these are often based on a tiny piece of information, fact or feature that the stranger happens to share with us. So, if that person went to the same school or college as someone we personally know and like, we assume that as they have one thing in common with our friend they naturally must share other common characteristics.

First impressions matter; logically we all know they shouldn't but they do. And once we've tagged someone and forced them into our own mental pigeonhole, it's not easy for us to alter our original opinion.

Blondes have more fun?

Altering our image can change the way people relate to us. Just ask any woman who has ever dyed her hair blonde!

Natural blondes are relatively rare: perhaps that's why being blonde attracts so much attention. Blondes are assumed to be dumb, sexy and yet, at the same time, strangely innocent. This paradox was epitomized by Marilyn Monroe who, despite all the sordid stories that surrounded her, always managed to retain a powerful image of innocence, naivety and purity.

One hair-colouring manufacturer conducted a survey to find out whether becoming blonde had any significant effect on their clients' feelings and lives. Eighty per cent said that while it made them feel 'lighter and more cheerful', other people's reactions to them changed. Some said they suddenly got more wolf-whistles from men in the street which they enjoyed, but many couldn't cope with the way in which they were suddenly taken less seriously.

The research also found that strong stereotype ideas about blondes were still prevalent and, despite the fact that most of the interviewees were fairly adamant that they *know* that being blonde didn't automatically mean a woman was dizzy or sexy, when asked to describe their ideas of what a blonde woman's bedroom looked like (as opposed to a redhead's or a brunette's), the images created were far more fluffy, childlike and self-indulgent than the rooms they imagined belong to women with other hair colouring.

Rock singer Kim Wilde, who used to be blonde before reverting to her natural colour, revealed in a recent interview that it was a strain living up to the bubbly blonde image that had been forced upon her, saying, 'The image was not something I was hung up on. But people must have felt disappointed as I'm not the bubbly type. People have very definite ideas of blonde personalities.'

One journalist (a natural blonde herself) tested the way people responded to hair colour by donning a brown curly wig for a day. The resulting newspaper feature reported that not only did men take less notice of her, but the majority of people who knew her as a blonde felt she looked a lot older, a lot harder and a lot less sexy, with the only positive comment coming from a colleague who said, 'I think men do notice blondes more but they would take you more seriously in a business situation as a brunette!'

And just look at the assumptions we all tend to make about redheads! Red-haired women are supposed to be volatile, hot-tempered and passionate, whilst the men, poor things, are generally viewed as everybody's favourite office boy (like Superman's friend, Jimmy Olsen) who never quite manages to get the girl! Though why this should be no one has yet satisfactorily explained.

Our preference for hair colouring can evolve over a number of years and for a variety of reasons. Some men avow they find blondes insipid and 'cold' while brunettes make them go weak at the knees! Some women find blonde men attractive while others go wild over men with ebony-black hair. All women loathe grey hair on themselves but adore a touch of it (or even a whole head of it) on men! Perhaps that has something to do with the fact that grey-haired men are considered to be 'distinguished' whereas grey-haired women are just considered 'old'.

When we examine the whole subject of hair colour objectively it's quite clear how ridiculous and ill-founded our assumptions and generalizations are. The problem is, it still doesn't necessarily help us become more objective when faced with our own personal preferences.

What's in a name?

The same situation applies with names. Some names have positive connotations, others have negative associations. Most of our assumptions about names are based on *personal personality theories*, but we're also conditioned by the media to associate certain admired or disliked characteristics with particular names.

When the popularity of the TV programmes *Dallas* and *Dynasty* was at its height, thousands of babies throughout the world were being christened Alexis, Blake, Krystle and Miles, presumably in their parents' vain belief that simply by conferring the name on their offspring their child would stand out.

The media, celebrities, royalty and even the fashion world create trends in popular names and often it's possible to estimate a person's age just by knowing their name. Few females in the UK have been christened Sandra in the last thirty-odd years and when I chose my daughter Gemma's name in the mid-'70s I'd only ever heard it twice (both women were actresses I admired – and, yes, I'll confess I wanted a 'different' name – so what does that say about me!). Now, when I hear the name being yelled at a grubby, snotty-nosed little kid, I still get a shock because what I'm seeing definitely does *not* live up to my expectations of the possessor of such a name (despite the fact that my own Gemma obviously went through that stage, too!).

Short names that convey an image of a wealthy, dominant, unusual or strong man are favoured for heroes of popular romantic fiction while longer, softer names are usually given to the heroines. Mills & Boon, the publishers of an enormously successful list of books in this genre, have conducted a great deal of market research into the public's perceptions of the characteristics associated with names and they are well aware that a hero by the name of Kevin, Timothy or Trevor wouldn't kindle *any* fires in the hearts of their enormous female readership, while Raoul, Jean, Paulo or even Blake or Charles would set more than a few hearts beating. But the more uncommon the name the better, because we have fewer negative assumptions about names that are unfamiliar.

Surnames can be important, too. After all, Krystle paired with Gusset, Bucket or Bloggs somehow doesn't quite conjure up the same imagery as when tagged with the surname of Carrington! Perhaps this is because there is a certain rhythm attached to names that trip and roll lightly off the tongue while those that don't can sound discordant and jarring.

Certainly, it's interesting to note that some of our greatest female stars and sex symbols used alliteration a great deal: Brigitte Bardot, Cyd Charisse, Marilyn Monroe, Diana Dors, and so on. And, according to one famous pop promoter of that era, many of Britain's male singers in the '50s and '60s were deliberately given a soft christian name (to suggest vulnerability) with a hard-sounding surname (or vice versa), denoting strength and a touch of untameable wildness. Cliff Richard, Marty Wilde, Billy Fury and Tommy Steele are four successful British examples that spring immediately to mind; though it has to be said that this may well have been a uniquely British phenomenon, as it is not so easy to think of American examples.

Sheep in wolves' clothing?

The clothes we choose to wear influence how other people respond to us. Women learn quite young how to use clothes as camouflage, as weapons, or to give off subtle sexual signals, while men tend to use them more to make statements about their status.

Psychologists say that girls who want to project bubbly personalities and a fun-loving image choose bright, primary colours while darker shades are adopted by people who wish to portray a more serious, intelligent and efficient personality.

Women on their way up the executive ladder recognize the value of power dressing in sharply tailored suits and are well aware that with such outfits they can convey the message that here's a person who means business: 'Ignore the fact that I'm a woman,' they're saying, 'just treat me like a professional and judge me on my abilities alone.'

Research has shown that people who wear the kind of clothes we associate with high status really do have more influence than those who wear clothes associated with low status. If you were stopped in the street by a person conducting a market research survey who was scruffily dressed in dirty jeans and a sweatshirt you'd be far less inclined to allow them to question you than if they were wearing a smart business suit.

Dr Peter Marsh, a lecturer in Psychology at Oxford Polytechnic, edited a fascinating book entitled *Eye to Eye – Your Relationships and How They Work*, in which he states that our choice of clothes may well betray our personalities. For example, men who are only interested in the practical aspects of clothes tend to be more cautious types who have low social motivation and a sense of dissatisfaction, whereas women with this attitude are more likely to be intelligent and confident despite the fact that they're reluctant to reveal too much about themselves.

On the other hand, men who are more interested in fashion are usually warmer, more helpful and very often a little bit impulsive, whereas the highly fashion-oriented woman is far more likely to have lower academic qualifications, generally holds more conservative views and is likely to be more religious.

However, Marsh also says that clothing is hardly an ideal personality test, as what we wear is largely dictated by our daily routine and also by the styles of our families, friends and colleagues. Despite that, we all know that our immediate impressions of someone dressed in, say, hippy gear would be quite different from those we form of someone who wears hand-made Gucci loafers and a designer-label suit.

Psychologist Glenn Wilson firmly believes that women, far more than men, use clothes as a social statement, to give themselves confidence, and to boost their morale. He also thinks that a woman's outfits are as important to her as her make-up. When it comes to men, however, he believes that, as they can't emphasize their sexuality with their, clothes business suits become their uniform. 'Men,' Glenn Wilson concludes, 'don't feel they have anything to prove because they already believe they are good enough.'

Of course, we all know of one situation in which a man *will* use clothes to express – *and emphasize* – his sexuality, and that's when it's essential to his image to promote that sexuality, such as with many of today's entertainment performers.

If Tom Jones appeared on stage in front of a house-full of screaming women wearing a kaftan or even a smart but baggy business suit the reaction wouldn't be at all what he – or his fans – were counting on! If he wore a suit at all it's far more likely that it would be of a shiny material with a tight-fitting waistcoat, trousers that moulded closely to the contours of his hips and thighs, with a shirt slashed widely open and minus his jacket. But more often than not, Tom's just as likely to don a snug, black T-shirt and skin-tight black jeans or leather trousers.

He's not silly, he knows his image has always been founded on his ability to convey an intensely macho, raw 'I-don't-give-a-damn' aura of sexuality that whips women into a frenzy and has them reaching for their knickers and offering them up as they would their bodies – if only they had the chance!

Legions of women love him for it; others just want to throw up.

Elvis Presley had the same effect on women, though fewer found him as offensive as some do Tom Jones. Perhaps that's because with Presley there always seemed to be an air of naivety and spontaneity, as though what he did and how he moved were somehow strangely beyond his control, whereas with Tom Jones one can't help feeling that his clothes and movements are a deliberate calculation.

One interview with the female proprietor of a high-profile PR company said that she definitely believed that dressing attractively made a difference to the way that people react, and openly admitted encouraging her senior executives to dress well but provocatively when meeting potential new clients.

Wearing clothes that make you feel attractive, sexy and more confident can't be wrong if you personally enjoy it. If, on the other hand, you feel – or are made to feel – uncomfortable in what you're wearing, then you shouldn't do it.

We all use clothes to make statements about our personalities, characters and status, but women have an added advantage in that they can also use clothes to send out subtle signals of their intentions – and enhance those signals with the use of cosmetics.

Gilding the lily

Both men and women have used make-up since the beginning of time. The Red Indians used war-paint when they went into battle to look more frightening and aggressive. Ancient Britons used a blue, herbal dye called woad on their faces and hair to achieve the same effect.

Cleopatra used make-up to enhance her beauty, and bella-donna – a highly poisonous plant substance – was widely used by women throughout the courts of medieval Europe to make their eyes look larger, brighter and more limpid in the belief that the eyes, more than anything else, signal our emotions, particularly in relation to love and attraction.

Lips

The British writer and anthropologist Desmond Morris has proposed the theory that when women use lipstick they're not doing so merely in order to increase their facial beauty but that such use also has far more primitive roots. [3]

According to Morris, female apes signal their sexual receptiveness by the swelling and reddening of their genital labia which, because apes move on all fours, are clearly visible to the male from behind. However, in human females, who stand upright (and today wear clothes which hide such obvious signals), sexual availability and readiness are far less easy to discern. And that, Morris suggests, is where lipstick comes in because it helps transform the lips into a 'mimic' of the genital labia by emphasizing their fleshiness and colour.

Sexologists have recorded that during sexual excitement both a female's genitals *and her lips* become more swollen and engorged with blood and, hence, much redder.

An investigation conducted in America many years ago into college men's attitudes to girls who wore lipstick certainly seems to bear out Morris's hypothesis. [4] A number of male students were introduced to six girls to whom they had to speak for an average of ten minutes. Three of the girls wore lipstick and three did not, though this was not pointed out to the men.

When asked to describe the girls afterwards, all the men decided that the three who wore lipstick were probably more frivolous, unconscientious about their work and more overtly interested in the opposite sex than the three who didn't. None of the men recalled noticing the lipstick and, equally, not one of them could come up with a rational explanation for his assessment which only serves to demonstrate the superficiality of the judgements we make when we first meet people.

Hair

The colouring, texture and quality of hair and skin are also important to our image and appearance. Of course, there isn't a great deal we can do to correct or alter our skin type and colour apart from using make-up to conceal blemishes, but there's a lot we can do with our hair to express our personalities, and sometimes even our allegiance to a particular segment of society. In the '60s long hair on men was an external declaration of affiliation to the hippy movement, while those young men who still wore their hair very short were perceived to be conservative, middle-of-the-road types.

Without doubt a woman's hair has always been seen as both adornment and a visual symbol of sensuality and even today many cultures and religions still have fairly strict rules about women displaying unbound hair.

Novitiates cut their hair when they become nuns – it's part of the symbolism of becoming a bride of Christ – in the same way that up till a century or so ago orthodox Jewish women were required to cut their hair (or to conceal it beneath a wig) when they became wives. In the Victorian era it was considered proper for young girls to wear their hair loose and flowing until they were deemed 'women', whereupon it suddenly became improper to wear their hair down anywhere other than in the privacy of the boudoir! For some reason hair and a female's innocence (and, therefore, virginity) have been inextricably linked for centuries.

Monks shave their heads, as do devotees of the Hare Krishna movement, as a symbol of self-abnegation and humility, while traitors, prisoners and other wrongdoers have often been forcibly shorn in order to mark and humiliate them in the eyes of the world.

Eyes

Although there is no doubt that hair is considered to be an enormously sexually attractive feature, it too – like our clothes – can be manipulated and altered to project the image we wish to convey to the world. The one thing we cannot do much about (apart from enhance and draw attention to with make-up) is the most prominent feature of all – our eyes; apart from their vital function of enabling us to see, they're also crucial in communication – and what they communicate is very difficult to fake. Some people possess incredibly expressive eyes that unconsciously transmit virtually every thought and emotion they have, while others appear to be cold and unreadable.

Because our eyes are such powerful tools for communication

a whole set of unwritten, though widely acknowledged, rules of etiquette apply with regard to the way we look at people and for how long. Whilst we might expend a great deal of time, effort and money on shaping, honing and refining our image, appearance, behaviour, speech and movements, if we ignore the simple basic techniques of communicating with our eyes to ensure that what our eyes reveal confirms what our appearance says, all our efforts will have been in vain.

Image projection

When we select certain outfits we are projecting an image. When people take that image at face value it is much easier for us to assimilate the value they place on us, too. Thus, when we look good we feel good, which in turn enables us to act good. And other people's reactions to the image we project actively encourage us to act out the identity role we wish to promote.

For whatever reason, Sue had long ago elected to project a certain image of herself and her choice of the figure-hugging Monroe number reinforced that image by not only suggesting that she had a supreme confidence in herself and her body, but also through its sexual signals which said, 'Look at me, guys, I'm all woman and as such I can fulfil every fantasy you've ever had; I'm feminine and vulnerable but I'm sensuous and voracious too.'

Hence, the image Sue projected was both a come-on and a challenge to every man in the club that night and it was designed to make her irresistible.

Clearly, image and appearance in the form of facial features, body shape, posture, voice, hairstyle, colour and dress all have a profound influence on the judgements we make about others and although most of us would maintain that physical attractiveness does not play a major part in how we react to the people we meet, numerous psychologists have proved us wrong.

Image projection is a vital component of sexual power. For example, when a person who wishes to create an aura of success and/or confidence becomes adept at projecting an image that conveys and convinces others that he or she really is successful and confident, they can actually create the very conditions that will more or less guarantee success.

Image projection is necessary if you wish to convince people that what they are seeing really exists. It's something that actors, actresses, film stars, rock stars and politicians use every day in their professional lives in order to stay in control of the way that we relate to them.

Of course, it's not only public personalities who use it, because we all use it too. The difference is that because we're not consciously aware of what we're projecting and how it might be interpreted, it's very much a hit-or-miss affair.

Adele was just 24 when she was hired as a personal assistant to the managing director of a leisure complex. Having only ever been a junior secretary before, Adele's title sounded so impressive to her that she would drop it into every conversation so that everyone would know what an important job she had.

Then things started to go wrong. For although she enjoyed her work, Adele sensed a certain amount of resentment in her colleagues' attitude towards her and a reluctance to accord the respect she felt her position was due. What then added to her sense of dissatisfaction was a gradual awareness that her boss rarely involved her in any of the really important or confidential tasks, with the result that she slowly began to feel unappreciated and undermined. Finally, she confided her distress to a recruitment consultant friend:

'I expected her to be sympathetic and agree with me, so it came as quite an unwelcome shock when she just said, "Well, if you don't like the situation, change it." I didn't understand what she meant.

'"Look," she explained, "if you want to alter the way people relate to you, you've got to first take a hard look at yourself, at the image you're projecting, which, from what I can see, is probably the source of your problem." She could see that annoyed me so she started explaining what she'd learnt in her profession.

'"If you want to be taken seriously, you've got to give people the impression that you take yourself seriously. I mean, just look at the way you dress for work – and then compare that to the way your boss dresses. He's in charge of the leisure complex, so he dresses in a way that lets everyone know he's got authority and that he's capable of dealing with it. You're good at your job, but that's not enough to impress people because you don't project the image that everyone expects."

'It took me a while to grasp her meaning, before it became clear. I had thought being efficient, capable and willing was enough. But it wasn't. Because she made me see that I was being paid to be those things, so, naturally, they were taken for granted. What I hadn't understood was that I was failing to meet any of the mental perceptions that people associated with the kind of person who was what I wanted to be. I didn't dress smartly, in fact, I dressed lousily. I didn't act comfortable in my role with other employees, which she said was why I made such a big thing about my status all the time.

'She then outlined what I could do to change things. "Start with new clothes, and a new, more relaxed attitude. You'll be amazed at the difference they'll make."

'And she was absolutely right. I spent lots of money on smart new outfits for work. I felt a bit self-conscious the first few days, but my boss complimented me so much that I soon began to enjoy wearing them. I stopped shoving my title down people's throats and gradually they began to treat me differently. They were friendly, but at the same time more respectful.

'As my confidence began to grow, things got a lot better. Instead of moaning about all the things my boss didn't give me to do, I started to use my initiative to make his life easier, and before too long, he started involving me in the more confidential aspects of the job. Now he's sending me on a management training course and talking about me hiring an assistant of my own! Which proves that my friend was right.'

Appearance counts

As Adele's friend pointed out to her, changing other people's attitudes to you begins with changing your own attitude to yourself. And whether we like it or not, clothes are an important and integral part of projecting the right image because they make such strong statements about who and what we are supposed to be.

A punk can't be a punk without the clothes and hairstyle that the rest of us associate with that particular group. Similarly, a bank manager wouldn't inspire much confidence in his customers if he didn't conform to the mental image they equate with the type of person they would entrust their money to.

This is what's known as labelling, and though we all know that initial impressions based on what people wear are largely superficial, few of us are capable of refraining from making judgements in this manner because it's too convenient for us to assume that people choose to dress in a way that reflects their personalities.

Appearance is a powerful method of communication. It's the

first thing people see, and the first they'll subconsciously use to stereotype us.

Appearance is also one of the easiest (though not necessarily the cheapest) ways to change your image. A new outfit that makes you feel like a million dollars will help you *look* like a million dollars, but a new outfit, no matter how expensive or flattering it might be, can also make you feel like a crumpled dollar bill if you simply 'don't feel right' in it.

Research has shown that people who yearn to be accepted by one particular group not only have to conform fairly closely to the accepted appearance code of their target group, they also have to be extremely careful not to under- or over-dress too far. Certain types of clothing immediately classify you as belonging to a particular class or profession. Barristers' wigs are one example; top hat and morning dress at Ascot another. In a courtroom, or at a society event, such items of clothing are acceptable and the person wearing them feels relaxed and comfortable. By changing the situation, though, it's possible to alter a person's frame of mind so dramatically that he will find the situation so difficult to cope with that he'd rather opt out of it all together. For example, just imagine how conspicuous a British barrister in full 'get up' would feel *outside* the courtroom.

If you feel a change of image could help you transform and improve your life, the first thing you must do is realistically identify an image you wish to project and work out what you can expect (or hope) to achieve by projecting yourself that way. If it's something as simple as a new job, respect, a softer image and so on, all you need to adapt is your attitude and then, if it's required, your appearance.

But if what you have in mind is a radical change, then more extensive research into what rules and restrictions might possibly apply would be required in order to maximize your chances of success. For example, a successful conman would achieve more success in passing himself off as a minor member of royalty if the person he was trying to convince had no connection with royalty than he would amongst those who have close acquaintance with it. Obviously, this is because there are so many subtle regulations that apply in royal circles that only those who were familiar with them would be aware of, whereas with anyone else he would merely have to conform to a stereotypical image to fulfil their expectations.

Status symbols

Symbols – particularly those associated with status – are another useful aid to projection. But, like the old school tie, or a badge that declares membership of a specific club, we know they're not worn because of what they are, but rather for what they represent – or, to be more accurate, what they can misrepresent! Because, of course, nowadays status symbols are so cheap and easy to come by, they're no longer a reliable indicator of a person's true status!

Where once accessories could be relied upon to provide an accurate visual indicator of status, with the advent of technology, it's now much harder to differentiate between fakes and the real thing; a man wearing a Rolex, for example, might have paid several thousand pounds for the privilege of sporting such a status symbol, but it's also feasible he could be wearing a fake. Few people know the difference, and probably fewer would even care.

The fact is, we meet so many new people all the time that we're far more likely simply to accept them at face value than to waste time questioning the image they project. Fundamentally, you see, people are honest, and they expect others to be honest, too, which is why conmen often find it so easy to hoodwink people. Another reason is that most of us are too polite to show disbelief openly.

Given this general attitude, therefore, if you were trying to change your image and present yourself as someone other than the real you, it's highly unlikely that anyone else would denounce you as a fraud as they're far more likely to make an instant assumption that either you're out of their league, in which case they'll forget you within minutes, or they'll accept you without question.

If they accept you but have no motive or reason to further the acquaintance, they'll then dismiss you without further ado, in which case you won't have a problem. But if they do have a motive, such as an assumption that interreacting with you can provide them with some reward, you'll still have no problem because by then they'll have advanced to the next stage – which means they'll be more preoccupied with worrying about the impression they're making on you!

Chapter 3

Eye of the Beholder

Sue's image and appearance were two of the aspects that contributed to her sexual power. But what about her looks? Sue was superficially attractive enough, but she could hardly be called beautiful.

So what role do our looks play in our lives and how much importance should we place on beauty?

Beauty, they say, is in the eye of the beholder. None of us would argue with that because I'm sure all of us have at some point in our lives become aware that the more we discover about someone, the more beautiful they can appear in our eyes. By this I mean, of course, that with familiarity we cease to be so consciously aware of physical imperfections in a person and often, when we really grow to like, admire or love someone, their inner qualities can even make them seem more beautiful to us, which explains why someone that we personally find attractive does not necessarily have the same effect on our friends.

However, certain types of people are universally judged to be beautiful because their facial features conform to a commonly held ideal. But who is the arbiter who decrees what that ideal should be?

The answer is no one single person but society itself, whose tastes are generally shaped and formed by fashion, films and the media: their tentacles of influence are so strong and pervasive that they affect us from the moment we are born. Thus, from the cradle on, our physical attributes play a vital role in the way other people react to us and also in the way that we perceive them; and the older we grow, the more deeply-rooted that influence becomes, reinforcing our subconscious ideologies in relation to how people look.

Evidence exists to support the theory that good-looking defendants in court cases are less likely to be convicted of crimes or, if found guilty, they are generally given lighter sentences[5] – unless, of course, the crime committed was one in which the defendant actually used his or her good looks in order to conduct the crime, as with confidence tricksters.[6]

There have occasionally been reports in some English newspapers supporting the theory that ethnic minority groups (who are rarely considered 'beautiful' by the Western world), such as black people and Asians, often receive harsher sentences and are convicted of more crimes in British courts than their white peers.

In job interviews, when educational qualifications and experience appear to be roughly equal, it has been noted that the most attractive applicant usually succeeds in getting the job. And once in the job, the attractive employee's work is generally evaluated more favourably than his or her less attractive colleagues.

While this unconscious process of a good-looking person being perceived more favourably than one who is not good-looking is prevalent with both sexes, women tend to be judged more on appearance by men – and other women – than are men themselves.

Attractiveness in the opposite sex is, it seems, more important to men than it is to women and, here again, research shows that a man with a physically attractive woman on his arm is generally perceived as being more intelligent, successful, wealthy and of higher status than a man accompanied by an unattractive woman: the reason for this presumably being that if a man ranks lower on the attractiveness scale than his partner, people assume that he must have other, more significant qualities if he can succeed in attracting a very beautiful lady.

Furthermore, there appears to be some kind of trade-off between women who are beautiful and men who are not. Usually, this takes the form of an unattractive man offering security, power, position and/or money in exchange for the woman's looks.

If this sounds unfair and depressing, you shouldn't worry unduly because research also proves that, though we envy and admire attractive people a great deal, when it comes to choosing our own partners the rest of us – who don't have a tradable commodity in terms of prestige, power, money or a remarkable appearance – invariably go for someone whose looks are more or less on a par with our own on the attractiveness scale. Other experiments have shown that a person's perceived place on the attractiveness scale may often depend on their attitude, style of clothing, presentation, cleanliness and other personal characteristics. After all, being perceived to be attractive does not rely solely on appearance. What is interesting though, is that while to others we might well rate a '5 out of 10' on the attractiveness scale, if asked to rate ourselves, most of us would tend to downgrade that rating.

Nowadays, because we have access to 'instant' information in the form of TV, films, newspapers and magazines, film-makers and advertisers have enormous – and almost total – power to shape our tastes. Consequently, cultural values, ideals and stereotypes amongst people of different nations tend to be more or less commonly-held, particularly in the Western world. This means, in effect, that beauty is bestowed by culture or society and it has now gone far beyond merely constituting an aesthetically pleasing feature.

Marketing men have long been aware that the presentation of their products alongside a good-looking model increases sales. And while we all like to think that we're far too intelligent actually to believe that buying the same washing machine or expensive make-up that we saw being advertised by a beautiful model will result in us becoming as beautiful as her, still the implicit associations take root on a subliminal level. Why else would car manufacturers *still* promote their latest models being driven by impossibly beautiful people with unrealistically successful, perfect lives?

Reflected glory

Good looks are used in advertisements and films to confer prestige and power on those who possess them, and this is a value that has been absorbed into our system. Good looks also confer – by reflection – power and prestige on those people with whom the good looking choose to associate.

Some years ago I was at a party given by a girlfriend when I spied, across the room, the most classically beautiful man I had ever seen. He was tall, blonde and muscular yet lean, and his face would not have been out of place on a portrait of a Herculean hero from ancient Greece.

'*Who is that*?' I whispered. 'That,' my hostess replied, 'is Geoff . . .

and he's my brother,' in a tone that revealed that she'd been playing this scene for as long as she could remember.

Of course I'd heard from other friends about the famous Geoff who had been away working on the cruise liners as a croupier, but none of the glowing reports I'd received could have prepared me for this veritable Adonis. Naturally, I didn't think I possibly stood a chance, but there was nothing to prevent me from admiring him from afar.

As things turned out, I obviously *did* stand a chance, because before too long Geoff asked me to dance and we spent the rest of the evening together. When the party was over he walked me home and asked to see me again. I was overjoyed and couldn't wait for our date.

Imagine! The gorgeous Geoff actually fancied little old me! Wouldn't the girls be green when they saw us out together!

Well, I had my date with Geoff, and several more. And it didn't take me long to discover that he was far from being a competent conversationalist. Truth to tell, he was so lacking in personality, in wit, in humour, in intellect – and almost everything else – that I very quickly became disenchanted and disillusioned.

Despite his deficiences, I saw Geoff a few more times, simply because, I confess, I was hooked on all the envious looks I got from other women who considered him such a catch. I mean, if everyone thought *he* was so wonderful, wouldn't they think I also must be something special to have landed him?

The novelty and the euphoria of massaging my ego by basking in Geoff's reflected (and totally without foundation) glory lasted but a short while before terminal boredom set in and I had to acknowledge to myself that if anyone had undergone a charisma bypass operation, it had to be he! The fact was, while any fool could see that Geoff had the face and body of a Greek god, he also had the mind of a Greek statue!

Now, I'm not suggesting that all handsome men – or beautiful women, for that matter – are 'Geoffs'; that would be grossly unfair and untrue. But my experience does illustrate the extent to which we can become blinded, both by what we see and what we feel we might gain from being the companion of a 'beautiful' person!

Beauty is as beauty does?

Because our society places so much value on looking good and tends to promote those who possess good looks far more than those who don't, the subliminal messages we all receive through the media, advertising and films shape the way we think and the manner in which we relate to 'beautiful' people. And owing to the manner in which our brains have developed mental shorthand to categorize unfamiliar people instantly, we then complete this conditioning process by ascribing 'beautiful' character traits to good-looking people.

Similarly, it would seem that certain faces, while not necessarily being perfectly proportioned, are nonetheless admired because we believe they have physical properties which we associate with the mental properties our culture admires.

Thus, we generally define some men as being handsome because, for example, they have a firm jaw (which we subconsciously equate with determination), a strong nose (dependability) or clear eyes (honesty). With women we will describe them as beautiful because they might have large, wide-apart eyes (which we associate with innocence), smooth skin (sensitivity), a full mouth and soft lips (sensuality) and a small chin, nose and ears (vulnerability).[7]

Sophia Loren is the perfect example of this. Many so-called experts agree that Loren isn't technically beautiful and does not possess the kind of regular facial features that constitute today's definition of true beauty. And yet, if you analyse a photograph you will note that what she does possess are the majority of those features described in the paragraph above.

Loren's eyes *are* large and well spaced (and she emphasizes this fact with make-up); her mouth *is* full, soft and sensuous and her skin *does* appear to be smooth and soft. Perhaps the only feature that might not fit into the category of definitions by which we judge true beauty is her nose. But then it doesn't have to, because by combining the features we do admire with our implicit assumptions about smouldering, fiery Latins, hey presto, we have someone that we all *accept* as sensuous, passionate, earthy and, therefore, infinitely beautiful and desirable.

If we add to that certain other qualities, such as drive (indicated by her rise from the slums of Naples to riches), beauty (implicitly conveyed by her marriage to a powerful film producer who, presumably, could have had his pick of beautiful women), and supreme confidence (her apparent refusal to change her style or looks to keep abreast of current trends), what we end up with is a very powerful and seductive confirmation of every one of our own implicit assumptions: that here is a woman who embodies every single component of glamour and sexual power.

In fact, a number of experiments conducted in the past have

shown that the most attractive and appealing face in a woman is a face in which the features most closely resemble a baby's![8] And what do babies have? They have large eyes, tiny button noses, shell-like dainty ears, pouting mouths and soft silky skin! Unfortunately, it would appear that in Western societies large faces are not considered attractive in a woman and small faces are not admired in men.

Oddly enough, some experiments conducted in the recent past have indicated that one of the most important requirements for good looks, far from being outstanding features, is in fact a marked *lack* of distinguishing features. This conclusion was, apparently, also reached in the late nineteenth century by Francis Galton, who was a cousin of Charles Darwin. Intrigued by the nature of ordinariness in facial features, Galton devised a method of creating composite pictures in which the features of different faces were superimposed over one another. The results, which were then rated by others, were that the composite pictures were 'singularly beautiful'. Galton went on to repeat his experiments and was so struck by the improvement, that he ultimately reached the conclusion that as it seemed to be the various irregularities in individuals' photos which were removed by superimposing other photos, it had to be a *regularity of features* that provided the yardstick for the visually most beautiful face.

Recently *The Economist* magazine reported that Drs Judith Langlois and Lori Roggman, both psychologists at the University of Texas at Austin, repeated this experiment with the use of computers which found that the greater the number of photos used in the composite, the more attractive the image became.[9] And although no one has come up with a definitive answer as to why this should be so, some child psychologists believe that it's because the most typical-looking people and objects are more easily recognized and related to, which suggests that familiarity, far from breeding contempt, as we're so often led to believe, might actually lead to a greater attraction.

In fact, familiarity has been the subject of a number of experiments associated with looks, several of which have strongly suggested that the more often we see a face, the more attractive it becomes. Ugliness is often only startling at first sight; once it becomes familiar we cease to notice it. The comedian Marty Feldman, who died several years ago, was generally acknowledged to be ugly. And yet, everyone who was exposed to him either in the flesh or on screen via his TV appearances and films, grew to love – if not his face itself – certainly something about the man, which in itself softened the impact of his 'ugliness'.

If you're not exactly blessed when it comes to facial features, it might be comforting to know that being beautiful can – believe it or not – have its drawbacks too.

Yes, I know it seems unlikely, and I can almost hear the myriad protests of the 'I wouldn't mind some of these drawbacks myself' variety, but think on this a little: because we tend to make the majority of our relationships with people who are more or less on the same attractiveness level as ourselves, those at the top of the 'good looking' scale often don't get half as many approaches as those of us further down.

Skin deep

Many people who were born beautiful receive so much un-justified attention, approval, admiration and envy that it's hardly surprising if some of them learn very young that their looks can represent an automatic passport to success, and, consequently, they never have to bother about developing their personalities or characters until much later in life.

Marie Helvin, the ex-model turned TV presenter and author who was married to photographer David Bailey, once said, 'It's a kind of game, in a way, to be able to use your looks or whatever, to get a man to do exactly as you want, and I like doing it. Maybe that's bad, but I do it.' And while I wouldn't suggest that she didn't bother to develop her personality, it does illustrate the point that many beautiful women are encouraged to believe that looks can get them anything they want.

The same can apply with beautiful men, too, though they seem to be more often regarded with deep suspicion by women who automatically label them as either narcissists or inveterate rogues, whereas the derogatory epithets applied to beautiful women (particularly if they are in a beauty-oriented profession such as films, TV or modelling) usually relate to the size (and capacity) of their brains.

And yet, beauty is still the one characteristic that we admire and envy above all others, particularly when we are young. As we grow older and mature we become more able to rationalize our feelings about it and realize that of all the things we could have, beauty is possibly the least important, simply because it's only skin deep. And besides, sooner or later it is bound to fade away.

Raquel Welch's beautiful face and body made her famous. But as she grew older she openly admitted her frustration with the

image that had been created around her, complaining, 'I feel
people are trying to bury me in a sea of C-cups,' which verifies all
the research which has shown that, more than anything else,
beauty is the biggest blinding factor to a person's true worth.

Meryl Streep's looks, on the other hand, do *not* conform to our
ideal of beauty, although she can often seem beautiful. About her
looks she has said, 'I was always the ugly kid with the big mouth,'
and, 'There seems to be a crime in this country in not being
beautiful. I don't think I have the kind of face that makes an
audience love you. I think I look like Dame Edith Sitwell. And yet,
I know I'm good looking enough to play any of the women I play
– individuals in the world!'

Meryl Streep is one Hollywood star who has never suffered with
a credibility handicap and maybe that's directly attributable to her
monumental acting talent. But it's also worth considering that it
might also be partly due to the fact that because she's *not*
classically beautiful she's been harder to stereotype; and not
being blinded by her looks we've been more clearly able to
recognize and acknowledge her genius.

Two people who have first-hand experience of the problems
associated with being good looking (and therefore not being
credited with a brain) are both British television presenters.

Nino Firetto is probably best known in the UK for presenting the
children's TV programme *Splash*. Nino is 28, half-Italian and
possesses the kind of dark, tanned, almost cute good looks that
people (and in particular the media) tend not to take too seriously.
In fact, Nino is a charming, intelligent and very talented presenter
who first established a name for himself in radio – a medium in
which how you look is immaterial and how you relate to your
listeners paramount.

As it happens, Nino has never rated his looks particularly highly
and certainly didn't believe they were of any significance when
it came to doing his job which involved conducting probing, in-
depth interviews with politicians and other prominent personalities and chairing serious discussion programmes on topics of
community interest and importance.

In his radio days, Nino felt that he was just a professional doing
a job that he found stimulating and enjoyable, and the awards he
won in recognition of his work were all the more gratifying
because they were an acknowledgement of the respect his peers
had for his professional abilities. It was only when Nino made the
transition to TV and became a 'face' as well as a 'voice' that he
found a strange paradox took place:

'I presented a programme on Satellite TV which was broadcast throughout Europe and, for some reason, I began to receive a lot of fan mail from Scandinavia. At the time I presumed that it was because I was very dark and, therefore, something of a novelty to Scandinavians.

'Then, when *Splash* were seeking a third presenter for their new series my agent sent my photo and biography to the producers. I was turned down. He then tried twice more and, eventually, when the producers had still not found a suitable presenter they agreed to interview me.

At the interview I acquitted myself well, was asked to test and, subsequently, was offered the job solely on my merits as a presenter.

'I later discovered that the reason I had been rejected on the two previous occasions was because the producers felt I looked "too pretty and lightweight" to be capable of handling the programme!'

Splash was a programme aimed at a pre-teen audience and, naturally, the content was primarily youth-oriented which meant that the presenters were often required to cover lightweight subjects. In one programme Nino was made to introduce a segment (apparently naked) from a bathtub. The studio was immediately deluged with fan mail and overnight Nino was labelled a 'teenage heart-throb hunk' by the tabloids and the youth press:

'Immediately people's perceptions of me began to change. Nino the serious presenter had suddenly become "Nino, the brainless-but-handsome tele hunk". I had fame, sure, but I'd lost credibility in the process – and all because of the way I looked!

'Scurrilous and untrue stories were being invented and printed and there was nothing I could do about it. One night I was sitting in Stringfellows [a London club] having a quiet drink and a bite to eat when Peter Stringfellow said to me: "Don't forget, every woman here is looking at you with the knowledge that you're worth £5,000 to them to sleep with!"

'That knowledge alone creates a tremendous amount of personal – and sexual – pressure. You have to learn to be very careful and extremely discriminating about your relationships; to ask yourself *why* a girl is flirting with you, and even if you don't feel she's the kiss-and-tell type, you're still aware that she has certain, totally unrealistic expectations of you; particularly between the sheets!'

When 'Nino the tele rat' stories were published in the tabloids, Nino found that his career began to suffer. For a while after *Splash* finished its run, the phone stopped ringing and producers suddenly seemed reluctant to offer Nino any work:

> 'Fortunately, for the last year or so I've kept a low profile, avoided the press and now, hopefully, I'm beginning to be judged on my merits as a professional again by those people who matter.'

Unlike Nino, Gloria Thomas's reputation hasn't suffered at the hands of the press. Nevertheless, while her looks gained her entrée to a glamorous life as an actress, TV presenter and former model, the way in which other people related to her beauty – and made negative assumptions about her intellect because of it – had a profound effect upon the way in which Gloria grew to perceive herself.

Despite being an ex-Bond girl and the only model to appear in *seven* of the most prominent and sought-after calendars of 1985, Gloria not only couldn't accept that she was beautiful, she also suffered from an incredibly low self-esteem which stemmed from being a target in her childhood for cruel jibes and taunts about her colour and origins:

> 'When you're half-Jamaican and half-Irish you're bound to get called a lot of unpleasant names by kids at school. As a result, I've always felt that I have to prove that I'm not just as good as everyone else – I'm possibly even better.
>
> 'I certainly never believed I could be beautiful; in fact, I've always had very low self-esteem. So, when a friend suggested I become a model, I only followed her advice because it seemed like a laugh at the time.
>
> 'The first few agencies I approached rejected me on the grounds that I was "too exotic and too beautiful". Of course I didn't believe them, I thought they were merely making excuses to get rid of me! However, the more people tell me no, the more determined and ambitious I become, so I joined a promotions company and gradually, through that, and my own efforts, I began to get modelling work.
>
> 'Then, at the launch party of the Lamb's Navy Rum Calendar, I was spotted by a photographer who hired me for the following year's calendar.
>
> 'When I got the part as a Bond girl in *View To A Kill*, I thought

it would be a stepping stone to much bigger and better things. I had a wonderful time travelling all over the world promoting the film but, in the end, it proved only one thing to me; and that was that being a Bond girl was *entirely* about beauty and nothing else – although, even then, I still could not accept that I really might be beautiful.

'After several successful years modelling, always striving to be bubbly and to make people laugh, it became apparent that I had to make more of an effort to get people to see that I had a lot more to offer than a pretty face.

'When I gave birth to my son – and almost lost him – I started to realize that looks just really weren't important and my whole value system underwent a fundamental change. I then found myself consciously playing down my looks. I've never been particularly clothes-conscious but I went through a period of wearing the same old pair of jeans and sweatshirt around the house, never bothering to put make-up on and just scragging my hair back in any old style, often without even bothering to brush it first!

'I was amazed by the difference in the way that people began to relate to me – they started seeing me as a *person* and no longer as merely a *face*. A lot of people didn't understand what was happening to me, but I was going through a crisis period in which I knew that there were more important things than me looking absolutely glamorous, but at the same time I didn't have *enough* belief in myself or my abilities to do something more significant.

'It was only when I became a Christian and then had vocational guidance which involved assessment tests that I began to discover more about myself. When my tutor told me that while I was never going to be a brain surgeon I was an extremely bright young woman, I just burst into tears because at last someone had acknowledged that there *was* more to me than an attractive exterior.

'Now, at almost 30, I have come to terms with myself. I can accept at last that I *am* beautiful, but it's not really important. I want to continue with my career as a TV presenter, to make the most of my abilities and my brain and to do something worth while.'

Nino's and Gloria's experiences aren't uncommon for people in the public eye and their comments only serve to underscore what we've already discovered about the way we *all* tend to first perceive and then stereotype good-looking people.

Perhaps it has something to do with the fact that we live in an era in which the media tantalizes and feeds our aspirations (often to unrealistic levels) and, by so doing, automatically create a negative culture of envy aimed at the few who do manage to achieve or become what we all secretly aspire to ourselves.

Certainly, these two stories aptly illustrate the fact that being blessed with good looks can, indeed, have its down-side too. A small crumb of comfort, perhaps, but there is also a great deal of evidence to suggest that while we all admire and envy beauty from afar, we often perceive it as being so far removed from ourselves that unless we feel we have something to trade, we don't risk rejection by approaching it (because that would be far too acute a reminder of our own physical limitations or inferiority) and, therefore, many beautiful people are often not approached by serious contenders in the romance stakes at all! And even when they are, their own experiences can lead them to suffer agonies of doubt about whether their attraction for others is purely superficial – which in itself can create enormous hurdles to the founding of a sound relationship.

Perhaps it's time we all recognized that possessing beauty – and having that beauty widely acknowledged – is not necessarily an automatic guarantee of self-confidence. Actress and model Twiggy, for example, has the kind of winsome good looks that most people admire and she's often been labelled 'beautiful', but that doesn't make it any easier for her to accept the things about herself that she doesn't like, if a recent comment about how much she hated her legs is anything to go by!

There are three comforting things that can be said about beauty. Firstly, it doesn't last, so those who have it eventually end up just like the rest of us and, presumably, when it does go they must agonize more over its loss than ever we did over its absence. Secondly, there are a number of things that can make all of us appear more beautiful, such as glowing good health, happiness, shining eyes and, of course, love! And thirdly, if we had it we probably wouldn't believe it anyway. Daryl Hannah doesn't believe she's beautiful. Nor do Glenn Close, Cher, Jane Fonda, Jessica Lange, Lauren Hutton, Sonia Braga, etc., etc. Need I go on?

Finally, we mustn't forget that beauty has nothing whatsoever to do with sex appeal or sexual power and everything to do with how *you* feel about yourself, for as the actress Angela Lansbury once said: 'If you visualize yourself as beautiful it will affect how others see you. That's important for us women of "a certain age" who've been brainwashed that men get more attractive with age and we lose sex appeal. That's ridiculous!'

Chapter 4

All Shapes and Sizes

Sue's body was certainly not the most perfect – or even the slimmest – female form I'd ever seen but, even so, one can't deny that it was part of her overall package; a package that had certainly seemed to work magic on an above-average number of men!

Is it possible that one could be less than physically perfect and still have sexual power? Let's take a look at the evidence – who knows, we could be pleasantly surprised!

Body shape

Body shape, weight and height are significant factors in the way that people perceive and relate to us. And in a society that is currently obsessed with appearance and the pursuit of physical perfection, those who can't conform to our current cultural 'ideal' have a very lean time of it (no pun intended!).

In the light of that statement it might seem a little pointless to pose the question: Can the fat and the short have sexual power? when it would appear that all the evidence suggests otherwise.

But does it? Has any research truly delved deep enough into the subject of weight, height and attraction to come up with any conclusive proof? After all, we're all aware of our society's aversion to fat, but all around us fat people are falling in love, forming relationships and living happy, fulfilled lives.

Similarly, despite the automatic preclusions they create when women say they only like tall men, many still end up marrying a man who's shorter than themselves!

So how much do the issues of weight and height really affect our lives?

According to the NACNE Report on nutrition and weight, published in the UK in 1983, 32 per cent of all British women were deemed to be 'overweight'. And yet, the British Royal College of Physicians' report on Obesity published in the same year, following exhaustive surveys, declared that a staggering 65 per cent of women in the UK were on a diet at any one time. That's 33 per cent more than *need* to!

Why is fat – or anything other than extreme leanness – such an anathema to us all? And why do we place so much emphasis on how our bodies look?

Physical perfection in a human being is exceedingly rare. Moreover, what constitutes the male or female 'ideal' to one generation, and in one particular society, is often passé to the next. Fashions change with looks just as much as they do with clothes, though, it has to be said, they appear to affect women far more than men.

Throughout the ages little has changed with regard to what women find attractive about a man's body. For a time in the '50s, there was a vogue for beefcake men, but that (thank heavens) was short-lived. That men's shapes have not been much affected by the vagaries of fashion perhaps owes much to the fact that women are not generally influenced by such inconsequentials when they are seeking a potential mate.

Sadly, the same has not applied to men.

In the early seventeenth century voluptuous Rubenesque bodies were very much the vogue. In the Victorian era – a time when women had little real influence – we were admired more for our 'womanly and motherly' qualities than our minds (indeed a woman who displayed any evidence of having a mind was an abhorrence to most men!). This was reflected in the popularity of styles that covered the female form from neck to ankle while emphasizing 'motherly' bosoms, 'feminine' hand-span waists, child-bearing hips and projecting derrières which were exaggerated to often alarming proportions.

In the '20s, women found liberation from their crippling corsets and the total autonomy of men both politically and socially as well as through fashion, which allowed them to revel in the androgynous look with short, shingled hair, an absence of waists and breasts, and slim, boyish hips.

The '40s and '50s saw a revival of the womanly shape once

more and those women who achieved celebrity by virtue of their 'Screen Goddess' looks, such as Rita Hayworth, Jane Russell and Marilyn Monroe, were considered by most men to be 'ideal' and the majority of yesterday's women judged themselves accordingly.

Fashions change every decade or so and with them our perceptions of what is considered beautiful and sexy change, too. Therefore, to come up with a role model for the archetypal 'beautiful' woman is no easy thing to do, though many have tried.

Body image

What is interesting is that psychologists have proved that so much of our own self-image depends on our satisfaction with our *body image*.

Surveys carried out both in the United States and in the UK have proved, time and time again, how much importance we place on our own appearance and on our bodies. And that satisfaction with our bodies can be precisely defined as the extent to which our perceived actual body deviates from our own personal ideals.

Of course, we don't really need sociologists and scientists to conduct surveys to tell us that most of us aren't really happy with our bodies. We only have to take a look at the number of slimming clubs, health spas, gyms and weight-watching magazines on the market to know that how we look and what we weigh is a multi-billion dollar business. According to a report published in *Marketing Magazine* in 1980, the total size of the UK dietary aids manufacturing industry was at that time estimated to be worth a staggering £200 million annually! In 1984, Mintel (a British market research organization) estimated that the market for products suitable for slimmers was worth £839 million! And we're even more obsessed by our bodies now, so heaven knows how much that same market is worth today.

So, because being overweight is extremely unfashionable, people strive all their lives to remain slim and if they happen to lose the battle they are often deemed to be 'different' and 'unattractive' to the world at large.

This applies just as much to children as it does to adults. In one survey carried out by the Royal College of Physicians into obesity, it was discovered that fat children are more disliked by their peers than either children with handicaps or those of a different race. The apparent reason for this is that handicap, colour, creed and race are considered to be beyond the individual's control. Being fat is not.

Therefore, once again, we make assumptions about the fat person based on what we perceive and our own in-built prejudices. For example, fat people are lazy, unintelligent, greedy and lack sufficient self-control. These are all characteristics which are definitely *not* considered admirable in our society, yet they are immediately ascribed to overweight people.

In fact, we've all got it wrong. Some fat people may be some of those things, it's true, but the majority of them are not.

Experiments carried out with women in relation to their own body image have shown that most women tend to see themselves as larger and heavier than they actually are. And, indeed, this was subsequently proven in one British documentary programme in which a number of women were invited to look at themselves in a specially constructed mirror (similar to those used in fairgrounds) which could be adjusted to make the women look larger or smaller.

Without fail, every single woman refused to believe the 'true' reflection of herself and, when asked to adjust the mirror themselves, only appeared to be satisfied when the mirror showed a reflection that was estimated to be at least eight pounds heavier than they actually were!

The problem is that each of us is acutely aware of *all our faults* – or imagined faults – and is hypercritical about them. What we tend to forget is that other people are not half as critical and because they invariably don't see beyond the surface image we present to the world, *our* faults are often genuinely not apparent to them. Furthermore, because most people are pretty self-deprecating and modest they generally feel obliged, when someone compliments them, to point out all the things that they feel are wrong with them. It's a huge mistake, but one we all make.

What then follows is that the self-fulfilling prophesy comes into play: we may feel that we're overweight so when someone compliments us on the way we look in a particular outfit, instead of smiling and accepting the compliment graciously, we feel duty bound to turn the compliment aside with a self-deprecating comment such as, 'Oh, but what about these awful thunder-thighs of mine – don't you think this skirt emphasizes them?' What we're really seeking is reassurance that we actually do look okay, but what we've done, in effect, is to draw someone's attention to the one thing that really bothers us.

If the person is polite, they'll probably say, 'No, don't be silly', but

if they're frank, they're just as likely to look a little more closely
and reply: 'Hmm, yes, I do see what you mean.' Result: we believe
we've got huge thighs and consequently, imagine that everyone
else believes so too. Then, because that person either hasn't
disagreed or, even worse, *appears to agree*, what little confidence
we might have had is shot to pieces, our worst fears have been
confirmed and what might have been a niggling little self-doubt
is then reinforced and helped (by ourselves!) to become a full-
blown, confidence-shattering complex.

In 1989, a British slimming magazine surveyed its readers in an
effort to find out: (a) how many were dissatisfied with their
bodies; (b) what they would like to change if they could, and (c)
whom they most wanted to look like.[10]

Twelve hundred readers, the majority of whom were in the
18–34 age group, responded with an overwhelming *YES* to the
first question. And what were they dissatisfied with?

Sixty per cent said they wanted smaller hips, 50 per cent
wanted a smaller waist, 71 per cent wanted thinner thighs, 42.5
per cent wanted longer legs and 17.5 per cent wanted a bigger
bust.

Given those percentages detailed above, perhaps it's not
surprising that the person who ranked top of the list of whom the
readers most wanted to look like was none other than the
exceedingly slender Victoria Principal! Second came Jamie Lee
Curtis and third was Jane Seymour. All three of these women are
slim, beautiful and have, at various times, been described as
having sexual power!

Interestingly enough, although 82 per cent of the readers
agreed that their self-esteem was directly related to the way they
look, 52 per cent of the total surveyed *also* believed that they were
confident, self-assured and had good self-esteem. Clearly more
than a few of the readers appear to be contradicting themselves!

The results of one American investigation exploring the dis-
crepancies between women's actual size and what they considered to be ideal revealed that the self-rated ideal size for body,
waist and hips was significantly smaller than the average
woman's measured size, but when it came to breasts, measure-
ments *larger* than average were considered to be ideal![11] These
findings seem to be totally consistent with the British women
surveyed above, which only serves to confirm the notion that the
cultural and social conditioning women undergo seems now to
be more or less universal.

What's interesting here is that one can't help suspecting that the attributes women perceive to be 'ideal' amongst their own sex probably stem more from what women think most *men* find devastatingly attractive than is actually the case.

In 1984 I published, along with my co-author, Caroline Buchanan, a book entitled *The Sensuous Slimmer*.[12] During our research we interviewed hundreds of women and men about weight and how they related to it. All of our own research revealed that being fat (or even just *thinking* you were fat) was a huge problem for the majority of women. This came as no surprise to us, but what did prove to be a revelation was that the majority of men over the age of 25 actually *preferred* their women to be well-covered!

One experiment carried out some years ago in Chicago attempted to discover whether there was a correlation between fat and sensuality in women. Thirteen pairs of fat and thin women were questioned about their frequency of sexual activity and then asked how that frequency compared to their actual needs and desires. While both groups of women testified to having sex roughly the same amount of times per month, it was the women in the fat group who admitted that they would like to make love a lot more often! The conclusion the researchers reached was that fat women are far more sexually responsive – and had keener sensual responses generally – than thin women!

Of course, a small test such as this can hardly be called conclusive, but our own research for *The Sensuous Slimmer* bore this out time and time again. And it's perfectly logical to surmise that if true sensuality does not confine itself to one 'sense' alone, then people who enjoy making love more than most will also enjoy food more than most.

In 1940 a psychologist, Dr William Herbert Sheldon, published a book entitled *Varieties of Human Physique* in the United States and coined three new words to describe human-body size and shape. Sheldon believed that the human physique falls into three basic classifications: endomorphic (fleshy, light-boned and well-padded), mesomorphic (muscular, broad-shouldered and skeletally sturdy) and ectomorphic (long-legged, lean and with a fragile bone structure).

Much has been written about Sheldon's theories since then and many investigations have been conducted to test his theories, the majority of which have shown that it is the endomorphs (the ones most likely to run to fat) who are the least flappable of the three types. According to Sheldon, endomorphs love comfort, company, warmth and satiety. He also firmly believed that they must therefore be the most affectionate and sensual of all!

Elizabeth Taylor has fought a constant battle with her weight for most of her adult life and yet it certainly hasn't stopped her from attracting men.

The jazz singer Bertice Reading is warm, witty and exceedingly large. But her size hasn't prevented Bertice from attracting – and marrying – a very handsome man who's not only a totally different colour but also happens to be less than half her age! To witness this happy couple together in a TV interview is to be totally confounded by the seemingly insurmountable barriers to their mutual attraction, and to be tremendously cheered by the evidence that love can, indeed, conquer all.

And if that's not evidence enough, take another look at Marilyn Monroe whose posters and photographs still turn men on today and ponder this: *Marilyn Monroe weighed a good twenty-eight pounds (12kg) more than is considered acceptable on a woman of comparable height today*!

And what about fat and men? Are men as concerned about their looks and bodies as women? The majority of the women who responded to the slimming magazine survey outlined earlier seemed to think not, as 68 per cent of them said that they did *not* think that men's self-esteem is dependent at all on how they look!

Again, my own research bears that out, too. Because men are not subjected to the same kinds of conditioning or the same amount of pressure as women, being overweight doesn't seem to present so many problems for them. That makes sense when you consider that we equate fat women with gluttony, idleness, carelessness and lack of pride. But we equate big men with power, strength and wealth!

Charlotte is a smart lady working in PR who absolutely adores big men – and what Charlotte calls big, the rest of us would term downright fat! So what is it about 'big' men that turns Charlotte on?

'I'm not sure I can put it into words, it's just something that's always been a part of me. I've always gone weak at the knees when I see a big man.

'Perhaps it has something to do with the fact that they command so much attention, that they're so noticeable in every way. I just love being with them. Maybe I also get a kick out of feeling so tiny and vulnerable beside this huge beast of a man when I'm naked in bed with him.

'I have to say, though, that while I adore looking at *all* big men, the only ones I would ever go out with, or have a relationship with, are the ones who have some of the accoutrements of success and power! I certainly wouldn't be attracted to a big bricklayer, or a refuse collector – they're hardly my type at all!'

It's interesting to note that Charlotte's penchant precludes those big men who lack the trappings of success and I'm sure that a psychoanalyst would have a field day trying to unravel the neuroses behind Charlotte's need to feel 'tiny and vulnerable' when with her men!

Perhaps there's an element of the primitive 'Me Tarzan, you Jane' appeal in Charlotte's relationships with big men. Indeed, who are we to criticize or comment? I merely offer the tale as an example of how women relate to bigness in men, and to suggest that it's a shame that men can't find similar ways to relate to big women.

Men, generally, have to be severely obese to be the butt of laughter or scorn, while women only have to be marginally overweight to receive derisive treatment – from other women as well as from some men. Obviously, we can't ignore the fact that men, generally, are that much taller than women and, therefore, can carry quite a bit of extra weight without it becoming too apparent.

But how do men themselves feel about their size and weight? Well, there is evidence to suggest that men do worry about their looks and bodies, but it would seem that the major source of worry for most men are the very things that women consider least important when selecting a potential suitor or mate.

Perhaps this is because men are encouraged to believe that they can always get a mate if they have something to trade (such as the evidence of wealth, power and position mentioned earlier), and also due to the fact that men appear to have their wires totally crossed with regard to what women like.

Despite all the evidence to the contrary, men *still* appear to be labouring under the misapprehension that, physically, women want hairy, muscular men with broad shoulders and large penises – but more of *that* in a later chapter!

The obsession with height

Physically, the other major worry men seem to have is related to height. And with good cause, too, because, here again, research has shown that in the eyes of the rest of us, height (particularly in men) assumes an importance out of all proportion to rationality – despite the fact that, logically, we all know height bears no real relation to ability.

Along with our aversion to those who are fat or ugly, one of our most blatant prejudices is directed against the short.

All male heroes are tall. Fortune tellers promise us that 'a *tall* dark, handsome stranger will come into our midst' as if, by virtue of his height, darkness and handsomeness, he'll possess the power immediately to solve every problem we might have! We also tend to refer to people we admire as being 'someone to look *up* to' and, though we rarely say so, we invariably look '*down* on' the people we dislike!

Height, or lack of it, is something I personally know a great deal about – I'm under five feet (1.5m) myself! The odd thing that I've noticed is that as I've progressed in my own career and learned to display confidence in myself, people *have* perceived me as being taller than I really am and are invariably surprised when I tell them what I measure.

Of course, lack of inches doesn't have quite the same implications for a woman as it does for men and society, as a rule, doesn't display the same prejudices to short women as it does to men. That's not to say that small men can't succeed – one only has to look at people like Dustin Hoffman, Woody Allen, Dudley Moore, Alan Ladd, Al Pacino and Elton John to realize that. However, research does show that it *is* that much harder to attain success, respect and advancement when you lack height and that small people *do* have to work much harder to earn those things.

One sociologist noted in 1971 that every American President elected since around 1900 was the taller of the two major political candidates.[13] Another found that our estimation of a person's height bears a direct correlation to the amount of authority that person is assumed to have.[14]

In one such experiment, American college students were divided into three groups and introduced in turn to a gentleman who was described to them in three different ways.[15] The first group were told that the man was of high status (a college professor), the second group were told he was of medium status (a college lecturer) and the third group were told he was of low status (a fellow student). Each group was then asked to estimate the man's height.

The students in the third group estimated 'the student's' height at around 5 ft 9 ins (1.75m); in the eyes of the second group (to whom he had been presented as a lecturer) the man had 'grown' to 5 ft 11 ins (1.80m); while with the first group the 'Professor' had shot up to an incredible 6 ft 1 ins (1.85m). In fact, the first group were absolutely correct in their estimation of this man's height.

The same experiments have been applied to women and these have also indicated that when someone is presented to us as being of a fairly senior status we generally tend to overestimate their height whilst when we meet people of junior or inferior status, we underestimate theirs.

Tall people are assumed to be successful and of higher status than short people. Tall people also command higher starting salaries than short people – and that's a documented, though grossly unfair, fact!

But why is this so? Headhunters and recruitment consultants say it is fairly common knowledge amongst their profession that employers usually decide within five minutes of meeting a prospective employee whether he or she is suitable for the job. Therefore, because initial impressions are so critical, physical appearance can be crucial.

One of the reasons for this is that most employers seek people who can convey an impression of leadership (particularly in executive positions) and, unfortunately, our stereotypical image of a 'leader' generally precludes a short person – though both Hitler and Napoleon were short!

As little children we naturally admire – and stand in awe of – adults who are, of course, much taller than us. Tall girls and boys are invariably elected as prefects in schools, although whether this is because they can intimidate younger children, or are more visible, or whether it's due to the fact that tall people are considered to be more mature, have more authority and can accept greater responsibility, is not entirely clear.

What is clear is that research shows that small people's self-esteem is adversely affected by their experiences regarding the way other people relate to them and, unfortunately, they're very often cast in a 'no-win' situation.

If you're short you have to battle that much harder for recognition (sometimes you have to wage a major war just to be seen!), but when you win the battle and increase your sense of self-confidence and self-worth through doing so, what happens? Tall people treat you as if you're arrogant, pugnacious and a 'little Hitler' for fighting that much harder, for demanding entitlement to the same amount of respect they take as their right, and even suspect your motives for wanting to succeed; seeing these as a sign of having a great big chip on your shoulder because you're small.

Most people, if asked, would admit to being dissatisfied with their height. Tall women invariably wish they were shorter and vice versa and most men (unless they're already over six feet) think that a few extra inches wouldn't come amiss.

Most research relating height to achievement and success has focused on men because, in the main, it wasn't considered to be a topic that affected women overmuch. Now, however, as women are increasingly competing in a male world and are being judged on male terms, it's not quite as acceptable as it once was to be 'petite'.

It's not easy for a small woman (or a small man, for that matter) occupying an executive position to have to remonstrate with, or give orders to, a taller subordinate. In the event that a female executive has to direct a tall subordinate who *also happens to be male* the situation can become almost impossible, because asserting your authority when you're small can come across as either pugnacious behaviour or as ludicrously funny. It's very difficult for small people to be taken seriously – I know!

When it comes to partnerships of the romantic kind, again, height can be an important factor – though actual height of the individuals concerned isn't nearly so important as the relative height between the two. Tall girls rarely want to be seen with small men and vice versa. A really tall man might feel a bit silly with an exceptionally short woman though this doesn't appear to form much of a stumbling block if the couple are really enamoured of each other.

All women, it seems, want a man of medium-to-tall height and, generally, it would appear that when specifying the actual height of the men they prefer, most women look for a man who is around six inches (15cm) taller than themselves, whereas men are generally looking for a woman around four-and-a-half inches (11cm) shorter than they are.

One interesting fact that has emerged from research into height is that the more dominant a man wishes to be, or considers himself, the more he wants to look down on his partner and, therefore, the greater the height difference he will seek when selecting a potential mate. On the other hand, those women surveyed who sought less of a height differential between themselves and their partners, were deemed more likely to be frustrated by the traditional woman's role and as seeking more parity in their lives, careers and relationships.

Naturally, as a small person myself, I couldn't possibly end this chapter without pointing out some of the benefits of being short – at least from a woman's point of view; and if you're a shorter than average woman yourself, this might be of some comfort.

While it's certainly true in my experience that people take you less seriously when you're short, once you do manage to overcome any obstacles (usually through sheer hard work and determination!), people tend to forget how short you really are and begin relating to you as if you're taller.

It's also true that men like to feel protective of small women. And, frankly, I'd say it's a wise lady who knows how to turn this to her advantage in a career situation – after all, if people aren't expecting you to excel, once you do, they're often so surprised that they never forget it!

And finally, smaller people are almost always perceived to be much more youthful than their actual chronological age! To be considered youthful and immature is not much fun, but when you are mature and have all the experience, wisdom and confidence that comes with age, to be considered younger can be a positive asset!

Besides, once you've discovered for yourself how to develop your own sexual power, the things you have no power to alter, such as beauty and height, will cease to be of importance – because you'll be in possession of something that's far more devastatingly effective!

Chapter 5

Charisma, Sex Appeal, and Glamour

Clara Bow was the original – and quintessential – IT girl.

Who said so? Not Miss Bow herself, but the writer Elinor Glyn, whose invention of IT proved to be one of her greatest claims to fame.

But what was – or is – IT?

Glyn defined it as 'a strange magnetism which attracts both sexes' and declared that in Clara Bow she had found the ultimate definition of it.

So greatly did Glyn's invention capture the imagination of Hollywood (and thus the world), that a film about 'IT' was immediately rushed into production in which Glyn herself appeared to explain – and then define her explanation – to the world. Having, or not having, 'IT' immediately became the biggest thing to hit Hollywood in years.

Did Elinor Glyn mean *charisma*? Was she referring to *sex appeal*? Or was 'IT' merely a euphemism for *glamour*? Perhaps a more interesting question to ponder would be: Did Clara Bow have IT *before* Glyn identified it? Or did she acquire it after the myth was born? And how much, if anything, do these three qualities contribute to sexual power?

During the course of my research I compiled a questionnaire which I dispatched to a number of people both sides of the Atlantic with instructions to make copies and pass them on to people of their own acquaintance.

While the responses that I received hardly constitute a representative example of mankind's opinions, they did reveal certain similarities of thought on a number of the issues raised.

In answer to the question: 'What, in your opinion, is the most attractive and sexually appealing quality a member of the opposite sex can have and why?' Kirk, a 28-year-old single man who works in the advertising industry in Chicago, had this to say:

> 'Assuming this means on first acquaintance, I don't believe an initial conversation may give an accurate representation of who or what a person is.
>
> However, the eyes tell all – where they look, how they move and how they "lock" with you. There is a sort of sparkle in the eyes of those who are most worth knowing. It can represent energy, lust, wisdom or wit, but the eyes are the best avenue to a woman's greatest sexual organ – the mind (contrary to popular male opinion)!'

Angie, a 24-year-old Personal Assistant from Essex, holds the same view:

> 'Although I believe attractiveness and sex appeal are a combination of qualities, I think eyes are the single factor. How someone looks at me, how long they maintain eye-contact for, what their eyes look like, these can hold me fascinated.'

Greg, a 42-year-old married businessman from Illinois, believes that sex appeal comes from sensuousness in dealing with the opposite sex, though he couldn't qualify his comments because he felt (quite rightly, it would appear) that the issue of sex appeal is an irrational subject.

However, when it came to the question: 'Would you agree that charisma and sex appeal are the same thing?', Greg said: 'To me, charisma is a function of either vivacity of mysteriousness, while sex appeal is good looks.'

Kirk, on the other hand, felt charisma and sex appeal were dependent upon each other, saying:

> 'Charisma is an element of sex appeal. No matter what anyone says, it is a combination of mental *and* physical qualities that maximizes sex appeal, and the impact of each is subject to a given frame of mind.
>
> Charisma can radically alter the effect of one's appearance and oftentimes physical appearance is indicative of how a person feels about themself. How can a person care for you if they don't care about themself?'

While Angie didn't think they were quite the same thing, she nevertheless felt that they were closely connected:

> 'To me, charisma is a quality which draws people to those who possess it, while to put it bluntly, sex appeal is a quality that makes people want to go to bed with you. You can be drawn to a charismatic person but you wouldn't necessarily want sex with them.'

Three very different people, yet with views that are remarkably similar. A small sample, perhaps, but time and time again when sifting through completed questionnaires, I was struck by the correlation of opinions on this thorny subject.

Can sex appeal, charisma and glamour be separated from one another?

If we acknowledge that Hitler is a prime example of a person who had charisma while not having even one ounce of sex appeal or glamour, then clearly there must be distinct dividing lines between the three.

John Kennedy, James Dean, Marilyn Monroe and Elvis Presley had all three. Jack Nicholson, for many, has all three. Mickey Rourke has two out of three: sex appeal and charisma; while Madonna and Mick Jagger get by with a different two out of the three: sex appeal and glamour. Joan Collins, on the other hand, has just glamour, but manages to make it serve her just as well as having all three.

The Queen ofEngland has glamour *and* charisma, but she doesn't have sex appeal. Paul Newman *definitely* has sex appeal *and* glamour, but he doesn't have charisma in the way that, for many, people like Mel Gibson, Mickey Rourke and Jack Nicholson do.

So, how do we define the difference between, say, charisma and sex appeal?

The dictionary defines charisma as 'a spiritual gift; an ability to inspire great trust and devotion; supreme gift for leadership; high artistic genius', which certainly goes some way to explaining why John Kennedy simply dripped with it, but isn't much help when you relate it to Jack Nicholson – well, would you *trust* such a gleefully wicked man as him?

Some sportsmen and athletes certainly seem to exude enough charisma via their sporting skills to inspire fanatical devotion: take Muhammad Ali and George Best, for example, but it's debatable whether they have the same amount of charisma off the field or out of the ring.

Madonna appears to have an abundance of sex appeal and now, because of her stupendous success, she has achieved glamour too. And although she's undoubtedly achieved superstar status, it's arguable whether she yet has sexual power, although if anyone knows how to *manufacture* sexual power, it is she.

Charisma is indeed a gift. It has its roots in total confidence and an ability to inspire attraction and devotion in both sexes. But it has little to do with sex itself. After all, Margaret Thatcher has, according to many prominent politicians, a tremendous amount of personal charisma, but I seriously doubt whether she's the secret fantasy of hordes of international leaders, all desperate to lure her into their Presidential beds!

Sex appeal, on the other hand, has to be exclusive to the opposite sex. Both men and women may recognize – and envy – it in their own sex, but they wouldn't be sexually attracted by it themselves. If a member of the opposite sex has charisma, then it's possible for them to have sex appeal for us, too. After all, when you meet it and recognize it, what better way to envisage absorbing it for yourself than through a close, intimate relationship with the person who has it?

Charisma

According to psychologist and author, Professor Ray Bull, while good-looking people seem to have a headstart in the charisma stakes, charismatic people aren't always good looking – they just develop their characters and social skills to make up for the fact that they're not immediately attractive.

According to many other psychologists, charismatic people are *born persuaders* who tend to be more dynamic, active and confident than the rest of us. Such people use hand gestures constantly, their body tone is far more alert and they're far more likely to be believed than people who are less dynamic.

Conmen very often have a great deal of charisma – and it's certainly no accident that the word 'con' derives from the word 'confidence'. To be charismatic, you not only have to *have* confidence, you also need to be able to persuade other people to have confidence in *you*. Because, deep inside us all is an innate *lack of confidence* or self-doubt; when we see evidence of confidence in others we can't help admiring and feeling irresistibly drawn towards it ourselves. That's why we admire great orators, politicians, public speakers and evangelist preachers – because they must have immense self-confidence in the first place to take such a platform alone and through their own beliefs persuade so many others that *their* beliefs are worth embracing.

Charisma can be – and has been – used to perpetuate evil as well as for great good. A lot of salesmen learn how to use charisma in order to close their sales. Some have reached the pinnacle of their professions and earned fortunes by being clever enough to combine charm, persuasiveness and confidence.

From time to time we read in the press about the dangerous, mind-bending techniques used by quasi-psychological self-assertion groups who prey on those who are lonely and insecure, promising that (in return for large sums of money) they will show them how to win friends and influence people. Some unscrupulous people have been known to take this process one step further and by labelling it 'religion' persuade others to forsake their homes, families, jobs and lives in order to 'serve' their charismatic gurus.

In the United States, there is the unique phenomenon of the 'evangelist' preacher whose message runs via television to millions of ordinary folk who happily hand over their dollars to their church or mission; and all because of the power of the preacher's persuasive personality.

Equally, there are people who have used their charisma only for good. Jesus Christ was reputed to have the most compelling character of anyone who ever lived. Gandhi, Martin Luther King and John Kennedy were three great leaders who could alter world opinion and move millions of ordinary people to tears. And though some might conjecture as to whether this was due to the power of their personalities or the humanitarian causes they publicly espoused, no one could be elected to lead any cause without having some ability to mesmerize and influence.

Throughout the world there are successful companies whose entire existence is based solely on the ability to teach ordinary businessmen and prominent personalities alike how to move, talk and 'sell' themselves more powerfully, effectively and convincingly. This proves that charisma can be learnt – and once learnt, can be developed and honed to perfection.

We've all met it or seen it in action. And we've all admired and envied it. What is it about Jack Nicholson that makes so many men smile appreciatively and causes hordes of women to murmur sentiments like, 'he could put his shoes under my bed anytime'? Nicholson isn't hunky, or slim. His hair is receding, he's far from being handsome and he definitely tends towards the paunchy. And yet few would deny that he undoubtedly has charisma.

Why?

Could it have something to do with that wicked gleam in his eye? Or the fact that he so obviously lives life to the full, indulging in devilish, headline-grabbing games with no thought for propriety or the potential damage to his reputation. Indeed, so great are the myths surrounding him that every misdeameanour only seems to add to his reputation, not detract from it.

One psychologist to whom I addressed that very question attributed Nicholson's appeal to the fact that everyone loves a lovable rogue, explaining it thus:

'Firstly, what we have to understand is that, with few exceptions, mankind as a whole no longer lives close to the edge. Life, certainly for those of us in the affluent West, is routine, ordered, fairly safe and, for the most part, predictable.

'We no longer live with the threat of predatory animals, or even hostile nations, endangering our security and for most of us life is bound by conventions.

'Danger can be a very exciting thing. We all know it releases adrenalin into the bloodstream and all our reactions and perceptions are heightened as a consequence.

'Human beings have an innate need for excitement and, to a degree, danger itself. But now that we no longer live with it on a daily basis, we manufacture it for ourselves. Witness the success of horror films and look how we all love to frighten the pants off ourselves by going on hair-raising rides at funfairs. We still crave our kicks, but now they're relatively "safe" kicks.

'Danger and excitement are addictive elements and while we all know that in order to protect ourselves and our lives we have to be sensible, still the *frisson* we get from these elements can be a seductive thrill.

'Whether Jack Nicholson, the man, embodies all these qualities is arguable; certainly the film roles he accepts usually portray something of the exciting, devilish, but largely non-threatening rogue. Because of this, I would suggest that these qualities have now been projected onto the man himself.

'Moreover, Nicholson himself is living proof that charisma and sexual power can be enhanced. When he first started out he made a number of films that achieved cult status but he wasn't a superstar and certainly didn't have the profile, status or image of one. In fact, I can recall watching a TV interview with him in those early days of his career and while I could certainly detect *something* approaching charisma in him, he certainly didn't display it to the level he does today.

'What I believe has happened is that over the years his career has blossomed and that has given him a certain elevated status. Whereas before he was more earnest about life, himself and what he wanted to do in films, he's now reached a fortunate stage where he's achieved everything he wants. He *has* attained superstar status, he *has* achieved a massive following and, consequently, he now *has* power, success and unlimited money. And because Nicholson the "star" has been hyped so much, every aspect of Nicholson the "man' seems larger than life.

'In a sense, that puts him in a position where he no longer has to give a damn; a position that each one of us secretly longs to be in. Moreover, the naughty, spontaneous, schoolboyish side of him has now been freed from all the restrictions of convention. Deep inside every man there is an intense longing to be totally irresponsible, to do whatever comes naturally, to live life to the full and to take full advantage of whatever comes his way. We'd all love to be a rip-roarin', fun-loving, womanizing rogue like Nicholson, which is why we admire him so much.

'For women, Nicholson's appeal is more complex. In the same way that men love tarts but only marry ladies, women love rogues. They can't *live* with rogues, because life would be far too insecure, but if you questioned every woman about her one, special, secret *grande passion* I imagine the man she'd describe would be something like him.

'Rogues are exciting, dangerous and untameable. Those very qualities that are so irresistible are the very source of their charisma to others.'

Sex appeal

Obviously, sex appeal is a subjective thing. Someone might have it for you, but they wouldn't necessarily have it for anyone else. We all have our unreachable heart-throbs and fantasy-figure heroes and we would defend our opinions to the death when debating the various merits of one sex symbol over another.

Some women are enormously turned on by the blatant sex appeal of Tom Jones; others just want to throw up when he goes into his crudely explicit 'bump-and-grind' parody of the sexual act. That's because we all seek different qualities in people, dependent upon our own needs, neuroses, personal personality theories and tastes.

But there seems to be a general consensus of opinion about various sex symbols, both male and female, that is more or less universal and that relates back to the fact that our conditioned 'ideals' are universally common, too. One man's opinion might not hold much weight, but the more people who hold a common view, the more readily we accept and adopt that view ourselves, particularly if some of those people are considered to be sex symbols too.

The curious thing about sex symbols is that very often those to whom we give the label don't see themselves that way at all.

Take Woody Allen, for example. Now there's a man whom few at first glance would hang a sex symbol tag on, but for Diane Keaton and Mia Farrow, Woody Allen has tremendous sex appeal. While for Allen himself, the greatest living sex symbol has to be Warren Beatty, of whom he once said, 'When I die I'd like to come back as his fingertips', which proves that even so-called sex symbols have difficulty recognizing their own appeal.

Humour

And let's not forget that humour can be incredibly sexually attractive. Certainly the American comedienne, Ruby Wax, places it very firmly at the top of her priority list in potential partners. And the man who turns her on more than any other is, yes, you've guessed it, Mr Woody Allen himself. 'I'd have Woody Allen's baby tomorrow. If he walked into the room this minute I'd have sex with him right away . . . And that's not to say I'm sex mad, I'm not. I don't need to have sex a lot but I do need to laugh a lot,' said Ruby in a recent magazine interview.

To have a sense of humour in common is a wonderful thing for a couple to share, for there's nothing like laughter for easing tension. It's almost impossible to hold on to anger when someone is making you laugh and, in fact, smiling and laughing has actually been shown to ease pain, promote healing, relieve tension and stress and generally make us feel happier and more contented.

Sharing a particular type of humour and little in-jokes can also bind a couple in a little conspiracy of togetherness that helps cement their relationship. Everybody loves a good chuckle or giggle, and anyone who can make us laugh is never without friends. It's not difficult, therefore, to see why so many women find funny men very sexy – and why so many men delight in the company of witty women.

Laughter, then, must be a vital component of sexual power and a sense of humour is something we would all do well to develop.

Heroes

The modern-day sex symbol, say some psychologists, has taken the place of the old-fashioned hero of yesteryear. The reason for this is that exciting acts of heroism are no longer enacted in real life, so instead we respond to those that are fabricated on the silver screen, and the glamour attached to screen heroes transfers itself to the actors and actresses who portray them.

Moreover, the more widely a person is known, the more global the consensus of opinion about that person is likely to be. It works on the same basis that marketing folk use when gauging percentage response rates: the bigger the audience reached, the higher the likely response will be.

Everyone who knows Sue would agree that she has sexual power. But the number of people Sue is exposed to is nowhere near the number who would be able to comment were she more famous.

Sexual power, charisma and glamour depend to a great extent on unavailability. The old adage, 'familiarity breeds contempt', was never more true than when applied to our heroes. Were our heroes to become accessible we would soon become disillusioned at the discovery that they don't lead charmed lives, they might have bad breath or body odour and they aren't as perfect as we imagine.

Our heroes must forever remain as they are *now*. That's why the ultimate hero is a dead one. Dead heroes can't change, they can't grow old, they can't disillusion us and shatter our dreams of perfection by becoming incontinent, mentally unstable or by sinking into a disgraceful old age. In fact, dead heroes rapidly transcend being mere heroes to become legends!

Marilyn Monroe, James Dean and Elvis Presley have possibly all become legends because they died young. The net worth of their respective estates has increased by millions since their untimely deaths, and despite the fact that in each case enough tales have circulated to rip their reputations apart and shatter every illusion or fantasy ever harboured about them, their cult followings go on increasing year after year and often include people who weren't even born when their heroes were alive.

We may read the gossip and the seedy scandals written about them with prurient interest, but they count not one whit against the powerful images we have of them.

Imagine, then, what Monroe, Dean or Presley might be like if they were still alive today. Would Monroe's breathless, girly naïveté appear a bit incongruous now in a woman of pensionable age? Wouldn't a petulant, permanently mulish attitude seem a bit silly in an ageing broody actor with whom many will have shared the best years of their youth? And what about Presley? Love him or hate him, would any of us really have wanted to witness the further degeneration of that famous voice – not to mention the man himself?

Heroes need to have a touch of human-ness about them to fuel our fantasies that we might someday become heroes too, but we don't want them to become too human or to show weakness or frailty in any way because that would be a betrayal of all our hopes and dreams.

Of course, there's nothing wrong with having fantasies about famous people. In fact, psychologists confirm that it's perfectly healthy and even necessary at times. After all, we all need the occasional escape route from the boring, routine aspects of our lives. The mistake occurs when we attempt to turn fantasy into reality.

The novelist Jackie Collins once cryptically commented, 'When I was a kid I kind of fancied Tony Curtis. And then one day I met him – never meet your idols!' Proof, if ever it was needed, that reality can never live up to our fantasies; for our fantasies are our own to control and direct – while reality isn't and never can be.

Glamour

Glamour has precious little to do with perfect good looks. Moreover, in some cases total facial perfection can even militate against it. That's not to say, however, that glamorous people *aren't* good looking because some obviously are, although it's also possible that glamour can provide the *effect* of memorable looks.

You don't need style or charm to have glamour – though once you're considered glamorous other people seem remarkably eager to attach these qualities to you.

Unlike other characteristics that we might be born with, such as beauty or talent, glamour can be cultivated and acquired through *assuming* the qualities or the lifestyle associated with it.

Money does help, of course, but serious contenders in the glamour stakes have been known to get by without it. Glamour can also rub off on you by association.

Glamour can come through the appearance of sophistication, style, taste, discernment – and, possibly, through being seen to associate with 'glamorous' people.

Bungalow Bill Wiggins now has glamour, due entirely to his association with Joan Collins. Previously he was just another property developer who was known only to like-minded people who enjoyed hanging out at trendy London clubs.

Ordinary people like you and me can develop charisma and sex appeal by developing our confidence, but because we only come into contact with a certain number of people, our powers will never be as widespread, or as widely acknowledged, as those of all the celebrities mentioned here.

Ordinary people can also have glamour, even if they lack the wherewithal to project the lifestyle that goes with it. For the *real* essence of glamour is mystique. Mystery and mystique convey the sense that what people are perceiving is just the merest tip of the iceberg; that beneath the dazzling exterior image lie such fascinating, unpredictable depths that all who come into contact with it will be consumed with an intense desire to plunder.

Consciously or unconsciously, glamorous people are adept at concealing much of their innermost thoughts and selves. Therefore, because mankind is essentially a problem-solving animal, whenever we scent a mystery we are intrigued. If the mystery is not easily solved, imagination steps in to complete the process. Suddenly, this mysterious, enigmatic person becomes the focus of our attention and we invent and endow them with all sorts of qualities that inspire fascination, admiration and awe.

Some professions automatically acquire an aura of glamour, particularly if they appear to contain elements of fascination such as the heroic, the dangerous or the exotic. Film stars and models seem to lead glamorous lives in comparison to ordinary folk; therefore they are glamorous. Fighter pilots, adventurers, secret service agents and explorers lead dangerous lives, and because danger inspires awe in those of us whose lives are fairly safe and monotonous, we accredit them with glamour. The same applies to anyone in a profession that incorporates travel, fast living or a seemingly exotic lifestyle.

However, given closer acquaintance with such people our exotic fantasies of the lives they lead will rapidly dissolve as 'mystery' gives way to reality because their 'glamour' is essentially an illusion. For example, you might think that the sexy, passionate new lover you've recently acquired exudes glamour and sex appeal from every pore, but would you still be inclined to think so if you discovered that in post-coital slumber she snores as loudly as a thundering juggernaut?

And what about that devastating man whom you can't wait to be seduced by? Will the fantasy remain intact when he kicks off his size 11 brogues in a passionate frenzy and a pair of Odor-eaters lands squarely on the bed? I doubt it!

In order to preserve their aura of mystique, truly glamorous people would do all in their power to ensure that such scenarios as those outlined above would never occur. The glamorous woman would fire her lover's fantasies about her sexy passionate nature and then deny him the opportunity to become disillusioned by leaving his bed before morning. And while the glamorous man might consent to stay the night safe in the knowledge that tousled hair and designer stubble are chic, he'd never make the mistake of wearing his socks in bed or displaying any other sign of fantasy-shattering ordinariness.

That's all very well, I hear you say, but what about us ordinary people? If projecting glamour means never risking a good old down-to-earth getting-to-know-each-other-warts-and-all relationship, doesn't that condemn us all to a lifetime of brief, meaningless affairs?

Well, if it's glamour, admiration, envy and awe you're after then I am afraid the answer's a resounding 'Yes', because it's impossible to found a real relationship on a lie. This is what happened to Josie when she tried it.

Josie is a 37-year-old divorcee who once fell madly in love with a 'glamorous' man in the recording industry:

'Or at least I thought it was love – until I had all my naïve notions about glamour shattered.

'His name was Mark and I met him at a cabaret dinner I went to with some friends. The group who were appearing were famous the whole world over – although they were getting a bit long in the tooth, hence their appearance at this particular place.

'I was sitting with my friends when I noticed some men at a nearby table who seemed more interested in conducting a business meeting than listening to the band. One of them kept looking at me and smiling in a way that told me he was interested. After a while, he sent a waiter over to my table with a magnum of champagne and a note inviting me to join him. I couldn't help being amused by the extravagance of the gesture – it was like something out of the movies – but I was secretly very pleased and flattered.

'We joined them and he introduced his friends. They were all from the group's recording company and they offered to take us backstage to meet the band after the show.

'Mark asked me if I'd have dinner with him one evening and because he was reasonably attractive, very self-assured and seemed, from what I had overheard, to lead such a glamorous lifestyle, naturally I accepted.

'He wined me and dined me as if it was going out of style and the more I saw of him the more fascinated and infatuated I became. His world seemed so different from mine and obviously that affected the way I saw him.

'He epitomized everything I had ever dreamed about in a man: glamorous, sophisticated, apparently wealthy, single, perfectly dressed and always immaculate without a hair out of place.

'One evening, he asked me to go to Cambridge with him to see a promising young student band he was interested in signing. I had a friend staying with me, which made things a little bit awkward, but when he said she could come too I was touched by his thoughtfulness.

'Well, the traffic was bad, he was late arriving and as I introduced him to Carol I casually reached up to smooth down his hair which, for once, was looking a bit windswept.

'I've never seen a man recoil so quickly! And from that moment on the whole evening seemed to go downhill, though I couldn't work out why. Mark seemed strangely tense and would hardly look at me, while Carol behaved very oddly and wouldn't look at Mark.

'The whole thing was such a disaster that when we finally got back home I wasn't surprised when he declined to come in, and though he said he'd call me the next day, for the first time I had serious doubts that he would.

'The moment he'd gone Carol fell on the bed, clutched her stomach and started laughing hysterically.

'"What on earth is the matter with you?" I asked angrily. All she could say was, "So *that's* Mr Wonderful! And to think I've been envying you for weeks!" I just couldn't see what she was trying to say, and the more she laughed, the angrier I got. In the end I was so mad I just said the first thing that came into my head which was something like, "Yes, it is, and if you hadn't spoiled everything I'd probably be having a great time in bed with him now instead of being with a demented moron like you."

'Well, that only seemed to start her off all over again. Eventually, though, she stopped laughing long enough to say, "Oh yeah? And what's he going to do with his hairpiece when it starts getting hot? Hang it on the bedpost?"

'I was so dumbstruck I didn't know what to say. First I refused to believe her. Then I was mortified. Eventually I could see the funny side, too. My dream man had finally appeared and swept me off my feet with so much sophistication and glamour that I hadn't even noticed he wore a wig!

'My infatuation died an instant death. Mark called me several times but I could never bring myself to see him again after that, and I never had the courage to tell him why.

'I know things like that shouldn't matter but somehow it just seemed to belittle him in my eyes.

As long as Josie *believed* Mark possessed the qualities she had projected onto him, her infatuation and her fantasies had room to grow. However, the moment he was revealed to her as just another ordinary human being (albeit in a 'glamorous' job), his glamour and appeal couldn't help but diminish accordingly.

While Josie's tale illustrates the fact that if you remove the mystique you can't possibly sustain glamour, this doesn't mean that all hope of acquiring glamour is denied to the rest of us. What it does indicate is that, if we wish to project glamour, we must learn the techniques that go with it.

Mark *did* have what seemed to be a glamorous lifestyle. He *could* have sustained his relationship with Josie and preserved that aura of glamour long enough to establish a firmer foundation if he had handled his own insecurities better.

He had all the advantages of money, lifestyle, image, acquaintanceship with fame (through the artistes he was connected with) and these, coupled with reasonable looks and a pleasant personality should have been more than enough to put him on a winning streak with Josie– and probably many other women too.

Unfortunately, Mark lacked the one single thing that's necessary if you want to project glamour – and it wasn't so much the toupée that killed his glamorous appeal, it was the fact that he lacked the *self-assurance* to be seen without it.

Without self-assurance and confidence, sexual power cannot exist.

So if sex appeal is subjective, charisma can be cultivated, and glamour nothing more than a bewitching dream, how much of what we find attractive is real and how much projected?

What pieces of the jigsaw lie hidden in the subject of attraction itself? Can it tell us what role chemistry has to play in sex appeal? Or how much of 'chemistry' is based on psychological factors such as our own subconscious, neurotic needs?

And what about the hypothesis that we are more like animals than we might like to think? Or that the gravitational pull we feel towards certain people might be caused by the invisible and virtually undetectable attractant scents (called pheromones) we all unconsciously emit, as some scientists suggest?

And what do all of these have to do with sexual power?

Chapter 6

The Aroma of Love

You're at a social gathering. Two members of the opposite sex walk into the room. One is obviously better looking than the other and yet, for some inexplicable reason, the moment your eyes 'lock' with those of the second person, you feel an irrational yet irresistible pull.

Is this love at first sight? The kind you never thought existed outside popular romantic fiction? Or is it merely something far more mundane that can be reduced to a simple chemical equation, as some scientists suggest?

Since attraction is something that affects us all, it's not surprising that this eternal enigma has proved to be such a popular subject of investigation for so many researchers. Whom we like, whom we loathe, and why, is a cause for endless fascination and speculation; and the hypotheses spawned as potential explanations are as varied and diverse as the types of people to whom we are ourselves attracted.

Some scientists suggest that attraction is based on a chemical reaction, while some psychologists claim that it has far more to do with our own neurotic needs than we might care to admit.

Romantic idealists, on the other hand, would hotly refute any suggestion of either, preferring to subscribe to the notion that attraction and love stem from a subconscious recognition of one's own spiritual soul-mate.

So wherein lies the truth?

In this chapter we'll examine some of the evidence that currently exists to support the theory that attraction has a great deal to do with pheromones, the name given to the known sex-attractant smells that motivate animals to mate, to see what what part aroma has to play in attraction. Then in the next chapter we'll take a look at some of the research that has been conducted in many of the other areas outlined above in an attempt to identify whether whom we love and whom we are attracted to is bio-logically and environmentally predetermined, or to what extent we might be influenced by chemistry, social conditioning and, of course, our own subconscious neurotic needs.

Follow the scent

The writer H.G. Wells was physically homely and fat. Yet he never seemed to lack women. Somerset Maugham, apparently curious to discover the secret of Wells' success, once asked one of the great man's mistresses what attracted her to Wells. Anticipating that she would probably attribute the attraction to something such as H.G.'s acute mind, or his sense of fun, Maugham was totally nonplussed when the lady insisted that it was none of those, but rather the fact that 'his body smelt of honey'!

Aroma, it seems, has a fascinating role to play, not only in attracting people to us, but also in cementing our relationships with them.

When we meet people for the first time we use our senses of sight and hearing to help us form opinions about them. What they say, how they say it and the timbre of their voice are allied with what they look like, how they dress and whether their appearance is pleasing or not. As we talk to them, all this information is being fed into our brain receptors. But what we're not aware of is the fact that our sense of smell is also hard at work 'sniffing out', if you like, other facts that might not immediately be apparent.

Of course, if a person smells obnoxious or repellent in some way, we couldn't help but be consciously aware of it, but as our society decrees that most naturally produced 'human' smells are taboo, it's uncommon to come across anyone who smells badly as we all go to such great lengths to eliminate this possibility!

Our obsession with ridding our bodies of their perfectly natural odours is relatively recent and stems mostly from the discovery of the relationship between dirt and disease. In primitive times mankind took such things for granted and showed no marked aversion to the body's by-products. Faeces were used as natural nourishment and replenishment of the earth (as they still are in some parts of the world) and urine – which, of course, is a natural (and cheap) source of ammonia – was used as a detergent.

Sigmund Freud maintained that young children display no shame or disgust about excretory products (it has now been established that below the age of five, children show very little aversion to *any* odours) and that our own aversion to bad smells is imposed on us by society which now decrees that anything associated with natural bodily functions is shameful, disgusting and should be kept secret.

To suffer from bad breath, sweaty feet, rank armpits or genital odour is to invite ostracism. Belching is permissible in public because belching has no odour. But the public passing of wind or gas (with or without an accompanying bad smell), which has to be the most humiliating thing that could ever happen to us, is not only considered to be crude, but is also virtually tantamount to social suicide. Sociologists have a term for this; they call it the 'fart taboo'. Why? Because anything emanating from this orifice is associated with shame, secrecy and extreme distaste – despite the fact that life would be exceedingly uncomfortable for *all* of us if we did not have one!

Freud took our resistance to bodily functions one step further by pointing out that because the genitals are so closely related to excretion, and because there are characteristic smells associated with these organs, our embarrassment about such smells is now inextricably entwined with our shame and inhibition about sex.

The nineteenth-century German neurologist, Richard von Krafft-Ebing, drew a direct correlation between the rise in smell-related fetishes and the growing interest in cleanliness and hygiene; noting that as soap became more widely available so the popularity of underwear, shoes, sweat, feet and even excrement began to feature more and more in sexual fetishes.

It's interesting to note that the words we use to describe someone we dislike – words like 'skunk', 'stinker', 'pig', and so on – are often associated with 'bad' odours and while few of us have qualms about pointing out other people's faults, we're all remarkably reluctant to tell someone that they smell, as this is perceived to be one of the greatest insults of all time.

Today's society is obsessed with smell. Virtually every other advertisement on TV and in the press is for perfume, deodorant or anti-perspirant. Indeed, every product on the supermarket shelf is launched only after years of painstaking research to ascertain the public's perception of how such a product *should* smell in order to make us feel confident that it will do the job we want it to do. Soap-powder manufacturers traditionally used to compete with each other purely on the basis of their product's amazing whitening powers. Recently, however, there has been a radical switch in emphasis to each product's remarkable ability to remove every trace of stale odour.

Our obsession with eradicating our natural human scents seems somewhat ridiculous when you consider that after we've done so, we invariably replace them with expensively packaged perfumes containing *the by-products of animal sex glands* in the hope that these will make us smell sweeter and more attractive to the opposite sex! The animal sex-glands so sought-after by perfume manufacturers as vital ingredients for their products all have one thing in common: they're all pheromone-producing glands.

The importance of smell

Pheromones (a term invented in 1959 from the Greek words *pherein* and *horman*, which loosely translated mean excitement communicator) are a group of chemicals secreted externally by the glands that are known to trigger sexual arousal – and to aid communication – in animals.

Aristotle observed and noted that moths and butterflies were attracted to each other on the basis of pheromones, a fact which was later confirmed by the French naturalist, Jean Henri Fabre, and modern-day scientists have long acknowledged that animals' sense of smell is exceedingly acute – as any woman who has ever been in the embarrassing position of having a dog's nose thrust up her skirt can confirm! Just one whiff of a wild boar's emittance of pheromone is enough to cause the female of the species to adopt the mating position immediately, while the male Emperor moth is capable of detecting the pheromones of a virgin female over a record distance of seven miles!

Experiments with sheep have shown that if a ewe's sense of smell is deliberately suppressed during gestation she cannot identify her own lamb. In the old days shepherds employed the trick of draping a dead lamb's coat over an orphan to encourage a bereaved mother sheep with an intact sense of smell to adopt the orphan as her own. Today, a man-made product called 'acceptone' is sprayed into a ewe's nostrils (which temporarily knocks out her sense of smell) to achieve the same effect.

Until fairly recently it was assumed that we had no pheromone-producing glands, although many scientists now claim that these do exist in humans. Certainly our human olfactory cells are identical in construction to *all* mammals and though we may not have them in the same quantity, we use our olfactory ability in exactly the same way. Furthermore, there is no doubt that our sense of smell is just as crucial to the information receptors in our brain as our other senses of sight, taste and sound.

One of the particular odours that humans are capable of detecting in infinitesimally small amounts is the chemical ethyl mercaptan which smells just like skunk and gives rotting meat its highly unpleasant odour. As the consumption of rotten meat could have such potentially lethal consequences, our extreme sensitivity to this odour can literally be a life-saver.

Smell can influence emotions. If we are on the receiving end of a disagreeable, noxious smell it can make us wince, gag, cough and, in some cases, even vomit or bring on other allergic reactions.

Our ability to link smells with people, places and experiences (our odour-memory) is far less affected by the passage of time than our visual or auditory recognition ability. It's debatable whether we would recognize someone we knew as a small child after many years had elapsed, although many of us have recollections associated with certain music or songs that can instantly be recalled on *hearing* those songs many years later. But just one whiff of a long-forgotten smell is enough to enable all of us to recall incidents and emotions we personally associate with that smell with remarkable clarity, no matter how many years have passed. The same smell may conjure up similar memories for a number of people (as with chalk, which invariably evokes memories of schooldays), or have entirely different associations according to the uniquely personal memories linked with it.

The fact is, when it comes to olfaction, we're far more like animals than we might ever wish to imagine and while an animal's sense of smell is still crucial to its survival (without it an animal would not be able to find food, identify other potentially threatening animals, or even reproduce), there is now a great deal of evidence to suggest that our own ability to smell is critical to our enjoyment of life.

But what role does smell have to play in human attraction and our sex lives?

Without going into too much technical detail, it has been established that when the olfactory bulb is stimulated, electrical impulses are relayed to the area of the limbic system that is directly concerned with our behavioural mechanisms and, in particular, those associated with sensory and sexual functions.

We all know that what we eat (such as a spicy curry) can have a dramatic effect on how we smell, but a nation's typical diet, even though it may not be particularly spicy or pungent, can also be an identifying factor. According to Ruth Winter, an American science writer who published a fascinating book called *The Smell Book* in 1976, Indians can sometimes smell like curry because of the heavy concentration of spices in their diets; South Sea Islanders have a characteristically fragrant smell of mingled fruit and palm; North Europeans often reek of cabbages and vegetables, while Americans 'smell like butter to the Japanese', who, in turn, have a fishy smell to Americans!

What we eat and how we live affects how we smell. But more importantly, the reason we all smell different culturally is due to the fact that we also have differing distributions of apocrine glands which produce our specialized scents.

The hair that grows in our armpits and around our genitals is designed to collect smells from the secretions of the apocrine scent glands. Our apocrine glands are small and relatively insignificant until we reach puberty, which also happens to be the same time that we begin to sprout hair in these areas. The apocrines reach their maximum size at sexual maturity and then gradually diminish with age (as does bodily hair growth). This is probably the reason why children rarely have a noticeable body odour and older people usually smell differently from younger adults. This discovery is also the reason why many scientists now believe that the apocrine glands in humans are, in fact, sex-pheromone producing factories.

The typical male odour produced by the apocrines has been described as 'musky', while the female odour characteristically seems to smell 'sweet'. If you doubt that, try smelling two discarded shirts, one previously worn by a man and one by a woman. Discounting the lingering presence of aftershave lotion, deodorant or perfume, you'll probably discover that it's quite easy to differentiate between the sexes. You'll also find that if you tried this experiment with several male and female friends, the men will all prefer the women's odours and vice versa, even though both odours may not be particularly pleasant. But then, pheromones *don't necessarily need to be pleasant* in order to attract the opposite sex!

Women, it seems, are remarkably sensitive to the male aroma of musk and it has been found that their sensitivity varies according to the menstrual cycle, reaching its peak around the time of ovulation. However, women who have had their ovaries removed are far *less* sensitive to musk, with the exception of those receiving Hormone Replacement Therapy which, of course, contains oestrogen. Research has also highlighted the fact that following the menopause, women who don't receive oestrogen replacement show a *decrease* in olfactory ability.

Musk is a chemical close-relation to the male hormone testosterone, whose levels control the sex drive in both sexes, although women produce only about 10 per cent of the level of testosterone as men. If a woman was to receive testosterone by artificial means, or if her body was producing too much of it, she might find her sex drive increased, but the chances are she wouldn't find any outlets for satisfying her ardour as it's likely she'd also experience a radical and unsightly increase in hair production!

According to Ruth Winter, there are too many established links between olfactory ability and the sex drive to be ignored. For example, the pituitary glands of rats that have been deprived of their ability to smell at birth produce lower levels of growth hormone, which not only results in stunted growth, but also in the formation of subnormal testicles. Moreover, aproximately 25 per cent of people who lose their sense of smell also experience a marked reduction in their desire for sex!

Such information obviously raises some interesting questions; for example, when we're suffering from stuffy head colds and attribute our disinterest in sex to the fact that we're feeling physically under par, could our loss of libido in fact be due to our diminished sense of smell?

Many years ago I heard a strange story which caused much mirth amongst my friends when someone said that the best cure for the common cold was rumoured to be oral sex! Nobody ever reported testing the theory (probably because it would have caused too much hilarity) but I've often wondered, since coming across the research detailed above, whether, in fact, the myth might not have become somewhat distorted from an original hypothesis which is, that if loss of ability to smell causes loss of desire, perhaps the logical way to counteract that would be by a much closer than normal 'association' with the very glands producing the sex-attractant pheromones!

Perhaps in years to come some scientists somewhere might like to put this hypothesis to the test!

However, there is increasing evidence to suggest that hormone production undoubtedly affects our ability to smell, just as smell seems to affect our ability to produce hormones.

The nerves relating to olfaction, and those relating to the ovaries in women and the testes in men, occupy the same area of the brain and research has established that animals' development of sex-gland systems and their olfactory bulbs are fundamentally related to the effects of hormones on the gonadal (reproductive organs) systems.

The mineral zinc is known to be a vital component for normal gonadal development, and the lack of it has been connected with an inability to smell in a number of patients (including anorexics who show no inclination for either food or sex), although treatment with large doses of zinc supplementation appears to be effective only in about one third of cases.

While there are many reasons why individuals may lose their sense of smell, taste or both – such as infection, disease, polyps, burns, head or neck surgery and even heavy smoking – many of these conditions also conspire to rob the body of zinc. Furthermore, it has been found that many women who do not recover their sense of smell after a severe dose of the flu (even with zinc treatment) experience an immediate onset of the menopause while some men find that permanent loss of smell can be accompanied by a decrease in beard growth!

We all produce sex pheromones, and among those identified so far, male pheromones seem to act mainly as an aphrodisiac to females, while female pheromones seem to announce our 'availability and readiness' to males.

A group of English researchers investigating this subject found that a woman's sweat and vaginal glands are stimulated to secrete odours by the hormones most plentiful in her bloodstream when she's in the maximum-fertility phase of her menstrual cycle. They also discovered that a man's production of 'attractant scent' is directly related to the degree of sexual arousal he experiences. Hence, they assert, if there was one aroused male (though *how* he might have come to be aroused the researchers didn't make clear!) at a mixed social gathering, and one woman at maximum-fertility phase, the woman could be subconsciously stimulated by the pheromones unconsciously produced by the man, thus providing the ideal situation for an irresistible attraction between the two – which might explain why Elvis Presley, Frank Sinatra, Tom Jones and so many other singers and rock stars could make a female audience go wild just by wiping a handkerchief across a perspiring brow or under a sweaty armpit and tossing it into the auditorium! It certainly makes you wonder whether they, or their image-makers, had some knowledge of pheromones – or whether it just came instinctively. It could also be an interesting technique for other young aspiring pop stars to employ in order to create a following!

That rats (whose sense of smell is extremely acute and crucial to their survival as a species) function in this way has been proved: for example, a female rat displays a marked preference for the scent of a normal male rat over that of a castrated rat. Female rats also prefer mating with a rat who does not smell of recent copulation than one who does. Male rats, on the other hand, are more attracted to the smell of a new female rat than one with whom they have recently mated, which is, when you think about it, perfectly consistent with the *raison d'être* of *all* male animals – including humans – which dictates that they impregnate as many females as possible in order to secure the survival of the species.

The female of the species

But it is the female of the species who possesses by far the most superior sense of smell, as it is most often the female who makes the decision about selecting her mate – as Charles Darwin noted long ago. The reasons for this are obvious. Men are capable, in theory, of impregnating a different woman at least once a day (although age, health, virility and opportunity can multiply his chances), while women can realistically only reproduce on average once a year and for only a limited number of years. Therefore, it makes sense that if nature is to minimize the margin for error with regard to physical defects she should not only endow the female of each species with a superior sense of smell, but also the right to make the decision with regard to selection of a suitably prime partner.

Many experiments have been conducted over the last twenty years or so to establish whether there really is a link between sex pheromones and attraction, but probably the most famous is the one popularly known as 'the dentist's waiting-room experiment'.[17]

As you might expect, this experiment took place in the waiting room of a Dental Health Centre over the course of several days (both before, during and after the filming of the actual experiment) and consisted of a number of chairs, a hidden camera to record actions, a spray of the male pheromone androstenone and about 850 people in total. Androstenone, which has no known physiological function (but doesn't appear to be a waste-product), is secreted by the adrenal glands, is excreted in urine and male axillary sweat and appears to be far more readily detected by women than men. The androstenone was sprayed on certain pre-selected chairs placed at random.

The results showed conclusively that women sat with increasing frequency in the sprayed-seat location while men showed an increased tendency to avoid it!

Nature gets a helping hand

David Craddock is a British entrepreneur who has made a lengthy study of the links between odours, emotions and attraction, as well as building a successful business based on the manufacture of smells which he supplies to industries throughout the world for varying purposes. He also has a small, but increasingly successful, sideline of selling male and female pheromones via mail order.

With David's help, I set up a tiny experiment of my own. While my own efforts could in no way constitute a representative sample of the human race, their results were extremely interesting (and amusing) for those involved.

My first experiment involved a spray of David's own product, Aeolus 7 + ('a blend of strong male pheromones', the bottle label stated), my son Danial and two of his friends, Matthew and Viv. All three young men are 18, good-looking and, on the whole, successful in their relationships with the opposite sex. The boys were asked to wear Aeolus 7 + and visit a nightclub they had never been to before and where it was unlikely that they would encounter anyone that they knew, and then report how they fared with the opposite sex.

All three 'got off with' the girls of their choice, they claimed, though I refrained (with great difficulty I might add!) from extracting the precise definition of this term on the premise that perhaps there are some things a mother shouldn't hear! Danial, it appeared, hadn't needed to make any moves at all because he was soon approached by a young lady who bought him a drink, asked him to dance, then immediately enquired whether he had ever been seduced!

Obviously, all three knew the supposed effects of what they'd been sprayed with, so it's conceivable that their success could have been due entirely to their confidence having received a 'chemical shot in the arm', as it were. On the other hand, as the smell was so revolting when first sprayed on (it really does smell like a combination of stale urine, old sweat and a distillation from a thousand unwashed jockstraps!), I wouldn't have been surprised if it had dissolved every ounce of their self-confidence before they were even out of the starting gate!

The next occasion came a few weeks later. This time, they were going out to a nightclub with a mixed party of college pals and they were specifically requested to make a mental note of any alteration they perceived in the behaviour of their friends towards them. What I was keen to discover was whether the pheromones would affect the attitude of any girls who might not have previously shown any particular romantic inclination towards any of them.

Again, all three 'scored', but only one of them with a girl who had previously appeared to dislike him, the other two receiving approaches from girls whom they already knew rated them fairly highly.

David Craddock describes male pheromones as being basically 'territorial' in that they are subconsciously used to claim a place or woman as a man's own particular territory, thus deterring any competition. Because men are considered to be the 'aggressors', David believes spraying a male subject with additional pheromones (to enhance his own production) is likely to attract women (who are supposed to be attracted to strong men provided they're not threatening in any way), but could have the opposite effect on men who, perceiving aggression but not knowing why, might in defence behave aggressively themselves. In the event, however, aggressive behaviour from other males – whether friends or strangers – didn't materialize in either episode described above.

Having concluded that little experiment (although the lads keep pestering me for more!), the next obvious step was to conduct one with women. And who better to start with than myself, I reasoned! I went to a nightclub in the company of two female friends, one who knew about the experiment and insisted on being sprayed with the female version of David's product, Aeolus 5 + (to help her on her 'scouting mission' for her fourth husband!) and one who was left in total ignorance of the whole exercise.

Unfortunately, the entire evening was not so much a disaster as a total non-event! My 'eager-to-be-wed-again' friend had several promising dances with a man she vaguely knew from her past, but he didn't ask to see her again. My other friend (who, by the way, looked very attractive in a tight leather mini-skirt) didn't even get spoken to by a man. And as for me, well, I got approached

all right – and by a cute guy who was at least twelve years younger
than me, too! The problem was, it wasn't my looks, my carefully
cultivated 'available look' or even the pheromones themselves
that proved to be the irresistible lure; for within ten seconds of his
opening line he'd disappeared . . . puffing on a 'borrowed' cigarette
– which was obviously infinitely more attractive than me!

But as I said before, my own little experiments were conducted
purely for the fun involved, therefore they don't really count.
However, none of us – doubting scientists or gullible consumers
alike – would deny that nature does appear to have harnessed the
power of scent to great effect, particularly when it comes to the
procreation of every living species. From the humble bee who
unwittingly cross-pollinates flowers in its insatiable quest for
honey to female pets who have to be locked indoors away from
the neighbourhood males of their species when they're 'in
season', the lure of that particular scent that signifies 'sexual
receptivity' is irresistible.

And a human being's susceptibility to scent manipulation has,
it appears, proved to be no different. Anyone who has ever
undergone the sensuously soothing experience of the ancient art
of aromatherapy in which essential oils distilled from plants and
flowers are massaged into the skin to treat ailments or to induce
feelings of relaxation or stimulation will attest to the remarkable
therapeutic powers such fragrances seem to possess.

Further proof that smells can manipulate emotions and moods
was found when experiments were conducted in cinemas in the
United States to ascertain whether it's possible to increase
popcorn sales by wafting the aroma of freshly-buttered popcorn
throughout the auditorium. Sales immediately doubled. It has
also been shown that plastic shoes and cars with imitation
leather upholstery show a sharp increase in sales when they're
sprayed with a 'real leather' scent. And most modern super-
markets which at one time bought in their loaves of ready-cooked
bread have now learnt the value of buying ready-made bread
dough and baking it in their own ovens purely because the aroma
is a formidable inducement to buy.

Our susceptibility to the subliminal, yet powerful messages that
scents convey is an exceedingly lucrative business for scent
manufacturers, many of whom have invested literally millions of
dollars on testing and proving that scents sell.

Following on from the success of many American direct
marketing companies' experiments in utilizing specific smells in
advertising and direct mail campaigns, David Craddock has used

his knowledge of pheromones and their likely effects to develop a spray that could, he says, prove to be the ultimate consumer-persuasive product. David's invention, which is based on the effect of human male pheromones when linked with mild aggression and fear, has already been subjected to a number of trials in Australia where it has been applied to letters sent to bad debtors to assess whether a slightly threatening subliminal odour could induce people to pay more promptly. The results so far have been so encouraging that David has taken out a patent to protect his product.

If such a method of painless and relatively harmless persuasion can conclusively be proved to work, it will provide yet more evidence that pheromones do indeed affect our moods, emotions, responses and behaviour in ways that few of us can even begin to comprehend.

However, the implications this could have for the unscrupulous future misuse of such scents could also prove to be too horrifying to contemplate. For example, it has already been suggested that mail order catalogues could be sprayed with an undetectable smell specifically designed to relax us, thereby making us more receptive to sales pitches. And American students, taking part in mock student elections set up to test whether pheromones can significantly affect the voting process, showed a remarkable propensity to vote in favour of a particular candidate when pheromones were used to reinforce the subconscious impression of dominance and leadership ability.

Take the concept one step further and the feasibility of mass mind-manipulation by unscrupulous dictatorships moves away from being thriller-book fodder and closer to reality!

Perhaps there's some comfort to be gained from the knowledge that in all the artificially constructed tests that pheromones have been subjected to, the one conclusive piece of evidence that keeps cropping up indicates that not all of us can be influenced by pheromones all of the time as so much depends on the concentrations used, the duration of the spray, the situation in which it is experienced, how individuals personally react and, at least as far as women are concerned, the concurrent phase of the menstrual cycle.

Nevertheless, that scents are a vital ingredient to our enjoyment of life cannot be denied. Nor can the fact that consciously or unconsciously our use of scents can influence how other people relate to us and, perhaps more importantly, how we relate to ourselves. So if the use of perfumes, aftershave and deodorants make you feel more confident about yourself, by all means use them. Particularly if your aim is to create a lasting impression in a personally important, though not necessarily sexual, situation.

Just as long as you remain aware that while artificially applied scents can be used to manipulate others' perceptions, when it comes to good, old-fashioned attraction, there's apparently nothing to compete with your own unique, natural scent which is potentially the most powerful attractant of all. For, as David Craddock says, 'Countless lives have been spent in search of the ultimate aphrodisiac when the answer's probably been under our noses all the time.'

Chapter 7

Love: Chemistry or Neurosis?

Love is something that, sooner or later, every single human being is likely to experience – and probably more than once in their lifetime.

We all understand the emotion of liking which stems from a positive evaluation of another person, and most of us can relate to the selfless, intensely forgiving love that a parent feels for its own offspring. But romantic love has so many different facets that it's often quite difficult for people to gauge how deep their feelings are for one particular person when measured against past feelings for others.

Few people know the difference between sexual attraction, deep lust, infatuation and love. All can arouse the same intense symptoms and often it's not until we've been freed from our obsession or preoccupation with the person who has aroused those emotions that we're in a position to assess the situation objectively.

Most people believe that it's impossible for anyone to be in love with two people at once, but ask someone who's in such a situation and they'd probably say only that each love is 'different'. The difficulty is that there is an essential dichotomy between sexual power and love inasmuch as it *is* possible to feel incredibly attracted to someone you know you do *not* love, in exactly the same way that it is possible to be strongly attracted to someone whom you do not even know and yet imagine that you love!

Conversely, we all know that it's feasible to love someone very much indeed and yet not find them sexually attractive any more.

This, unfortunately, is a common lament in many marriages when the sheer practicalities of earning an income in order to support a home, lifestyle and children can erode every trace of the romantic ideals a couple start out with. I've personally seen this happen many times with young couples who are inseparable, deeply in love and so certain when they marry that nothing will ever undermine the feeling they have for each other, only to find a few years and a few children on that the daily grind and constant pressure have effected a startling deterioration in their relationship.

Someone once commented that love was one of the worst reasons of all for marrying! And yet, certainly as far as the Western world goes, marrying for love is still one of our major goals. The question is, should we marry when we're still heavily influenced by the newness and wonder of being 'in love', or would we (and the divorce rate) do better to take a more pragmatic approach and refrain from committing ourselves until we're able to take a more objective view of our prospective partner? On the other hand, if lovers *were* able to be more pragmatic, wouldn't this mean that they're possibly not as much 'in love' as they'd like to think?

The many faces of love

Dr John A. Lee, an American sociologist, believes there are three primary and three secondary types of love which he has named according to their own typical style.[16] The first of the primary types – and the most intense – he has termed *eros* because it is both passionate and predominantly sex-based with a powerful sexual chemistry that draws people together in an all-or-nothing relationship. *Eros* relationships are often intensely exclusive and highly-charged emotional affairs in which the couple tend to idealize each other a great deal. *Eros* types are, apparently, sensuous, tactile, open and sincere individuals who are inclined to be verbal and get a great deal of enjoyment from experiencing intense emotions and sex.

Dr Lee has named the second type *ludus* (Latin for play or sport!) in which love is seen as fun and not to be taken too seriously. While *ludus* relationships are based on sexual chemistry too, it's usually not as strong as the *eros* kind and the pair tend to avoid becoming too involved or making any commitment to each other, preferring to keep their options open, to keep each other guessing and to be allowed to flirt and have affairs with others if they wish. *Ludus* types prefer casual, mutually enjoyable relationships but would rather steer clear of intense emotions and having their privacy intruded upon.

The third primary form of love, *storge*, Lee likens to a deep, caring friendship in which neither partner is totally preoccupied with the other, though they may well share many interests, hobbies and other pursuits. Couples who have this type of love usually have a great deal of mutual trust and gain most of their pleasure from sharing things such as building a home and raising a family together. *Storge* types tend not to become too preoccupied with their partners, often don't feel or show strong emotions and can be fairly shy about sex.

The three secondary types of love are identified by Lee as *mania* (meaning, quite literally, madness), *pragma* (practicality) and *agape* (charity and selflessness).

Mania lovers are possessive, jealous and very often obsessive (just like the character Glenn Close portrayed in the film *Fatal Attraction*). They're also highly insecure and anxiously dependent upon their partner, constantly fearing the possibility of rejection to which they may well respond with illness (either real or feigned). *Mania* types are usually highly jealous lovers who swing from being totally euphoric to utterly miserable, often for no good reason. But, if love fails to make them feel like this, then they are unlikely to believe they're in love at all.

Pragma lovers are often highly realistic people who tend to love through expediency rather than romanticism. These types usually choose the 'right' person from the 'right' background because they are likely to 'fit in', make a good parent or can bring other, highly-valued aspects to a potential union. *Pragma* types know what they're looking for and when they find it they rarely allow it to affect their lives unduly; they're sensible, dislike emotional scenes and, I'm afraid, tend to feel that no one is worth a great deal of sacrifice.

And finally, there is the *agape* love (probably the rarest of all!) who lives only to make his or her partner happy. Such people are totally selfless, genuinely expect little in return and will sacrifice all their own interests for their partner's; which, I suspect, is fine if the *agape* lover is a woman involved with an ambitious, powerful man, but, perhaps, not quite so desirable for men if it were the other way around!

But who's to say which type of love is right or wrong? Certainly many of us will come across a variety of them during the course of our lives and each will be equally important at the time for a variety of prevailing reasons. But the one we ultimately settle for in a permanent relationship will probably be the one that suits our own needs. And the basis of those needs will often have its roots in our upbringing, environment, social conditioning, experiences and, ultimately, in our unconscious needs for validation of the 'self'.

Few of us ever bother to examine or question how or why attraction and love begin and none of us are immune from its devastating effects, though most of us share the common assumption that the better looking are likely to be on the receiving end of love far more frequently than the rest of the world. And though we only have to look around us to see evidence that this isn't so, how many conversations do we still begin with, 'What *is it* that he sees in her?' or, 'How on earth could *she* be attracted to *him*?'

What man, on losing out in the love stakes to an apparently inferior example of overweight manhood with a beer-gut and balding head, has been able to accept qualities such as sense of humour, thoughtfulness or warmth as an explanation for a beautiful woman's preference for a less than attractive rival? Or, for that matter, what woman rejected in favour of a seemingly dumpy, frumpy specimen of femininity could ever comprehend the nature or the power of her rival's hidden charms to lure a man away?

Scientists explain love as a chemical chain-reaction while psychologists maintain that what we call love is merely a physical manifestation of our own subconscious neurotic needs. The fact is, there are probably as many theories to explain why, whom and how we love as there are types of love itself.

One theory put forward by Professor Fred Meeker who has recently completed a study on romantic involvements with students between the ages of 18 and 40 at California State Polytechnic University is that love is no more than a 90-day affair. He found that in the average romance passion starts cooling after an average of 90 days; he also found that the average length of most love affairs is just eighteen months and that with each 90-day period the strength of the initial passion is halved and halved again until, eventually, there's nothing left!

Well, that's a disillusioning thought for those of us who love being in love! However, to counteract that, there are some more comforting aspects that the experts have come up with. And one is that love keeps us healthy. According to Dr David McCleland of

Boston University, being in love can ward off coughs, colds and sneezes simply because the experience of being loved has been found to raise the concentrations of munoglobulin in our bodies – and munoglobulin is, apparently, the body's first line of defence against chest infection!

Many psychologists say that we all have different reasons for falling in love at different times in our life, but the most important factor that governs how, when and with whom we fall in love at any particular time depends on how ready we are at that given moment and how much we might be *expecting* it. For example, most single people's thoughts turn to romance when they're on holiday. That's because holidays are one of the few occasions when everything synchronizes; we have the time, the conditions are right in that we're warm, comfortable and relaxed, we're away from home enjoying a new experience (which, presumably, an enjoyable little dalliance would round off quite nicely) and, of course, we've got the inclination because we *anticipate* that something exciting should occur on holiday.

And that's why we often fall in love with totally unsuitable people whom we probably wouldn't look at twice back home! One reason for this might be the novelty factor; for example, it's easier to fall in love with a foreigner because they're so different from anything else in our experience that the interest factor is high. It's also much easier to contrive fantasies when the person seems to be exotic and to lead a totally different lifestyle from our own. If they don't speak our language very well, this can be an added excitement in that: (a) it can make us feel more powerful and in control; (b) it helps release our inhibitions, and (c) we can indulge ourselves in all sorts of flights of fancy and actually even mislead our lovers a little without any danger of them ever finding out!

Another reason might be opportunity. What happens here is that if the conditions are right and we're in the mood for romance but the choice of available men is limited, we'd rather lower our expectations and standards than miss out altogether.

In his book *Loving and Loathing* Dr David Lewis relates how this was put to the test some years ago by Dr James Pennebaker of the University of Virginia Psychology Department who asked a number of people in a bar to rate the attractiveness of members of the opposite sex. As the evening wore on and it got closer to closing time each individual was asked to rate the same people again. What Dr Pennebaker found was that the nearer they came to losing an opportunity to strike up a relationship, the higher they rated the available members of the opposite sex![16]

There's the theory of like attracting like and, to counteract it, the theory that opposites attract. There's a theory that we all have a hidden agenda based on social conditioning, early experiences and environment, and yet another that simplifies the subject by relating to it biorhythms. Astrologers believe love and attraction are in the stars, while Freud maintained that love is merely neurosis – an effective way of sublimating a sex drive which can never be wholly satisfied in a civilized society.

But theories do not alter the fact that the pursuit and experience of the 'big encounter' is one that consumes us all and that we all perceive the possession of true and lasting love as possibly our lives' single, greatest achievement. And yet, each theory could be worthy of greater inspection to anyone who wishes to understand where sexual power comes from and how it can be used.

Love is a drug

Several American scientists examining the subject of love suggest that the way we experience romantic love is often affected – and possibly even pre-determined – by biochemical activity involving the brain; that how deeply we fall in love and how long our relationships endure could ultimately be controlled by the levels of particular chemicals our brains produce. And that even the painful, recurring syndrome of loving too quickly and selecting the wrong people which can prove so psychologically damaging can be explained by the brain's production of a chemical they call the 'love drug': phenylethylamine (PEA).

Whilst conducting investigations into our neuro-chemical reactions, these scientists observed that when we meet someone we are attracted to and fall in love, certain chemical factors come into play and the intense passion we feel in the early stages of love can have exactly the same effect on our brains as a powerfully addictive drug. Or, as one eminent American professor of psychology described it, 'attachment is essentially an addictive phenomenon involving opiods'.

Opiods are the brain's equivalent of opiates, and experiments conducted with young animals have revealed that the symptoms of separation anxiety that would normally be displayed upon enforced removal from their usual habitat can be prevented by the administration of two types of opiates: clonidine (a drug used to reduce withdrawal symptoms in addicts) and beta endorphins, which are believed to be an inhibiting factor on the neural circuits connected with anxiety arousal.[17]

These findings provide the basis for the notion that attachment in humans might somehow be connected with an addiction to certain chemicals or 'drugs' that our brains produce when 'love' is experienced. This idea is not only intriguing, it also seems to carry quite a bit of scientific evidence to back it up and, if proven, could certainly provide one logical explanation as to why love causes us to indulge in totally bizarre and unpredictable behaviour, and also why we feel such deep emotional anguish (and sometimes even physical pain) when an affair ends.

That incredible feeling of tempestuous excitement which causes our hearts to pound, our legs to become like jelly and our mood to swing from wild euphoria to deep depression is, according to the 'drug' theory, entirely fuelled by the hormone adrenalin and the chemicals dopamine and norepinephrine. The latter two chemicals are, apparently, the main stimuli that excite the limbic region of the brain (which has been identified as the definitive 'pleasure centre'), thus causing us to produce more phenylethylamine. The more these chemicals are produced, the greater their subsequent 'drug-like' effects.

Anyone who might ever have experimented with amphetamines (or even 'slimming' pills) in their youth probably knows only too well that the rapid pulse, sudden compulsion to talk, excitement, anticipation, sleeplessness and lack of hunger one experiences with these drugs are remarkably similar to the effects of being in love. Moreover, it has been suggested that emotion depends on two distinct processes: firstly, the body has to be aroused physiologically in some way through hormones, drugs, exercise or even shock and secondly, once emotion has been aroused, we tend to classify it according to the situation we're in at the time. So, if our emotions are stimulated when we're watching a scary movie, we put it down to fear. If they're stimulated when somebody is telling us off, or making us feel guilty about something, we put it down to shame. But if they're stimulated when we're with an attractive member of the opposite sex, why then we call it love – or sexual attraction, depending upon how romantic, pragmatic or cynical we might be. Either way, or bodies respond with an increase in production of phenylethylamine (PEA) and adrenalin.

Adrenalin, sometimes called the fight-or-flight hormone, is produced by the adrenal glands in times of extreme stress, excitement or danger. It's also known to be highly addictive (as has been found with athletes and joggers who say they're hooked on the phenomenon known as the 'runner's high'). When they're secreting adrenalin, the adrenal glands also release cortisone which, when prescribed medicinally, has the side-effect of producing an increased sex drive and feelings verging on wild euphoria.

Dr Max Lake, a retired Australian surgeon and author, claims that love should be separated into three phases and that each of these phases is accompanied by the body's production of chemicals.

First comes the initial attraction and discovery of emotions of love which, he maintains, are fuelled by adrenalin and PEA. The second phase occurs when the initial euphoria has worn off, leaving the couple to settle down into a period of calm, romantic love. Chemically, this phase is accompanied by a flow of enkephalins (chemicals associated with comfort) which help to increase our capacity for illusion and lessen our experience of pain. Finally, there comes the established, loving relationship accompanied by the brain's production of endorphins, which, in turn, are associated with feelings of intense pleasure.

The chemical substances our brains release throughout each of these three phases are all known for their addictive qualities and, as with any addiction to a drug, our bodies are devastated when, for whatever reason, they are withheld.

Phenylethylamine is a chemical produced in the brain that has exactly the same effect on us as amphetamines. When we fall in love, or even when we simply receive approval, it has been found that the production of this chemical is greatly increased. Which could provide another explanation for the fact that an abundance of approval and love are such vital factors to our sense of happiness, emotional security and well-being.

Are chocaholics loveaholics?

The New York psychiatrist, Michael Liebowitz, also likens the euphoria of love to having a shot of amphetamine (the risk being that one can easily become 'hooked' on both) and believes that if we could only be educated and encouraged to understand how our own body-chemistry affects us we could all learn to form better, more loving and more enduring relationships.[19]

Curious to investigate these links between amphetamine-like responses and PEA, Dr Liebowitz administered a mono-amine oxidase inhibitor (an anti-depressant drug which suppresses the breakdown of PEA) to a volunteer whom he had previously diagnosed as a 'love-junkie'. After just a few weeks, Dr Liebowitz found that his patient's reactions to love were far less extreme and he no longer got so swept away with romance. In other words, the man's *urgent need* to be in love all the time had disappeared.

According to those who have researched the chemistry of love, even our most romantic and seemingly spontaneous gestures are not necessarily what they seem. For the greatest natural source of phenylethylamine is said to be found in chocolate and also, to some extent, in roses – two of the first things we tend to buy when we wish to express our love! This could also mean that women who indulge in a chocolate-eating orgy to comfort themselves when they're disappointed in love aren't just being pathetic, self-indulgent pigs (as so many people accuse them of being); they're merely instinctively providing themselves with an alternative source of the chemical their bodies need!

Whilst the link between chocolate and emotional responses may initially seem lighthearted and laughable, Michael Liebowitz and Dr Donald F. Klein, Professor of Psychiatry at Columbia University and Director of Research at the New York State Psychiatric Institute, have identified an affective disorder condition (hysteroid dysphoria), which largely – though not always – affects women, in which the regulation of PEA has proved to be a vital and integral part of the treatment.

In a paper jointly published by Liebowitz and Klein,[19] hysteroid dysphoria was defined as a 'chronic non-psychotic disturbance' involving repeated episodes of abruptly depressed mood in response to feeling rejected'. Characteristically, it appears, these women show a greater than average vulnerability to loss of love, spend much of their time seeking attention, approval and praise (particularly from romantic attachments), display a marked in-tolerance to personal rejection and, when depressed, dramatic-ally overindulge in chocolate and sweets!

Liebowitz and Klein noticed that the symptoms of increased energy and elation in response to approval, and the low energy levels, increased need for sleep and greater appetite common to these individuals are remarkably similar to the effects of stimulation and withdrawal from amphetamines. Therefore, they reasoned, it was entirely feasible that hysteroid dysphorics might simply be suffering from an unstable control mechanism that is incapable of efficiently regulating their levels of PEA.

Though research is still continuing, a pilot study which included double-blind trials indicates that hysteroid dysphorics do indeed respond remarkably well to treatment with certain mono-amine oxidase inhibitors which are known to regulate PEA.

However, for the benefit of those of us who have occasionally succumbed to the wild excesses of a chocolate binge (and who hasn't?), such behaviour shouldn't immediately be construed as an indication of a personality disorder like hysteroid dysphoria, as so many other extreme factors would have to be taken into account; it's probably far more likely to mean that in common with the rest of the world, you've just simply acquired a taste for the irresistible stuff!

Michael Leibowitz's research has not yet been able to crack the 'chicken-and-egg' conundrum of PEA inasmuch as he still hasn't been able to identify whether it is the *presence* of large amounts of PEA in the brain that *creates* a greater propensity to fall in love, or whether the *falling in love itself* creates the immediate *manufacture* of PEA. What is clear, however, is that the effects of PEA on a newly-in-love couple appear to be remarkably similar to the effects experienced by people who take LSD or Ecstasy, in that each partner often experiences an urge to break through their own normal ego frontiers in order to feel unity and oneness with the other.

To reduce the euphoric state of newly-found love to a chemical equation seems somewhat cold-blooded, unromantic and prosaic. But is it any worse than looking at love through the analytical eyes of psychologists and psychiatrists who maintain that that wonderful new man or woman who's just swept you off your feet and declared undying devotion is merely responding to a neurotic need to re-create a familiar pattern from their own childhood?

Love as neurosis

Love and relationships are, so psychologists say, our chief identity fixers. Through them our identities are validated and we receive clear evidence that we are worthy, acceptable beings.

We all grow up convinced that what we want and need is a secure, loving relationship that will ensure commitment, fidelity, warmth, friendship, understanding and support – but what we often experience is something quite different. And yet for many people, a series of similar damaging relationships indicates a recurring pattern of being attracted to the 'wrong' kind of people who treat them badly, let them down and fail continually to satisfy expectations or meet any of their needs.

Why? The dichotomy occurs, it appears, because there is a division between our conscious mind, which dictates our expectations and draws up our checklist of what we want, and our unconscious mind which retains the hidden agenda compiled by the unintegrated and unacknowledged part of our psyche.

Dr Robert Young is an American psychotherapist currently living and practising in London, who firmly believes that when we first fall in love, we are actually in love with an internal object or fantasy:

'Most people, when they marry, are marrying someone who is a manifestation of something in their inner world; it could be a negative thing but it *is* a figment of their unconscious.

'The important thing is what occurs when they discover that their partner is *not* the person they had imagined them to be. What usually happens is that they either learn to accommodate themselves to who that person really is, or all hell breaks loose.

'In most committed relationships, such as marriage, surviving the accommodation process occurs. But because we don't marry *real* people – we marry an unconscious fantasy person – so disillusionment is a natural prelude to either the maturation of the relationship, or a living hell, or divorce.'

Bob Young believes that in many cases people will do their damnedest to become what their partner needs or desires and this is when the modification process usually comes into play. But modification can be either a positive force, as when people begin to examine themselves and come to terms with reality as opposed to ideals, or a negative force as when they try so desperately to become what they think their partner wants that they lose all sense of 'self', as with co-dependency.

Co-dependency, a word that has been coined to express a person's elusive search for self-esteem, exists when a person looks to a potential partner to fulfil all the hidden needs that they have not fulfilled within themselves. In other words, when a person has little self-esteem or a low sense of self-worth, they can become so isolated from their own feelings that they will spend all their time looking to others for clues as to how they should behave in order to give *them* what *they* want, and in doing so become more lovable themselves.

We all know people who change their personality, their appearance and their interests with each relationship they have, in the vain hope that if they become what their partner wants the relationship will last. Usually it doesn't, but the pattern goes on repeating itself until the subject loses touch with himself or herself and settles for a relationship that confirms their own subconscious feelings of worthlessness, or begins the process of attempting to understand *why* they needed to submerge their own personality in someone else's in the first place.

For many of us, our patterns are learnt in childhood. How we are perceived and treated by our parents and families influences how we perceive ourselves. What then happens is that each relationship we pursue is a subconscious attempt to re-create a familiar pattern which, while it may not be ideal, does provide an element of security in that it is one we can recognize and, in a bizarre way, feel comfortable with. For example, a man who grew up with a domineering mother may state that he detests domineering women and is looking for a submissive wife, but then wonder why all the submissive women he meets fail to turn him on.

In fact, what's probably happening is that the 'internal' pattern he has learnt to feel comfortable with is exerting a subconscious influence by ensuring that he's *only* attracted to dominant females. So while he's busy blaming his failure with relationships on the fact that he can't find a submissive female who appeals, his own subconscious is actually *preventing* him from finding them appealing.

This pattern of subconsciously-conditioned repetitive behaviour is, psychologists say, the reason why so many daughters of alcoholic men end up marrying alcoholics themselves, despite all their vows to steer clear of such men.

One theory about love that nearly all of us can relate to is that of like attracting like, and the reason we're prepared to give it more credence than other theories is because we only have to look in the newspapers to see the evidence.

Couples such as Don Johnson and Melanie Griffith, John McEnroe and Tatum O'Neil and even Prince Andrew and the Duchess of York, all bear such a physical resemblance to each other that they could more easily pass for brothers and sisters than husbands and wives.

So what is it that attracts us to people who look like ourselves?

Mirror image

Psychologist and author Dr David Lewis agrees with the notion that a scale of attractiveness exists and that as we all have a very good idea of our own place in the pecking order, we're more likely to select a partner who ranks alongside or close to us on this scale because it enables us to justify our own right to look the way we do.

Moreover, in choosing a 'mirror image' of ourselves, we are also selecting a partner with whom we can feel more comfortable, on the assumption (albeit subconscious) that if a person shares our physical characteristics, they're far more likely to share other characteristics, too (sterotyping coming into play yet again!).

Similarity, it would appear, has a very important role to play in determining just who we become attracted to and numerous experiments conducted over the years have confirmed that the people we learn to like the most are those whose attitudes, opinions and outlook most closely mirror our own.

Our processes of attraction to potential lovers and partners are remarkably similar to the processes we use when selecting our friends and though it cannot be denied that appearance is the first step towards attraction, once acquaintance has been made it is similarity of attitude that is often a deciding factor when it comes to pursuing a relationship.

In cultures that place little emphasis on love (such as those most commonly found in Asian countries) parity of background, status, religion and views is considered to be paramount. Interviews with subjects of marriages arranged under these conditions not only confirm the importance of this belief but usually illustrate that when these conditions are met, love often follows.

Love with the proper stranger?

A similarity of background, views, opinions and attitudes not only makes life that much easier and more comfortable, it also reaffirms *us* and what we believe in.

If we get chatting to strangers, perhaps at a party or some other social gathering, after we've exchanged polite chitchat and established some sort of base from which to make an opinion of the other person, we very often move on to discuss fairly non-controversial issues in which we exchange views and opinions. If we find that the other person shares many of our views, we feel the meeting has been a positive and rewarding one. If, on the other hand, we find that we are diametrically opposed in many of our beliefs and opinions, we tend to view the person negatively. What then happens is that we'll either get involved in a lengthy discourse in an attempt to justify our beliefs and perhaps alter theirs or, being the polite people we are, we'll decamp at the first opportunity. The whole experience will then be viewed by us as positive and stimulating, or negative and off-putting.

If, on the other hand, we're incredibly sexually attracted to the person, we might not let our opposing attitudes interfere with the possibility of a short-term relationship because our goals are not necessarily such that would seriously affect us in the long-term.

If a primarily sex-based relationship such as this does become more important in time, depending on how involved our emotions are, we'll often dismiss the dissimilarities by cloaking them in fantasy and thus fooling ourselves into placing little emphasis on what our partner really believes because, at that stage, we can't handle the hidden implications of acknowledging those beliefs.

Love at first sight

Fantasy can play a large part in love and sexual attraction and many people have gone in hot pursuit of someone who physically fulfils their fantasies only to count the cost later when things go wrong – as they invariably do.

Brigitte Neilson captured 'Sly' Stallone simply by sending him a photograph of herself. Within a short time they were married – and within an even shorter time they were divorced.

Rod Stewart has openly admitted that Britt Ekland was a fantasy figure of his youth. When she became reality he couldn't help but follow his dream – and we all know what happened to them! Similarly, when Stewart saw Kelly Emberg in a TV commercial he just had to pursue her.

The actor Terence Stamp fell in love with the model Jean Shrimpton when he saw a photograph of her when she was at the height of her fame in the '60s. He chased her, she duly fell in love with him and they had a relationship, but it didn't last.

Simon Le Bon fell in love with his beautiful international-model wife Yasmin just from a photograph, saying 'her face just got to me'.

Michael Caine first caught sight of his wife Shakira in a coffee-bean commercial on TV and immediately decided that here was the woman he wanted to spend the rest of his life with. They're still together and, from all accounts, are still madly in love and blissfully happy.

Richard Gere fell in love at first sight with his current girlfriend, model Cindy Crawford, at a barbecue given for Elton John. 'When I first caught sight of her I was stunned. I thought she was absolutely gorgeous. Since that day we haven't been separated at all', raved Gere, who's so smitten with Cindy that he's talking about marriage and fatherhood *and* he's taken the proprietorial step of banning her from baring all for *Playboy* magazine because he can't bear the thought of other men ogling his property!

Orson Welles fell for Rita Hayworth at first sight, Prince Rainier of Monaco did the same with Grace Kelly and more recently Princess Diana's brother Viscount Althorp fell head over heels with, and married, model Victoria Lockwood.

It has to be said that men tend to fall in love at first sight far more than women. Whether this is due to the fact that women are more reticent about chasing men they like and are, therefore, more reluctant to make their infatuations known, or whether they're more pragmatic about their infatuations and don't try to turn them into reality, is not quite clear.

I personally know two men who claim they fell in love at first sight *and* 'knew' immediately that the object of their respective affections was going to become their wife! Statistics lay great odds against that one, but what's interesting about both these examples is that the odds were doubly compounded because *both* men met their future wives on a continental holiday – which is all the more surprising as holiday romances are considered the *least* likely to last! Twenty years later, however, both couples are still happily together.

So how do the experts explain this phenomenon of falling in love with the visual image of a person and how high do they rate their chances of lasting success?

Well, the evidence does suggest that men *are* far more likely to make decisions based on what they *see*, and because their fantasies about females are more visually-oriented, when they see someone who comes close, they're more likely to get hooked. There also seems to be some truth in the notion that, as men see themselves as the dominant sex, a woman's personality is far less important – presumably because they believe they can always mould her to their taste! Which might explain why so many older men fall for the young brainless bimbette types!

The singer Billy Joel, who married top model Christie Brinkley (once labelled 'the most beautiful girl in the world'), supported the theory that looks are far more important to men than women when he said: 'Men don't have to be devastating. They don't even have to be good looking – look at me. Women have to be attractive. Men are so much shallower; they go for surface things, they go for a beautiful body and beautiful face.'

Perhaps looks aren't that important to women because so many are brought up to look for 'other qualities' such as strength, reliability, kindness, etc. (probably because they've had it drummed into their heads for centuries that they're the passive sex and, as such, they're likely to be at the mercy of their men so their future happiness depends more on these qualities than looks!), so they're less likely to get carried away by a romantic ideal.

Women also have another reason for not chasing men too hard, of course, and that's because when they do men assume that the conquest has already been made so consummation automatically jumps to the top of their agenda, while all a woman really wants at this stage is an opportunity to get to know him better.

Some men have a propensity for a certain 'type' of physical appearance, like Rod Stewart whose ladies have all looked as if they'd sprung fully formed from a remarkably similar mould, while others appear deliberately to embark on a process of moulding their woman of the moment into an exact replica of a previous love. Stranger still, a few have even been known to turn their women into replicas of themselves.

Elvis Presley, for example, fell in love with his wife, Priscilla, when she was just an adolescent and then began to dictate the way she should dress, how much make-up she should wear and even the colour and style of her hair. Pictures released of their wedding reveal that Priscilla Presley looked exactly like a feminine version of her husband! And when David Bowie was married to his wife Angie, it was almost impossible to tell them apart. Which seems to take the mirror-image effect to the ultimate conclusion of narcissism.

Film-maker John Derek chose to have relationships with identical women not twice, but three times: the three major loves of his life, Ursula Andress, Linda Evans, and latterly Bo Derek, are all physically and facially remarkably similar. As did French film director, Roger Vadim, who fell in love with a cover photo of the very young Brigitte Bardot and then displayed her on screen in such a provocative way that millions of other young men around the world fell in love with her, too. When that marriage ended his next two loves, Catherine Deneuve and Jane Fonda, bore such a close resemblance to Bardot that the world's press wondered aloud whether Vadim was reliving his youth.

Perhaps he was. Because psychologists do explain this propensity towards 'cloning' as a subconscious method of attempting to recapture earlier fond memories of positive emotions. These might primarily be of parental or familial origin or even stem from a physical similarity to a significant early love. And though in some cases the resemblance might not be obvious to the people involved, it doesn't go unnoticed amongst those who know them well.

All the world loves a lover. And everyone loves the experience of being in love. There's nothing quite like love for making you feel good about yourself, or for awakening the senses. Somehow, everything seems so much more real when you're in love; colours are brighter, sound has more clarity, food tastes so much better (when you're past the stage of not being able to eat at all, that is!) and everything seems so much more sensuous and enjoyable. We're also much nicer people when we're in love.

So what are we trying to achieve by analysing it? It can't take the pain away when love dies, and it certainly can't make the experience of love any better than it already is. Loves come. Loves go. And if analysis helped eradicate the pain, would we be any happier? Particularly if, in eradicating the pain, we also removed all the pleasure.

There's only one thing we should do with love – experience it to the full for as long as it lasts, and simply enjoy it! And if it should last, why then, we should all be very careful never to allow ourselves to lose sight of *why* we fell in love with that person in the first place.

Chapter 8

What Men Want from Women – What Women *Think* They Want

Men and women spend their entire lives labouring under mis-apprehensions about what the opposite sex finds sexy and what they want from each other, both in and out of bed. It's not surprising really, when one considers that we've never been very good at communicating with each other; preferring to believe the powerful messages the media promote than to confront the very people we all work so hard at attempting to understand.

Even before we are old enough to be affected by the subconscious conditioning processes of media messages, we have our parents, our siblings and our peers all quietly influencing our minds with stereotypes, ideals, false assumptions and subliminal preconceptions about the opposite sex.

Is it any wonder, therefore, that we grow up with such damaging, *fixed* notions about what *they* want from *us* and what *we* expect from *them*? To look at our history, to observe the two sexes both together and separately, to eavesdrop on conversations in all-male enclaves or on women's-talk in powder rooms, an alien could be forgiven for believing that men and women really don't *like* or even *respect* each other very much; or for marvelling at the sheer effort and energy we expend trying to get physically close to each other in an attempt to merge our thoughts, our lives and our hearts.

Psychologists, scientists and authors have carried out years of research, analysed literally millions of questionnaires and published whole libraries of works devoted to engendering within us all a deeper understanding that goes beyond the merely biological reasons for attraction between the sexes. And yet still the myths and misconceptions are passed on down through the generations to confuse, to exasperate and, ultimately, to frustrate us all.

The simple, unremarkable and incontrovertible truth is, men and women were born to seek, love, nurture – and procreate with – each other. The fact that still, after centuries of doing precisely that, we have not yet found a way to break down the barriers of communication and discover more *about* each other, must surely be due to the enormous social and political pressures that ensure we believe what we are told and deny each of us opportunity to prove otherwise.

So, what *do* men want from women and how does what they want differ from what women *think* they want? And what do women want from men? This chapter and the next explore both sides of the great divide between each gender's needs and desires and the common assumptions each sex makes about the other. Hopefully, both sexes will benefit from the information provided and both will gain greater understanding of each other. For understanding and knowledge are the vital keys both need in order to have sexual power and to give each other what they want.

A mutual need

Men and women have always known they *need* each other. That's a basic, fundamental fact of life. But the other beliefs each holds; where do they come from and how did they begin?

Men have always believed at heart that women just want to capture them, spoil their fun, control their lives, rule their homes, take charge of their possessions, and spend their wealth. And they are convinced that the tools women employ to ensnare them are their bodies and their inherent female weakness.

Women are brought up believing that they are worth nothing without a man whom they can live through, who will protect them and provide for them while they go about the vital business of mistressing their homes and bearing and mothering their children. And women are conditioned to believe that the only tools they have at their disposal to ensnare the opposite sex are their bodies which *are* men's weakness.

Or, to put it another, cruder way: women are taught that men want sex and the price they pay is love and marriage; women want love and marriage and the price they pay is sex.

In these assumptions, men and women are, of course, perfectly accurate. For that is how we have both been biologically programmed. In the primitive days of pre-history when the survival of the species depended solely on the three basics of food, shelter and procreation there was no conflict. Man, being physically stronger, was assigned the role of hunter and protector, so food and shelter fell within his brief; woman, because of her sole ability to bear children, thus became the nurturer dependent on man to provide the necessary food, shelter and protection.

Nowadays, despite the fact that there is much evidence to suggest that many women are totally eschewing marriage and motherhood in favour of a career, the majority of men still seem to persist in the belief that all a woman wants is a wedding ring on her finger and a husband on her arm.

The paradox is that sociologists have long known that marriage can actually damage a woman's health while men seem positively to thrive on it! Married men live longer, are generally happier, and are far more likely to be judged as mentally healthier than single men; whereas married women fall sick more frequently than their husbands, are often less fulfilled than their single working sisters *and* are twice as likely to be the motivators of divorce than men! And it is men who are more likely to fall apart emotionally when their marriages break down.

What women *think* men want

Most women, if asked to draw up a list of what men find physically sexy in a woman would probably produce a list not too dissimilar to this:

- A sensuously long, preferably blonde mane of hair (that never needs the benefit of curlers).

- Large breasts that will always retain their upright firmness (without benefit of a bra).

- Long shapely legs, slender thighs with well-defined muscles (and no cellulite!).

- Come-to-bed eyes.

- A pouting mouth and sexy lips (that never emit sounds unless they're cries of ecstasy or murmurs of assent!).

- An impossibly perfect, shapely but very slender figure that's fashionably and sexily (though decently) clad (but with erotic lingerie worn underneath for the benefit of *his* eyes only).

And the other qualities men seek in wives? Well, many women subscribe to the view that *all* men want a woman who is:

- Bright (but not so intelligent that she'd argue with his views).

- A cordon bleu cook.

- A whizz at home-making.

- Permanently headache-free.

- Always ready and eager for sex.

- A perfect mother (who nonetheless *never* forgets that her husband's needs must *always* be paramount).

- Totally supportive.

- Ever understanding.

- Capable of multiple orgasms.

- And who never – and I mean *never* – ever nags!

You don't believe that? Jerry Hall does – unless she had her tongue tucked behind one of her perfect, million-dollar cheekbones when she said recently: 'There are three secrets my mother told me. Be a maid in the living room, a cook in the kitchen – and a whore in the bedroom. I figure as long as I have a maid and a cook I'll do the rest myself. You can only do so much in one day.'

If you're still not convinced, try putting that list in front of a group of men you know, and then a group of women and compare the results.

What men want

And when you've done that, try comparing the men's responses to the results of a survey conducted with young men and women in the United States, which sought to establish a list of potentially desirable attributes in a prospective partner, which revealed that the average (American) man's list reads (in order of priority) something like this:

- Physical attractiveness.

- Ability in bed.

- Warmth and affection.

- Social skill.

- Home-making ability.

- Dress sense.

- Sensitivity to others' needs.

- Good taste.

- Moral perception.

- Artistic creativity.

Whilst it's probably true that most women *hope* that men rate other qualities as highly (or almost as highly) as they do the physical, it's also true that if they found one who said he did, they'd have great difficulty actually *believing* him. Which is not surprising when you look at that list!

And who can blame them when the myths and misconceptions have been instilled into them from the cradle and society has only served to reinforce them? And the situation isn't helped by the young boys and men they first come into contact with, who (though *they're* only responding to their *own* particular brand of conditioning) tend to spend most of their adolescence chasing their own private fantasies before experience, maturity and, of course, reality modify their views.

For reality, as we all know, is very different from fantasy and while it is certainly true that, in general, men do display a strong physical attraction to overtly sexual women, when it comes to choosing a potential mate they are a darn sight more selective – which is precisely what our mothers have always told us!

This was borne out by the results of an experiment carried out in the USA in which a number of men were requested to rate a selection of women in photographs as potential wives.[21] While all the men confessed to being attracted to the sexier women photographed in skimpy bikinis and provocative poses, when it came to rating the same ladies with a permanent relationship in mind, they opted overwhelmingly to give higher ratings to the photographs of women who were attractive though less spectacularly sexual and more conventionally dressed.

The experimenters concluded that what a man finds attractive in a woman is not biologically determined, but depends on his age, social class, personality and *what he wants the woman for*. But women have always known that anyway!

Women's roles within society have changed far more dramatically over the last thirty years or so than have men's – a fact which has, quite understandably, led us to challenge and question all our preconceived notions with regard to what we've always *believed* women want versus what they now *seem* to be demanding. Granted, much has also been written about 'the new man' who seems to be less afraid of showing the gentler side of his nature than his forebears and is prepared to become more fully involved with domestic matters, but many women who've been looking report that they're still not easy to find.

However, there is no doubt that change is slowly occurring in the way men and women are beginning to relate to each other but, as the popular saying goes, 'the wheels of change grind exceedingly slow'. And change can also be a terrifying prospect. So for every man who welcomes women achieving equal status in the working environment, there are probably two who feel deeply threatened by this prospect.

Time and again when I asked male interviewees whether women who were powerful in business turned them on, I received a very definite 'No' for answer. And few women will be surprised to hear that the ones who *did* admit to finding powerful women sexy were usually older, more successful in their own careers and, therefore, presumably confident enough not to feel threatened by the competition.

In 1989 *Cosmopolitan* magazine conducted a survey of 500 men between the ages of 20 and 35 to discover what the modern British man thinks and feels about love and marriage today.

The survey results indicated that the majority of younger men do now appear to have more respect for women's rights, are more aware of women's sexuality than anticipated and feel far less threatened by it than most people imagine. Moreover, these men were romantic, wanted to fall in love, marry and have children when the time was right and displayed a positive attitude towards working women.

In response to questions about initial attraction, while 34 per cent of the men said they were first attracted to a woman's face and 18 per cent her figure, a further 34 per cent agreed that personality was more important. Older men, it appears, are more likely to emphasize personality and younger men are less likely to be eyeing a woman's breasts than assessing her style of clothes.

When it comes to bodies, however, the findings definitely appear to reinforce the view that men's predilections come in a variety of shapes and sizes, with 31 per cent expressing a preference for tall, slim women, 28 per cent favouring the short and petite, 14 per cent opting for the athletic look and a further 14 per cent liking them 'rounded and curvy'. Although it's interesting to note that the ones who preferred the latter type tended to be older!

Many women believe that men want women to dress sexily – unless they're married to them, in which case a woman is allowed to dress sexily *only* for her man and only then, of course, in private. So how did *Cosmo*'s 500 men vote on that one? Surprisingly, over 40 per cent said they found 'provocatively dressed women' a turn-off, although another third admitted they would definitely be attracted. When it came to overall appearance, including make-up, the overwhelming majority stated a preference for the natural look. But what they said they disliked most of all are women who smoke and drink a lot!

However, the survey also revealed that the one subject the sexes still seem to have disparate views on is sex. Here, the good news was that as many as a third of the sample confessed they were looking for a long-term relationship, while the bad news was that 41 per cent just wanted to have a 'good time'. And this, despite the fact that over 90 per cent expressed the belief that love and sex go together!

Of course, statistics and surveys often don't prove very much at all, particularly when the random sample taking part is such a small percentage of the male population as a whole. But what this particular survey highlights is that while men (or at least, those surveyed) definitely *do* eventually seek commitment in a relationship, they still see nothing wrong in sowing their wild oats with a multitude of one-night stands along the way. And women really don't have the right to blame them or hang labels upon them for it, because they're only responding in the way in which they have been *biologically programmed*.

The problem with making generalizations about men (and the same does, of course, apply to women), is that once a consensus of opinion has been formed very little allowance is made for the evolutionary process. By that I mean that none of us stay the same for ever, and what we believe and how we behave during adolescence and early adulthood is subject to change as we grow older, mature and, naturally, have further experiences. The truth is that the cherished myths we absorb from those who influence us when we're young (which are usually reaffirmed by some of our early experiences with the opposite sex) may well not apply later on in life.

Yes – it appears to be true that men, for the most part, *are* influenced more by their balls then their brains during early adulthood. And, yes – it's equally true that their powers of perception and discernment are clouded by the need to compete with their peers and to prove themselves in an acceptable – and stereotypical – macho manner. But let's not forget that it's precisely *because* they live and function in a man's world and have been subjected to their own social pressures and role-defining conditioning processes that they find the predominantly female ideology of commitment and fidelity so alien and unimportant to them – *at that stage of their lives.*

Nowhere are men and women further apart than when it comes to their fantasies about each other. Ask a man to describe his favourite fantasy and it would undoubtedly begin with an incredibly beautiful, erotically nubile woman whose sole aim is to seduce him. This fantasy figure will possibly take him by surprise and probably take all the initiative too. She'll be sexily clad in basque, suspenders, black stockings and the briefest of panties, and the things she would do to him would incorporate every sexual dream he'd ever had. She'll be eager, voracious, have multiple orgasms and undoubtedly praise him as the best lover she's ever known.

And here's where we get to the interesting part – because when they're asked to describe what happens *afterwards*, most men *can't*! Why not? For the simple reason that there *is* no *afterwards*. Men's sexual fantasies are complete and entire in themselves and they concentrate exclusively on the sexual act itself.

Mention the word 'hormones' to the average man and he'll probably recoil in horror at what he considers to be a matter relating exclusively to 'women's internal plumbing'. But men's behaviour is governed as much by their hormones too. The hormone that governs the male sex drive is testosterone, and while this hormone does also regulate a female's libido to a small extent, the levels to be found in the female body are far less significant. Testosterone is the likely cause – though not necessarily an excuse – for a male's ability to separate the physical act of sex from his emotions. Certainly it is understood that women are far more likely to be unfaithful when they are feeling *emotionally* deprived; whereas the root cause in men is usually *sexual* deprivation.

Furthermore, it also appears that the amount of testosterone present in males determines how aggressive they will be, not only in the bedroom, but also, surprisingly, in the boardroom, and (social conditioning and opportunity factors aside) experts say that it is this, probably more than anything else, which accounts for the fact that men still – and perhaps always will – outnumber women at the highest levels of any given profession.

With age everyone inevitably matures and experiences a redefinition of their attitudes, goals and values. Hence, the selfish, chauvinistic young stud will often mature into an enlightened, more sensitive older man. The danger is that, by the time this metamorphosis occurs, a woman's initial preconceptions have usually had ample opportunity to become permanently fixed, or at the very least, difficult to shift.

Women's assumptions about men

Men and women, thank God, *are* different and neither sex should hope or imagine that it will ever be otherwise. All we can ever hope for, and work towards, is a deeper understanding of why and how each sex thinks, feels and reacts in the way they do – and then learn to make allowances for the differences in behaviour that naturally stem from the way each has been programmed to *be*.

So let's now have a look at a small sample of the most common assumptions many of the women I interviewed made about men, and then at any evidence that may exist to prove them wrong.

1   Men prefer women who are hard to get.
Surprising at it may seem, all the studies that have put this idea to the test have proved that this is rarely so. What has been found is that men tend to prefer women who prove to be *selectively* hard to get, i.e. *hard* for everyone else, but *easy* for themselves.

2   Men prefer to be the initiators of sex.
Some do, most don't, although a lot of the time it depends on whether the relationship is in its infancy or whether it's been established for some time. The fact is, men are just as susceptible to self-doubt and fear of rejection as women. Therefore, if a woman makes an obvious play for a man it can be immensely flattering and it doesn't always automatically mean he'll 'have his way' and then dismiss her as 'loose' either. Men need to feel loved and wanted, particularly when they're in a committed relation-ship and a woman's persistent failure to initiate sex can make a

man feel guilty and ashamed of having a sex drive, that he's being manipulated in a way that he cannot comprehend and maybe even cause him to question his own abilities.

3   Men get married just to please their women.

The major misconception (held by both sexes) about marriage is that men see it as something that can only enhance a woman's status and can only demean theirs. Men may resist the *idea* of marriage for a time but there is no doubt in the minds of sociologists that whether they agree with the institution or not, marriage not only *suits* men's emotional needs, it actually provides positive benefits in terms of their mental and physical health as well as their average life expectancy.

And if that's hard to believe, one only has to look at the statistics relating to divorce and second marriages to learn that most divorce cases are brought by *women* and that 41 per cent of divorced men remarry within two and a half years as opposed to only 25 per cent of divorced women.

4   Men don't have the same emotional depths or needs as women.

Wrong again. Men may not *display* their emotions as openly as women, but only a fool would suggest that they don't possess them – a fact which has been borne out by several surveys, which have revealed that as many as eight out of ten men cry when they're emotionally upset or moved.

5   Men are essentially polygamous.

Whilst it's true that men were biologically designed to be polygamous, there is increasing evidence to suggest that once a commitment is made, today's men value fidelity very highly indeed – though it has to be said that there is still a dichotomy between their hearts and their loins that may never be fully resolved. It's not that men can't *see* how much infidelity hurts their partners, it's just that they sincerely believe that if the loins are engaged, but the heart's not in gear, infidelity doesn't count!

It seems unlikely that women will ever change their minds on *that* one, but it *could* prove easier for us to understand if we were able to view men as dispassionately as sociologists and psychologists do; accepting that though men are highly advanced animals, they are still motivated by primitive passions in the same way all animals are. And most male *mammals* are naturally polygamous in that when their sexual activities are confined to only one member of the opposite sex their libido often shows a marked decline.

6   Men are nothing more than grown-up little boys.

A tricky one, this; for example, few women can ever understand a grown man's love of sport (particularly when he still insists on turning out every week to play football when it takes him a week to recover from the exertion), as it seems so juvenile and – well, non-productive. Women are also outraged at being termed the weaker sex when most men will faint at the thought of childbirth and take to their beds with the slightest cold! Suffice it to say that men hate the patronizing attitude most women display towards men's favourite sporting activities, their periodic bouts of ill health (which women call hypochondria) and they particularly dislike being referred to as 'overgrown boys'.

Satisfying men's needs

Alexandra Penney, who wrote the book, *How to Keep Your Man Monogamous*, maintains that men don't necessarily stray because of something their partner has or perhaps has not done so much as to fulfil certain basic, primary needs within themselves that are not being met. These range from a need for acceptance and a need for variety to intense sexual frustration, sheer boredom or simple curiosity.

She's also firmly of the opinion that it is within the power of every woman to satisfy all her man's needs (if the desire is there) through simply feeding and nurturing 'man's hungry ego'.

A volatile statement, indeed! So, before a chorus of female voices is raised in protest at the suggestion that it's up to the woman in a relationship to assume the mantle of guardian and become 'keeper of the flame', let me state now that *their* turn to be heard and represented comes in the next chapter.

Personally, I feel the only, and to my mind the most fundamental, problem with men is other men – and, of course, women. But in order to clarify that statement, it's necessary to look even deeper into the structure of society itself where it all began.

We know that men are biologically programmed in a different way from women. We know that society places different, and possibly even harsher, pressures on them than it does on women. But how many women have seriously attempted to understand what makes men the way they are? Or, for that matter, encouraged and allowed them to be the way many of them would secretly like to be?

From the moment boys are born they are virtually denied the right to have emotions. They're taught to be competitive, manly and tough. They're encouraged to believe that 'winning' and 'scoring' are the name of the game, that overt displays of emotion are signs of weakness (and therefore to be abhorred) and that to take their rightful place and stand shoulder to shoulder (or even head above) their peers requires that every one of them conforms to precisely the same rigid standard of what represents 'true' maleness as dictated by society and all other 'true' males.

Denied from boyhood the kind of expression that is actively encouraged in girls, it shouldn't surprise us if, by the time they're grown, many men feel isolated in – and very often from – their inner emotions when almost the first lessons they learn are how to dissociate emotion from reason, then emotion from sex and, ultimately, emotion from love. Winning, whether it be at sports, in business or with women, rules their lives, not necessarily because they *want* it to, but because they have been taught that it's the only stick they can use to beat insecurity and anxiety into submission.

Cut off from their emotions, afraid (and denied the right) to express their more vulnerable inner selves, perhaps we shouldn't question why some men turn their eyes towards women with fear and mistrust, but rather pose the question: Is it women they fear and mistrust? Or is it that they fear and mistrust what a woman might lead them to discover about their own vulnerability?

Believe it or not, men are romantics at heart. What women mistake as thoughtlessness or pragmatism is often just diffidence in disguise, and though many men might think to send their lovers flowers and buy chocolates it often genuinely doesn't occur to them be more wildly extravagant or imaginative. What women fail to recognize is that very often a man's most practical gestures, such as cleaning our cars or fixing up our homes, are *to them* romantic in their origin, because they stem from a desire to please. Okay, so they often get it wrong, but how are they to know what women want and need if we don't spell it out?

Clearly, there's enough material to write an entire book on the subject of men, but fortunately (or unfortunately, depending upon which side of the great divide you hail from), there simply isn't room. So let's just finish this chapter by taking a look at what seems to turn the majority of men off – and then what turns most of them on!

What not to do – if you want to wield sexual power over men

In response to the question, 'What turns men off?', I received such a wide variety of responses that, rather than list them all (and give a large number of women a massive complex in the process!), I've selected the most common annoyances and irritations:

'Constant nagging,' said Paul, a 35-year-old bricklayer from the north of England, who interprets his wife's nagging as dissatisfaction with what he's doing and how he's behaving. 'It's criticism, isn't it? And no man likes that.'

'Women who say yes when they really don't want to,' said Peter, a single American writer from New York.

'Women who seem to be eager for sex and then act as if they're *only* doing it for *my* sake, or worse, that *I* ought to be grateful,' complained Joe, a single Canadian who is currently working as a barman to earn enough money to continue his travels around the world.

'Women who kiss and tell – publicly or privately,' stated Neil who, as lead singer in a band which once had a minor hit, became a victim of gossip. 'Women complain about guys who boast about their conquests to all their mates, but women can be just as bad. Some of them think nothing of spending hours on the phone with their girlfriends analysing and discussing their intimate moments with their boyfriends and comparing notes on performance!'

The other men I spoke to also claimed that they were turned off by women who are:

- Neurotic
- Strident
- Insecure (because they hate having to give constant reassurance)
- Constantly putting themselves down
- Manipulative – playing them off against other men
- Needy: 'if you loved me you would . . .'

- Vain (even though they're often vain themselves)
- Moody
- Emotional blackmailers (in order to get their own way)
- Obviously upset, yet say 'nothing's wrong'
- Cold and unresponsive
- Fond of talking all the time about *other* men
- Always saying 'I love you just the way you are' but never cease trying to change them
- Unable to cope when the going gets tough
- Gold-diggers and obvious heart-breakers
- Superior

How to turn men on

All men are far more easily – and instantly – influenced by the visual; they're naturally more turned on by the sight of bodies than women are. And the body that turns them on doesn't have to be perfect, it just needs to conform fairly closely to their individually conditioned ideals.

All men love sexy underwear, soft and slinky fabrics, stockings (particularly when they're black) and suspenders – though quite why this should be few women really understand.

All men are attracted to women who display an interest in them – possibly because they perceive the interest as a signal that they're less likely to be rejected.

Most men are attracted to feminine women, though not necessarily to clinging vines and whilst it's true that strong, successful, outwardly capable women can frighten some of them off, if they discover that beneath such a woman's cool, independent exterior lurks a softer, more vulnerable streak, the combination of ice and warmth will prove remarkably appealing.

Most men can't help melting when faced with the Monroe type of vulnerability and wide-eyed navïeté, particularly if they perceive a potential for eroticism and sensuality.

Many men have a preference for long hair over short (and soft, natural hair over starched coiffures) because they believe it implies softness, sensuality and, possibly, even abandonment (probably a legacy of adolescent fantasies woven around the famous cliché-scene in which Miss Prim and Plain removes her specs and hairpins to allow a cascade of luxuriant hair to transform her into 'My God, Miss Jones, you're beautiful!').

All men prefer well-cared-for women to the unkempt (except when the well-cared-for woman tumbles unkempt from *his* bed after a night of glorious passion). Most men do *not* appreciate a woman emerging from the same scenario looking untouched and unmoved.

Some men who are turned on by power, and strive hard for it themselves, find successful women sexy but it's fairly true to say that manual types and those lower down the socio-economic scale would be frightened off.

Contrary to popular opinion, bimbos and bimbettes appeal to only two types: those who'd be frightened off by successful women, and opportunists who look no further than the next lay.

All men find it incredibly sexy when a woman is spontaneous, honest, unafraid and unashamed about her sexual needs.

All men like women who have a sense of humour, who don't take themselves too seriously and who aren't afraid of laughing at themselves.

And finally, all men are turned on by a woman who is *obviously turned on by them.*

Chapter 9

What Women Want from Men – What Men *Think* They Want

Ask any man to tell you what he thinks women want from men and his first response would probably include a number of tired old clichés such as marriage, money, control, etc. etc., *ad nauseum*. If pressed further, his second response would undoubtedly include much demented flailing of arms and perplexed scratching of the head, followed by a comment along the lines of: 'God knows! Women are unfathomable and it's beyond the capabilities of *any* man to understand how their minds work!'

Sounds familiar to all you nonplussed men and frustrated women out there? You bet it does! Because men seem to be in a permanent state of puzzlement when it comes to women, and women simply cannot comprehend why. As far as women are concerned, you see, their needs are amazingly simple and providing they're being met they're perfectly content to behave like pussycats. The problem is, most men are intensely suspicious of pussycats, as they're all too well aware that felines have a nasty tendency to unsheath their claws precisely when it's least expected.

To counterbalance that viewpoint, many women feel they're victims of a sinister conspiracy specifically designed and orchestrated by males to ensure that every male takes as gospel the hoary old myth that women are unpredictable, illogical, dangerously emotional creatures who are best kept at arm's length.

What's more, they also feel it's a conspiracy that's constantly being perpetuated in male society through frequent gatherings together in pubs, bars and locker rooms; by brief indulgences in the ancient ritual (no doubt passed down by their fathers) of raising their eyes to heaven, shaking their head in puzzlement and repeating the chatechism quoted above, before the enigma of women is resolved and ruthlessly relegated in favour of the latest – and far more interesting – football scores.

What women want

The very *first* – and the most important – thing women want is for men to take the time to *listen* to them. Not with a head buried in the sports pages, not with half an ear open and one eye on the clock because they're late for the office or a drink with the guys; but to listen *seriously* and *understand* what they're trying to say – *in spite* of the fact that what they're saying might sound incomprehensible, overemotional or just plain silly to a man's ears.

And the very *last* thing a woman wants from a man is to have what she's saying wrongly interpreted as hysteria, criticism or downright stupidity.

Women, you see, are born communicators when it comes to their emotions and they have an intense need to discuss their feelings. They also have one advantage men don't possess: the advantage of a highly-developed intuitive sense that allows them to 'know' when something's right or wrong. Women rarely criticize men without very good reason (at least not to their face), because most of them have inherited their female antecedents' belief in the fragility of the male ego which they've been programmed to guard with the utmost compassion and sensitivity.

The real difficulty between the sexes arises out of our misguided wishes that men could be more like women and women could be more like men. It seems strange that after thousands of years of living and loving together we're still hopelessly incapable of realizing how impossible that would be.

It's not my intention to upset any radical feminists, because I've personally never subscribed to the view that either sex is superior to the other, but I do believe that we're *different*. And everything I've ever read and learnt has only served to confirm and strengthen that view.

Quite simply, men and women have different basic skills, different modes of operation, different methods of digesting and dealing with information and different ways of responding. Whether this is due to social conditioning, as some schools of thought maintain, or whether it's something more fundamental than that, such as the way in which our brains themselves are programmed from conception, who can say? The fact remains that intense research has shown that there are *many* unalterable variations between men and women – apart from the obvious ones.

Science has acknowledged that women generally have better hearing and memories than men. They also learn to speak and read earlier, are more fluent, have more patience and compassion and are generally much tidier than men.

In fact, when it comes to anything to do with the senses, it has been found that women out-perform men in almost every area. Which is why they're so much better equipped to deal with matters relating to intuition, communication and relationships, whereas men outshine women in virtually everything to do with things, theorems, abstract thinking and spatial ability.

The other basic differences are that men are innately more dominant, more decisive, more aggressive, more mechanically-minded and better at judging distances and space. They're also more interested in sex than romance and more money-orientated than women. Women, though, are naturally better at judging people's characters and managing others, are far more interested in people than money and seem to need love and romance more than sex.

Neither sex is superior to the other, we just have different specializations, different strengths and weaknesses and different mechanisms that dictate the way we think, act and respond. If we add to that list men's and women's different biological mechanisms, different types of hormones and different social conditioning processes, it becomes obvious that we're wasting precious time wanting them to be more like us and wishing we could be more like them when what we should be doing is finding a way to understand each other better.

What men *think* women want

Most men seem to think that when it comes to physical attraction women *still* want broad shoulders, hairy chests, well-developed muscles and, of course, that large penises are the main attributes to be found at the top of most women's shopping list.

Not surprisingly, they're wrong – particularly when it comes to the size of the penis, which has *never* been considered even remotely significant by anyone but themselves. And that's *not* because women are uninterested in sex, but because women are wise enough to know that size has nothing to do with satisfaction.

Even as impressionable teenagers, women don't pay much lip-service to a man's looks – image, yes, clothes, certainly, street-cred, absolutely. If a young guy's got those three, then looks are immaterial. And though I'm not denying that women do find handsome men attractive, it's more likely to be due to an objective appreciation of symmetry and beauty (or even envy) than out of desire for the man himself. Because, believe it or not, most women are deeply suspicious and mistrustful of beautiful men.

What women want

Not surprisingly, therefore, the female equivalent of the list of desirable attributes sought in prospective partners that was outlined in the previous chapter reads something like this:

● A record of achievement

● Leadership qualities

● Skill at his job

● Earnings potential

● A sense of humour

● Intellectual ability

● Attentiveness

● Common sense

● Athletic ability

● Good abstract reasoning

The first thing you'll notice about this list is that looks don't feature anywhere at all – it reads more like a well-thought-out shopping list for a potential husband than a quick résumé of what women find attractive in men generally. That's because when women think about their ideal man they are, of course, thinking about the man they want to spend the rest of their lives with and not a temporary fixture (the list of qualities sought for *that* being of an entirely different nature – as we'll find out in due course).

Because women mature much earlier than men, by the time they reach their early twenties (even though they may not necessarily be seeking marriage in the short term) they have very clearly-defined ideas about what they'll be looking for when they are. Something which men don't normally establish for themselves until much later on.

Women are far more interested in the qualities of a man than in his external appearance. And although they are often influenced by looks while they're looking, when it comes to marriage they seek more practical, solid qualities that they know they can depend on. That's why women can, and often do, fall in love with an outwardly unattractive man – a fact which few other men understand.

Women, it has to be said, place far greater emphasis on character, kindness, dependability and sense of humour than men ever give them credit for.

Of course, it's equally true that they're also programmed sub-consciously to seek a strong, healthy specimen who's in a position to make life comfortable and secure for them so that they can create the right environment in which their children can grow up safe and protected. Which possibly explains why some of them are capable of putting practicality first and marrying for comfort and money instead of love.

A world of difference

When women and men first meet, their aspirations, thoughts and expectations are quite different from each other's. Several years ago a British TV documentary programme investigated this very subject. The camera crew had special lenses fixed to their cameras (similar to rifle sights) that demonstrated the precise spot the subject's eye was focused on. What then ensued was an amusing illustration of the first points on a female's form that the male subjects' eyes were drawn to, and likewise the other way around.

Men, it was demonstrated, tend to look briefly at a woman's face, then travel lingeringly over the body to take in the legs; back up to the breasts, where they'll pause for several seconds and finally back to the face – for a while. At several intervals during conversation a man's glance will briefly repeat the exercise, unless he's standing so close that to do so would appear too obvious.

When tracking a woman's gaze at men she finds interesting, the technique illustrated that women tend to look first at the face and particularly the eyes, then flick briefly over the body but quickly return back to his face, the major source of interest being a person's eyes.

Of course, when we first meet someone of the opposite sex, we have no idea whether or not they're likely to become permanent fixtures in our lives so at that stage any opinions or thoughts we might form will be of a purely speculative nature. And this is where the sexes differ, because at this precise moment of the encounter we can only react to our biological programming.

What happens on a mutually attractive first meeting, therefore, is that the thought uppermost in most men's minds is likely to be: 'Could I get her into bed?', rapidly followed by: 'How soon?' Whereas the kind of thoughts that run through women's heads are: 'Mmm, I wouldn't mind getting to know him better', and, 'I wonder what sort of person he really is?'

The problem is men tend to base their behaviour towards all women on the assumptions they all commonly hold and on instinct. They also tend to act before they think. They can no more help the way they respond and react than they could give birth to babies, so they really shouldn't be criticized so harshly for thinking base thoughts because, as we've surely digested by now, they're only responding to primitive biological programming which dictates that they impregnate as many women as possible throughout their fertile years. But what we *can* hold them responsible for is their easy acceptance of – and strict adherence to – the notion their society fosters that while women may be both decorative and useful, they are essentially *objects*.

Women, however, who have been designed to seek one exclusive long-term relationship because they are only capable of being impregnated every twelve to eighteen months or so, are motivated by the need to ensure that their chosen mate will stay with them long enough to shelter, protect and provide for their progeny.

With easy access to contraception, neither sex has cause to worry any longer about untimely or unwanted impregnation, but centuries of subconscious programming cannot be eradicated overnight and we can't avoid being unconsciously motivated by such deeply ingrained, innate primary processes.

The truth is that for the majority of men sex will *always* funda-mentally be a *purely physical act*. And their orgasms are centred totally around the penis. That's not to say that a man's emotions are never involved in the sex act because clearly they often are, particularly when he's making love to a woman for whom he cares deeply. What it does explain, however, is why men find it easier to succumb to the temptation of infidelity than most women.

Jerry Hall publicly acknowledged that fact when she said, 'I think men can have sex with anyone. For them it's like changing the TV channel, like a toy, something to pass the weekend.' But, as we all know, acknowledging a fact intellectually and accepting it emotionally are two quite different processes. Perhaps the next time Mick Jagger steps out of line we'll find out whether it's Jerry's intellect or her emotions that govern her response!

For most women, fulfilling sex only occurs when their emotions are involved and, therefore, sex is a deeply intimate, *personal* event, and whereas men's orgasms are primarily centred around the groin, a woman's has the capacity to encompass her entire body *and* her 'self' – physically, mentally and emotionally. That's why, when women fantasize, they focus mainly on situations with which they can identify such as relationships, etc. While men, who tend to be far less discriminating, can hop from one fantasy object to another and rarely, if ever, include relationships in theirs.

Unlike the typical male fantasy (outlined in the preceding chapter) which begins and ends with seduction and the sex act itself, women's typical fantasies tend to be woven around a whole complex scenario that will involve romantic encounters, prolonged seduction, intensive foreplay followed by ecstatic love-making and the (possible) requisite declaration of eternal love. And if they don't end with a hand-in-hand stroll into the sunset, they'll probably extend right up to the church door itself.

For the most important thing women can never get enough of is romance. And the second thing they can never get enough of, is passion – particularly when it's wrapped up in love and romance.

The only other type of fantasy women enjoy is the one in which they're swept off their feet and caught up in the unexpected maelstrom of a passion over which they have no control, because that gives them permission to strip away their inhibitions and really let themselves go – which is something that many women clearly still find difficult to do.

Shirley, a 34-year-old wife and mother who works part-time in a record store, thinks men (including her husband) are basically selfish animals who find it impossible to understand why women aren't as rampant, ready and raring to go as they usually are: 'I can't believe that they really don't know that it's virtually impossible for women to automatically turn on at the sudden tweak of a nipple and quick grab of the groin.'

Sadly, there are still a lot of men around who fail to understand that apart from the crassness of such an approach, a woman's biggest enemy in bed is time. Men can switch on to sex in seconds. Unfortunately, women can't. Men can become aroused on their way home from work by a sexy voice on the radio, a glimpse of mini-skirt on the street, the sight of a pretty girl, or even by something totally unconnected with sex itself. And they never seem able to understand why the wife they drag into bed to satisfy a need she had no part in inducing seems unwilling or unable to respond.

Women very rarely enjoy being taken unawares. And while they can be spontaneous, for them to function normally they often need to feel that it's *they* who have turned the man on, and even then they often need to be stimulated to arousal by displays of tenderness and plenty of foreplay. It's not something they can control, and they're not deliberately putting the moment off just to torment a man; they simply can't help having a much longer fuse. For a woman sex is definitely more cerebral than physical in origin.

For a woman to be truly fulfilled by sex, she doesn't necessarily have to be in love, but she does need to feel relaxed, safe, confident in her choice of partner and to know that he has some form of positive feeling for her. That's often why when women sleep with a guy on a first date, it's rarely because they find him irresistible and more likely to be because they don't know how to – or don't like to – say no. Particularly if they imagine (or hope) there might be a future in the relationship.

Professor Hans Eysenck and his colleagues have recently compiled a great deal of evidence about sexuality and the sexes which confirms that no matter how far we have come in terms of liberating women in sexual terms, nothing can ever alter the fundamental, biological differences between women and men.

Men are more motivated by physical feelings such as lust, while women are more motivated by emotional feelings like love. Men think about sex between one and six times an hour, while women tend only to think about it when they're confronted with the prospect. Men can get obsessed with sexual gratification, women don't because for them it's not so much physical as emotional. Most men would be unfaithful given the opportunity (and a guarantee that they wouldn't be found out) and are turned on by novelty, while women can't understand why a man should want to stray if their love life is happy. Women can enjoy sex as much as men, but the conditions have to be right inasmuch as it has to be at the right time, in the right place and with the right (for 'right' read 'special') man.

Men, I regret to tell you, will always be able to disassociate their emotions from sex, but women probably never will. That's why men can have one-night-stands, but if women do they usually want more. Men can also sleep with strangers, but the very thought would probably give most women nightmares.

Evidence to support this came from one American experiment conducted with college students to assess how many of them would be prepared to sleep with someone at first meeting: 75 per cent of the men approached with an offer accepted, while all of the women declined.

Professor Eysenck's research further revealed that on average men's sex drive is 12 per cent greater than women's and they're also generally more interested in unconventional love-play than women. Women, on the other hand, receive greater pleasure when they are playing the role of passive partner being stimulated totally by foreplay. No matter how liberated we feel after more than thirty years of the Pill, women still have a sneaking suspicion that the old double standard will always apply and that we'll eternally be damned if we do and yet still be damned if we don't.

Old habits die hard; particularly the old habits acquired at our mothers' knees. They didn't mean to be unkind or to confuse us, we know, but even so, the legacy their mothers passed down to them which they, in turn, passed on to us still influences our subconscious minds when it comes to the subject of men and how they like their women to be. For centuries women have been taught by their mothers that it is wrong to contradict or compete with men. Men, they warned, don't find strong, opinionated women attractive.

Farrah Fawcett, who has, in her time, been rated as one of the most beautiful women in the world, confessed in a recent newspaper interview that the reason she won't marry her long-term lover, Ryan O'Neal (with whom she has a four-year-old son) is because 'there are certain rights a woman loses when she becomes a wife and vows: "I will obey my husband." ' As a child growing up in Texas, Farrah Fawcett was taught that women should never be outspoken and though she excelled at athletics, her mother would often warn her that she wasn't supposed to beat men at sports! So deeply was she influenced by the 'little Southern woman' ethic that she's only recently admitted that when she was married to Bionic Man, Lee Majors, she actually allowed a clause to be written into her own working contract stipulating that she had to be home in time to have her husband's dinner on the table! Not surprisingly, as she matured and gained enough confidence to reject the idea that women were born to serve men, she and her husband drifted apart and, eventually, they divorced.

However, despite her persistent refusal to marry O'Neal, they are, she said, a committed family unit. She also acknowledged the fact that it was O'Neal's supportiveness, sense of humour and deep sensitivity which not only drew her to him in the first place, but still underpins the fabric of their relationship.

Supportiveness, sense of humour and sensitivity are undoubtedly three of the most potent attraction-factors for the majority of women. It doesn't matter how handsome the competition is, or how well he performs in bed, when it comes to choosing a mate for life and a father for her potential kids, these three qualities will win a woman over any time.

Of course, if we're not talking about permanency in a partner, then for a large percentage of women almost *anything* can prove to be fatally attractive – from a man with a roguish sense of humour and laughing eyes, to a little lost boy whom they can mother for a week or two. And the more closely he resembles the very kind of man our mothers warned us to avoid, the more tempting it is to take our chances and have our once-in-a-lifetime wild fling. (Though at the time, we won't believe it's just a fling!)

And quite rightly so, too. For in my opinion, every woman should try the forbidden at least once in her life, because in doing so she'll learn more about men than her mother would ever want her to know.

Men find it very hard to understand how women can be so attracted to 'bastards', particularly if they've been brought up to treat women with consideration. So the other thing about women that men ought to know is that there is nothing more appealing to a woman's ego than the notion that *she* is the only woman who can reform a rogue.

Women want the perfection of the early days of a romance to last for ever and because they put so much more effort and emotion into their relationships they can often feel bitter and disillusioned when it doesn't. On the other hand, they can also accommodate themselves remarkably well to settling for warmth, understanding, affection and respect in marriage when the romance is gone. Contrary to what many men believe, women have a very practical streak in them. They're also far more realistic and much tougher when it comes to ending unsatisfactory relationships.

Men often accuse women of being fickle, which probably is true some of the time. Certainly research has shown that, before the age of about 20, women fall in love much earlier and far more often than men, but once past this age, it's the men who *fall in love* more easily and the women who fall *out of love* quicker!

Pauline, a 42-year-old housewife and mother of two small children, told me that, in her opinion, men and women ought only ever to come together in order to procreate: 'After that I think the men should live on their own and leave us free to bring up the kids. When you consider how little involvement some men have with child-rearing, we'd probably all be far better off!'

Pauline's list of things she'll never understand about men would, if printed, cover several sheets, but the thing she dislikes the most, she says, is their arrogant, patronizing attitude: 'Why is it that when men gather together it's called having a "discussion", while when women gather together it's called "gossiping"? I really hate that attitude, particularly when we all know that they love gossip, too and, in fact, are every bit as fond of bitchiness (though they refer to it as back-stabbing) as they claim women to be.'

It's true that mature women tend to look upon men as little boys, but when you consider that the majority of women find maturity through motherhood, perhaps it becomes easier to see why. Men become fathers, too, but the change this makes to their lives is not nearly as radical. They've always felt responsible for their wives, and to add one more responsibility doesn't have such far-reaching effects. For a woman, the consequences of motherhood and the intense devotion she often feels for her offspring can have overwhelming and far-reaching consequences in her attitude to *everything*.

Power, or the lack of it, is something else that affects women's feelings strongly. And when you consider that as a rule they're brought up to *wait* politely to be asked, and discouraged from being assertive, aggressive or pushy in their approach to men, it's not surprising that many women say they feel as if they have none.

Nineteen-year-old Katie, who's training to be a computer

programmer, said that she disliked intensely 'the idea that when we meet an attractive man we have to wait for him to make the first move. Sitting by the phone waiting for calls that often don't come can be really humiliating.'

In virtually every stage of the dating and mating game women feel that it's men who have control. Many also complained that they were 'expected' to make love 'for his sake' even when they didn't feel like it; although, to be fair, when questioned closer on this subject, more than a few admitted that they didn't actually *know* whether their men 'expected them to make love', or whether the guilt feelings came from within themselves.

Several women mentioned how much they love to be cuddled (and so do some men, of course), but many also said they got annoyed when their men got aroused, seeing cuddling as a natural prelude to love-making.

With regard to the workplace, most women said they don't want to compete with men, they just want to be given the same opportunities. They also said they don't want to be patronized or pawed by the men they work with, and they particularly don't want to be treated like their bosses' wives; it's surprising how often women found themselves in a situation where, no matter what position they occupied, they were still expected to make the tea!

Most of the working women I spoke to were in agreement on the subject of respect for their abilities and still found they weren't accorded anywhere near the same level of respect that is given to men – though they encountered this attitude amongst younger female employees too! They also felt that it was grossly unfair that there's still so much disparity between salaries.

Women dislike the double standards that are applied to certain qualities that are respected in men and often derided in women. If they're energetic and dynamic, they don't want this interpreted as tough and pushy. If they show compassion they don't want to be treated as soft, and if they're firm, they don't want to be called hard. And when they present new solutions born out of their lateral-thinking approach they don't want them to be rejected out of hand as 'crazy female logic'.

Women don't want to take over, they just want to be allowed in; but if they're capable of taking over, they'd just like to be allowed to do so in peace and with all the respect due to them for their knowledge, experience, qualifications, ability and superiority – not over all men, but obviously over the ones with whom they work.

Men's assumptions about women

And now for some of the more common assumptions that men tend to make about women:

1   When women invite a man in for coffee, they're really inviting you in for sex.

Sorry, guys, you're wrong. Some women might use coffee as a euphemism, most don't. The fact is, women worry a great deal about what men 'think they mean', which probably does more to inhibit them than anything else. If a woman has enjoyed her evening out with you, it's just possible that she'd like it to continue a little longer. It's also possible that the invitation means only that she's ready to proceed to the next stage which, to her, consists of kissing, cuddling, maybe even a little petting, but not necessarily sex.

2   Women who dress sexily do it to tease men.

Wrong again. Women often dress provocatively to please them-selves and to *attract* men, but there's a world of difference between teasing and attracting. Of course, it's also perfectly possible that they're wearing sexy clothes because they have sexy bodies and showing their bodies off makes them feel good. Another reason to consider is that women dress more for other women than they ever do for men!

3   When a woman says she has to stay in to 'wash her hair' she really means she doesn't want to see you.

Again, not true. Some younger women may make excuses rather than hurt a man's feelings, but not many grown-up women would use this childish excuse. Besides, you might believe them and ask them out again, which means they'd have to make up another excuse. No, most women, if they wanted to put a guy off per-manently, would be far more inclined to drop some comment about her 'fiancé' into the conversation so that he'd think she was already spoken for.

4   Women *need* men.

Some do, some don't. Certainly when Germaine Greer said. 'I'd like to have a man around – a very small one. He'd be about 18 inches tall and I could keep him in a cupboard and bring him out when I needed him,' she was echoing what many women have said to me, which is, 'the only man worth having is a disposable one'. And as we've already learnt, there are enough statistics around to indicate that women get by perfectly well without a permanent man in their lives. I think, therefore, it's time this one was modified to: 'Women don't necessarily *need* men, but they *do* like to have them around somewhere.'

There are, of course, many more widely-held assumptions men make about women (as indeed there are the other way around), but if we started to list them all, this would go on for ever. On the other hand, there's a whole series of books just waiting to be written about what men want and what women need . . .

So, as with our chapter on men, and in the hope that the men are still reading, let's conclude with a look at what turns (most) women off – and then what turns them on.

What not to do – if you want to wield sexual power over women

The overwhelming majority of women I spoke to are turned off by men who are:

- Arrogant
- Surly
- Chauvinistic
- Disrespectful to women
- Cold
- Humourless
- Crass
- Badly behaved
- Patronizing and treat all women as lobotomized bimbos

They're also turned off by men who want them to be clones of their mothers, though they don't mind occasionally mothering them; by men who take them out to dinner and then expect 'payment' before dawn; by men who say, 'I'll call you' when they don't; by men who break dates at the last moment; by men who treat them as useful accessories in order to boost their own egos in the eyes of other men, and by men who ignore them when they're with their friends.

In addition, they're turned off – and confused – by men who translate their signals of interest into an automatic assurance that they'll jump into bed or who insist on interpreting plain friendliness as a sign of something more; by men who sulk but won't discuss what's upset them; by men who give them the silent treatment; by men who carp and whine; by men who *assume*, and by men who boast about their sexual conquests to all their friends.

Women are turned off by weak men they can manipulate, by wimps, by overly-vain men (it was Coco Chanel who said, 'Hell hath no vanity like a handsome man'), by dirty men, by meanness, by 'mother's boys', by obvious men, untrustworthy men and men who compliment too much too soon.

And finally, here's a warning that all men should take to heart: women are *totally* turned off by any man who's unbelievably stupid enough to utter the immortal words, '*How was it for you*?' Because if he doesn't know how it was for her, then he couldn't have been paying that much attention!

How to turn women on

Women can be attracted to almost anything – the colour of a man's eyes, the shape of his hands, the timbre of his voice, his sense of humour, the way a man moves or his experience, knowledge and/or intellect.

Women are turned on by tenderness, by conversation, by communication and by the knowledge that a man is *really* interested in them.

Women are turned on by men who appear to possess strength of character, power, authority and control wrapped up in an aura of unattainability – and they'll go weak at the knees at the first glimpse of softness and vulnerability in a man, particularly if they feel that the only chink in his armour is for them.

Women can be turned on by touch, by smell, by a gesture or even a look. They're also turned on by compassion, by understanding, by subtlety and by warmth.

Women adore men who make them laugh or who are artistic, creative or poetic. They also have a weakness for generosity – not because they're acquisitive (well, maybe some of them), but simply because they're truly delighted when they receive evidence that they're appreciated, loved and thought of.

Women are turned on by romantic men who'll hold their hand in the street, whisper sweet nothings in their ears and do all the things that show they're not afraid to tell the world they're in love with them.

And, finally, every woman's dream man is a man who acknowledges her views and opinions as being important, who takes the time and the trouble to understand how she feels and thinks, who *really listens* to her (that's vital), who worries about her, comforts her, cherishes her, adores her, protects her, indulges her, remains faithful to her and desires her passionately and possessively yet *still* treats her as a worthy, independent, articulate, interesting, intelligent and *equal* partner. Particularly if he also happens to be caring, considerate, sensitive, romantic, passionate and yet infinitely tender in bed!

But if she fails in her search to find this elusive paragon she'll invariably settle for warmth, fidelity, consideration, respect, reliability, humour and good sex. And be content with her fantasies for the rest!

Chapter 10

Power, Money, Men and Status

Power, the kind that controls corporations, heads dynasties and influences world leaders, is immensely attractive and infinitely seductive to women. But whether this is because it signifies absolute omnipotence and immeasurable confidence, or simply implies the possession of limitless resources and incalculable wealth has never been quite clear.

Most women, if asked what they find so compellingly attractive about powerful men, would probably refute the suggestion that it's money or the status that counts, although how they can say that is beyond most people's comprehension when it's virtually impossible to find an instance where one appears without the other two.

For wealth, as we all know, can purchase power and powerful people invariably generate wealth. Which is why even the most underprivileged can scale the social heights if they are prepared to work hard in the pursuit of power and accumulation of money.

For the same reason, struggling pop stars who have no clout before a mega-hit can instantly find themselves welcomed in places they were thrown out of the day before, courted by people who previously considered them *non grata* and suddenly deferred to and hero-worshipped by all who, but for their new-found power, wouldn't even give them the time of day. The possession of power, however little, can not only elevate one to the status of demi-god, but also dramatically increase one's own sense of self-esteem.

Men chase power as if it were the crock at the end of the

rainbow, and many women, given half a chance, would too. Powerful men, for some strange reason, also appear to be incredibly highly-sexed. But is it the high sex drive that also spurs them on to score in every other area of their lives, or is it the acquisition of power that fuels the libido?

John Kennedy's sexual appetite is reputed to have been gargantuan (and the seemingly never-ending procession of women who happily passed through his arms and quickly in and out of his bed is legendary), a fact which he not only appeared to take for granted but was apparently able to dismiss as of no consequence by explaining that if he didn't have a woman for three days a terrible headache would ensue!

Senator Gary Hart's libido proved to be the death of his political career, while Donald Trump's not only contributed to the break-down of his marriage but rocked his entire empire, too.

Tycoons like Onassis and Khashoggi were famed for their ability to attract beautiful women who were often powerful in their own right, too. And it's not only the corporate and political sectors which seem to be afflicted by this phenomenon, because stories abound about all kinds of successful men – from artists such as Pablo Picasso and Salvador Dali to judges, film directors, rock stars and writers. And even religion provides no protection, as was demonstrated by the evangelist preacher, Jim Bakker – a man who, perhaps more than most, should have been aware of the dangers of succumbing to the flesh!

Such compelling, dynamic sex drives are the last thing we would expect in men whose working schedules are so tightly-packed and require so much more energy and input than the average man's, that we could more easily understand the reverse effect on their libidos.

To many women, power is the ultimate aphrodisiac, but does the same apply to the men who wield that power?

It's tempting to explain it by saying that no man, however rich, powerful or successful, when faced with a constant stream of available, willing women would be able to resist. But that can't be the answer, because sooner or later the novelty-aspect would surely begin to pall. And even if the brain remained eager and willing, the very fact that many of these men are past their 'sexual peak' ought to ensure that the flesh should inevitably become weak.

The chemistry of power

The fundamental key to these men's prowess in the battlefields of the boudoir and the boardroom is, it seems, to be found in the levels of the male hormone testosterone. For testosterone is not only responsible for making men male, it also governs their libidos and their aggressive streaks. Hence, when a man experiences a sense of accomplishment or achievement, as when he scores a winning goal or pulls off a major business deal, testosterone levels in his bloodstream will rise and so also could his desire for sex.

What happens biologically is that when a man faces danger, stress, threat or any other potentially stressful situation, adrenalin floods into his bloodstream to provide him with the impetus for fight or flight. If the conditions in which he experiences threat persist for any length of time the effect is likely to drain his energy, upset his nervous system and could even lead to illness or depression. In these prolonged circumstances, sex will be the last thing on a man's mind, as has been proved in cases where men faced with constant stress, redundancy, financial pressures or other threatening situations have complained of temporary impotence and/or partial or total loss of libido. But when the stressful situation is short-lived, and the man emerges victorious, adrenalin is then replaced by the hormone noradrenalin, which has been found to have an effect similar to a spark plug in that it stimulates the brain's pleasure centre and sparks off the production of testosterone.

The more dangerous, competitive and frightening the situation, the more adrenalin, noradrenalin and testosterone a man will produce.

Which could explain something that has puzzled most ordinary folk for years: such as how come so many celebrities, VIPs and recognizable people stupidly take chances in their personal lives that could potentially have such disastrous repercussions on their public lives? And why, when they're aware that the tabloids will go to any lengths to expose the moral failings and sexual peccadilloes of the rich, powerful, important and famous, don't the potential victims do everything in their power to avoid being caught out?

The respected judge who's a closet transvestite, the pop star who's gay or bisexual, the politician with a mistress or three, the captain of industry with a penchant for corporal punishment, have all become clichés because they're exposed so easily and with such monotonous regularity that the public could be forgiven for becoming bored with their sordid scandals and for muttering the time-worn phrase, 'they should avoid playing with fire if they don't want to get burnt'.

Though no one excuses such behaviour, perhaps now we're more able to understand why, if their actions truly are governed by such wild fluctuations in their hormonal patterns, powerful prominent men have little power to control it – although it's rather ironic when you consider that the very power that gives them their competitive edge could also be the ultimate cause of their downfall!

A man cannot necessarily control the production of adrenalin, noradrenalin and testosterone, as the body will naturally produce it in response to external situations. But it is possible for a man to 'switch on' his own body's production at will, through several means.

The first, and the most obvious, way would be to deliberately invite and encourage competition. That's not to say that he should provoke aggression or confrontation because that could only lead to negative and possible even harmful behaviour. What he can do is encourage competition through playing sport with other people, or even through exercise which he can do alone. Apparently even cold showers and swimming in an icy cold sea will do the trick, as shock is another means of flooding the bloodstream with noradrenalin.

The influence of power

Women unfortunately, don't have access to the same facility to generate an instant 'turn-on' within themselves. Nevertheless, many women do get turned on by the evidence of power. Some psychologists say this is connected with Darwin's theory of evolution which ensures that only the best and strongest of the species survive and with women's primeval instincts to select the most superior specimen of malehood as a mate. And what better way to demonstrate superiority than through a display of dominance and power?

While this theory may be based on fact, it's hard to believe in this post-feminist age that the majority of women are still more turned on by the prospect of a powerful man than by the notion of achieving power for themselves. Or, for that matter, why so many women still allow themselves to fall into the trap of falling for their bosses.

Shelley is a 31-year-old Australian journalist who recently found herself in a situation that challenged all her beliefs about dominant men and the kind of relationship she had always imagined she wanted:

'Perhaps it's not surprising that I grew up a feminist when you consider that the country I was born in is predominantly dominated by chauvinistic attitudes. As my mother is American, I also got to spend a lot of my holidays with her family in the States, so maybe that influenced my attitudes as well.

'I came to England partly because I wanted to travel more and partly because I was fed up with the types of men I was meeting. But I hadn't even been here a month when I found all my ideas about myself being turned on their head.

'What happened was that I fell in love with my boss. And, yes, he was married. I can't explain what happened, I only know that he seemed to be so powerful and knowledgeable and so very much in control, not only of himself but of everyone and everything, that I just melted in the face of it all.

'Pretty soon we were having a full-blown affair and everybody knew about it. He took me to restaurants and shows, showered me with gifts and made it quite clear that only the best was good enough for me. I loved every minute of it.

'The funny thing was, he was hopeless in bed. His technique was non-existent and as for stamina, well, forget it – four minutes was a marathon for him! Despite that, his appetite was incredible. I used to call him my Martini-man, you know, "any time, any day, anywhere", because that's how he was. And me too. I couldn't understand how he could turn me on so much when he never delivered the goods!

'We continued like that for about eighteen months, but it really began to affect my work. In the end I had a breakdown. He wouldn't leave his wife, didn't want to make it permanent with me, and I just felt as though I'd lost everything. And for what? A fat, ugly, middle-aged man with money and power.

'It took two years of psychotherapy for me to see what he really was – and he *was* stout, he *was* in his late forties and although he wasn't exactly ugly, he wasn't an oil painting either.

'I hate arrogant domineering men and I've never been attracted to the "me Tarzan, you Jane" type, so I find it hard to understand now that I'm free of him how and why I allowed him to have so much control over me – or how I allowed his position and power to seduce me into losing all sense of proportion.'

What lay at the root of Shelley's relationship (and, incidentally, what lies at the root of all power) was the one emotion that all of us fear: fear itself.

Firstly, she was alone in a strange country, and therefore vulnerable – which created fear. Secondly, she was faced with a new job, in unfamiliar surroundings with strange people who would undoubtedly reserve their professional judgement until she'd proved herself – a situation which contributed to her experiencing more fear. Thirdly, she was flattered by her boss's interest in her – which probably caused her to feel gratitude and immense relief from fear.

If we add to that the man's position, his wealth and his obvious power, not only over her, but many other people, too, one can see how Shelley found it so easy to give up all personal control and allow him to assume the responsibility for her.

One of the biggest arenas where power battles are so often fought is in the bedroom. Traditionally, a woman's refusal to allow her husband his conjugal rights was grounds for divorce. This led to many women believing their husbands had total power over their bodies while they had none. And though those days are long gone, still many women feel that when it comes to bed they do not have the power or the right either to refuse their man, or to initiate sex with him.

Whilst there's something incredibly compelling about power, there are also times in a person's life when giving up all responsibility for themselves proves irresistible – which makes them more susceptible to powerful people.

So what does power actually convey? To be seen to have power is to convey the sense that one's arrived, that one's untouchable (though we know that isn't really true) and that one can command. Absolute power, when abused, can be used to manipulate and exploit, thus corrupting all who come into contact with it. But when treated with respect and handled with a sense of responsibility it can only enhance the holder's life and the lives of all whom she or he controls.

But what is it about power that makes us all strive so hard to attain it?

The motivation of power

The pop star Madonna, for example, has achieved success, wealth and superstardom on a scale that few of us will ever attain and yet the one thing that still motivates her is power. As she admitted in a recent interview, not only has she been pursuing it all her life, but even now that she has it she would still go on competing and fighting to maintain it and acquire more, adding, 'I think that's just the quest of every human being: power.'

So what can power give us that we don't already have now – apart from money and status, that is?

Keith (the pseudonym of a very well-known entertainer) has power, lots of it, and having once been without it, his new mission in life is making sure that he never loses it. He's in his late forties, has been happily married for over twenty-five years and possesses few of the physical attributes that turn women on. And yet, he gets more offers than he can cope with. So I asked him: is it the power of being important, the money or the name?

'Before I became well known my success rate with women was low. I had no confidence in myself personally, though I had bags of it professionally. When I became famous, I had women falling over themselves to get at me. Initially I thought it was the groupie-syndrome, you know, the one in which everyone wants to say they slept with a star.

'When I became rich, I thought it was the money. Now I know that I don't get women for any of those reasons – but, indirectly perhaps, *because* of those reasons. I get them because I now have personal confidence that's so unshakeable and supreme, it attracts them like moths to the proverbial flame.

'And the reason I'm so sure about that is because I've put it to the test when I've been abroad to places where my face and my name mean nothing.

'Fame, power, wealth and success are responsible for developing my confidence. And the ridiculous thing is, I now know that it's possible to have none of those things and yet still be confident and score with woman.

'They say nothing succeeds like success, but they're wrong – because I say that nothing succeeds like confidence and, more than that, nothing will succeed *without* confidence.'

Some people believe that confidence is a by-product of success or money and power. But Keith redefines that by saying that it's the other way around.

Perhaps he's right, who can say? Certainly, unbelievable things have been achieved with confidence, but then the unbelievable has also been achieved with money and power. What does seem clear is that mankind's quest for power, like his quest for love, seems to be fuelled by his need to justify his position in society. What then spurs him on to greater heights could well be a sense that power means nothing unless it is acknowledged by others.

The use of power

Everyone experiences power to some degree and everyone uses it themselves, often without even realizing it. Parents use their power over young children to make them behave in the way they want them to and the implicit threat that reinforces their power is that they may withdraw their love if the child doesn't learn to behave and do as it is told.

Every single relationship has power somewhere at its base. The guy who doesn't ring when he says he will may genuinely have forgotten, or he might never have intended to in the first place. On the other hand, he might be exercising his power to demonstrate his lack of concern and make a woman feel more concerned.

A boss wields power at work, and the man he wields it over will often go home to wield it in turn over his wife. If he's wielding it over her, she can't wield it over him so she wields it over the kids instead. Older brothers and sisters use their power over younger siblings who in turn will demonstrate their own power over the baby, the cat, the dog, or failing those options, probably their toys.

Couples in love use their power over each other, often shame-lessly. The downtrodden wife who feels she has no power may resort to using whatever power she can over her husband, whether it be the power of emotional blackmail or the power she has to grant or deny him sex.

Sometimes a relationship can start off with both people feeling that they have equal power, and before one of them knows it, the balance has shifted and they're left with none. This often happens in relationships in which one partner becomes complacent and almost blasé about being loved or adored and often mistakenly imagines that their mate would be totally lost without them. However, should the complacent partner suddenly discover their other half's infidelity or some other form of duplicity, the balance of power will rapidly shift in the other person's favour. Which indicates that one can't have or retain power without having a sense of security and supreme confidence.

The power of money and status

Separating power from money and status is virtually impossible. However, there are people who have sufficient status and money to make life comfortable who, while not necessarily having power over a large number of people, *do* have power over those who are attracted to them *because* of their money and status.

Claire openly confesses that she has always been motivated by status and money. Furthermore, despite having risen as high as her professional capabilities will take her in her own industry and having acquired a certain amount of status and a very good income of her own, she freely acknowledges that the only way she can ever acquire enough to satisfy her is to marry it. Claire divorced her first husband, Glen, who was a shopkeeper, when she met Michael, an investment consultant, through her job:

'The first thing that attracted me to Michael was his position. I was born poor and my father always drummed it into me that it was just as easy to fall in love with a rich man as a poor one.

'Glen was from the same social background, but when I met him he had his own shop. That was rich to me, so I married him. However, I soon learned that one shop was enough for him. I pushed him and through my efforts his business grew, but he didn't like the extra responsibility and the amount of time he had to devote to it.

'His lack of ambition frustrated me and soon I began to despise him for it. I had several affairs with rich, successful – and mostly married – men I met through work. Glen never knew. Then I met Michael.

'Michael was single, five years younger than me and also from a much classier background. Those factors made him infinitely attractive and when he showed an interest I responded. Eventually we had an affair, he broke off his engagement and I left Glen to move in with Michael.

'After my divorce we got married. I loved him, I enjoyed his friends who were all so very different from mine, and I thoroughly enjoyed being spoilt and indulged by him. I wanted a big house, so he bought me one. In fact, he gave me whatever I wanted and for a long time we were incredibly happy – except for one thing. Michael had rather strange tastes in bed. Some of the things he wanted to do seemed strange, some of them were downright weird, if not actually perverted! Still, it wasn't anything that I couldn't put up with. What annoyed me far more was his totally cavalier attitude towards money and possessions. Because he had always had money it meant nothing to him and he couldn't see why I should get so steamed up about his generosity to other people or his disregard for the value of things.

'I was also very disillusioned when I realized that Michael didn't have any real ambition to progress further either. He'd fallen into his job straight from university through a friend of a friend of his father's. He was content earning a very good salary and enjoyed doing what he knew well. But I couldn't get him to use all his specialized knowledge to invest our money, no matter how much I nagged him.

'Eventually, I found myself hating him. I went off sex, couldn't bear to sleep in the same bed as him and I was so *angry* all the time that it was all I could do to be civil to him.

'The inevitable happened. He had an affair, I found out and then all hell broke loose. Now we're getting a divorce. I can't bear the thought of losing the house and I've begged him to come back, but although he insists he still loves me he refuses. He says we're so fundamentally different that it would never work. He also thinks I only married him for his money. But that's not true. Whenever I see him now I go weak at the knees with wanting him. We've slept together a couple of times since and each time he has said he has never loved anyone the way he loves me but he still won't come back. I love him so much I just don't know what to do.'

One might be inclined to believe Claire if it wasn't for the fact that she keeps insisting that if she can't get Michael back, she'll only allow him to divorce her if he gives her the house, pays off the mortgage *and* provides her with a sum equivalent to half his current net worth!

The curious thing is that Claire really believes that she *does* indeed love Michael, and yet, when a friend suggested she prove it to him by giving up all claim on their house and his wealth in a last-ditch attempt to get him back, Claire's spontaneous response was: 'Why should I?'

Unfortunately, for some people (Claire included) status and money have such an incredibly powerful allure that it's virtually impossible for them to separate their intense desire for these things from their emotional responses to the person who possesses them. When Michael had everything Claire desired he had power over her. When Claire had won Michael's love, she had power over him. Now the situation's reversed once again and both are the losers because for Claire, power will always equate to money and status, whereas for Michael, power can only ever equate to love.

The powerful tyranny of the weak

There's another side to power which we often fail to take note of and that is the power that ordinary human beings wield over each other in order to fulfil their own needs.

And power doesn't necessarily lie with the person who *appears* to be in control, either. For one sometimes finds that the very person who seems powerless actually uses their weakness to gain control, as with those who allow themselves to appear emotionally hurt when things don't go their way, or when someone uses physical illness or a disability to evoke feelings of sympathy, shame, guilt and/or a compelling need to make amends in a partner, friend or relative.

I long ago discovered that there is such a thing as the 'tryanny of the weak', which is something most of us have been subjected to at some time or another. There are certain people (and all of us know one or two of these types) who seem permanently to be depressed, miserable and helpless. Things are always happening *to* these types and they often appear to us to be the unluckiest souls we've ever come across.

One typical example is the man or woman who is always being 'put upon'. He or she will often go out of their way to make friends with strangers, to do them 'favours', to be accommodating, selfless and helpful, but there's always a price to pay. And the price extracted usually takes the form of crying on the shoulder of someone stronger. This type of character is very fond of the wry smile, the puzzled, helpless shrug of the shoulder and phrases like: 'I don't know why it always happens to me. I must be the biggest mug in the world. I'm always putting myself out for people and look what happens – I'm the one who ends up getting trodden on.'

Every one feels sorry for the emotionally weak, and none feel more pity than those who are emotionally strong themselves. And because they're strong, they also feel guilty. So they allow the weak person to call on them at all hours, to cry on their shoulder over every mishap and if they occasionally feel impatience or frustration, they bury it beneath a profound sense of shame, feeling they *ought* to drop everything to comfort their weak friend and to spend hour upon unproductive, boring hour listening to the same litany of complaints that they've been hearing for weeks, months and sometimes even years.

Janine spent several years caught up in just such a relationship with her friend, Nina:

'Nina was always getting mixed up with the "wrong" kind of men. I used to feel so sorry for her. She'd been abandoned by her wealthy husband with three small kids and very little money. She wasn't much to look at and her personality was rather humourless and dour to say the least.

'We were introduced by a mutual friend who felt that as we were both divorced we might like to go out together to some singles' clubs and help each other out with childminding, etc.

'Nina always seemed pleased to help me out and before too long I was so in debt to her "favour-wise" that I felt the only way I could repay her was to always be available when she needed someone to pour out her troubles to.

'The problem was, Nina's life was one long spell of trouble. She was always moaning about how all her men let her down, how her kids were so naughty and unappreciative of all the sacrifices she made for them, how her ex had got off scot-free, how sooner or later everybody in her life let her down, etc., etc.

'I found myself breaking dates because she'd ring me at the last minute in a depression or because she just had to get out of the house and needed someone to go out with. I spent hours with her working on her hair and make-up because she was always going on about how unattractive she was compared to me. I even found myself playing down my own looks and not wearing make-up when we went out to give her more of a chance!

'I'd get so frustrated with her, and then, of course, I'd feel guilty for losing my patience. Then one day it just hit me that I'd been doing this for years and nothing had ever changed – except that it was me who was losing boyfriends, me who was passing up opportunities and me who was feeling guilty about being more fortunate, being younger and being better looking. And the incident that finally opened my eyes was an argument she had with her son in which everything she said to him seemed deliberately calculated to make *him* feel guilty because *her* life was so rotten.

'At that point I got out. I felt terribly guilty but I knew if I didn't, I'd end up giving up my whole life for her – and still she wouldn't change because in a funny way she actually seemed to enjoy playing the eternal victim and being the underdog.'

Janine was lucky. Some people never recognize that *they* are the ones who are being manipulated (albeit often unconsciously) by a weak person who has become adept at using the strong person's sense of guilt as the ultimate weapon of power. Beware the tyranny of the weak – and if you're in a situation in which your sense of guilt is being manipulated by such a person, ask yourself which one of you is *really* the weakest!

Chapter 11

The Silent Language

Imagine you're an unseen observer watching the following scene. The setting is a party – a casual, informal affair at which several different groups of people are mingling in a relaxed atmosphere.

Two newcomers, both women, enter the room at the same time, though they're obviously not together. One is so beautiful that immediately there's a hush as each man's eyes are transfixed admiringly on her. The other woman is reasonably pretty, but the effect she has is negligible when compared to the first woman.

The beautiful woman, whom we shall call Lynn, appears slightly embarrassed – or could it be annoyed – at being the focus of so many strange eyes. One man in particular, Paul, is staring in such a way that the impact Lynn's looks have had on him is immediately apparent.

Paul continues to stare, eventually his eyes catch Lynn's and after a few seconds he gives a small smile. Refusing to acknowledge Paul's interest, Lynn averts her gaze, moves quickly across the room towards the bar and turns her back on the entire room as she slowly pours herself a drink.

When she turns around, she sips her drink slowly as her gaze sweeps rapidly around the room without pausing to linger on any one person in it. A brief flicker of irritation frowns her features (perhaps because she cannot locate her hostess) and then she moves away from the crowd, crosses to the far corner and seats herself in an armchair.

Meanwhile, the other girl, whom we shall call Jill, who also doesn't know anyone there, is still standing alone by the door.

When people look at her, Jill's eyes return their gaze with openly expressed interest. After a few seconds, she smiles briefly before she, too, crosses towards the bar where she positions herself in such a way that she can pour herself a drink without cutting off the people in the room.

Jill then stands in front of the bar and sips her drink while she echoes Lynn's attempt to catch a glimpse of their hostess. Unlike Lynn, however, Jill smiles slightly and allows her eyes to lock for small moments with each individual who returns her gaze. After several moments, her eyes meet Paul's who, after a brief interval, detaches himself from the group he's with and joins Jill at the bar.

By the end of the evening, Jill, who goes home having made lots of new friends, is so buoyed up by the wonderful evening she's had and the prospect of her forthcoming date with Paul that she immediately rings her best friend to share her excitement and joy at having attended 'the best party she's been to in years'.

While Lynn (who, having registered Paul's admiring stare and secretly anticipated an approach is now at a loss to understand how she lost him to Jill) goes home in such a thoroughly miserable mood that she has to ring her best friend to tell her all about the 'worst party she's been to in years'.

Two different women with two different attitudes leave the same party with opposing views of the people they met and the kind of time they had; while Paul and the rest of the guests discuss their opinions about each girl. As you would expect, the general consensus about Jill is enthusiastically positive, while poor Lynn is dismissed as a cold, arrogant, superior and unapproachable, though beautiful, girl.

Have you any idea why?

The answer is to be found in the secret way we all communicate. Every time we are in the company of other people, even if we do not exchange one single word or glance, we are secretly communicating with them. And they are communicating with us.

When people speak, we listen to what they say and, without being aware of it, we're also subconsciously watching everything they do; how they move and stand, what gestures and facial expressions they use, how often they shake their head or nod, and, in particular, what they are communicating to us with their eyes. Because no matter what people say with their mouths, their body language will always secretly transmit the vital messages that give their thoughts away.

A knowledge of body language can be useful in every area of life. In business, it can be used to guide you successfully into closing a vital deal or as an early-warning device to tell you when to back off. It can be utilized to enhance your professional status and increase respect. In relationships with friends, family and acquaintances it can help you sidestep confrontations or steer you through all the right moves to make people relax more. While with people you'd like to impress, it can be used to make them more receptive to you or equally to warn you when you're in danger of going too far.

For example, we all know it's rude to stare, therefore when we look at strangers in the street, on a train, bus, or any other place we might encounter them, if their eyes meet ours we quickly look away. We do this for a variety of reasons that range from a simple reluctance to 'get involved' right through to embarrassment that our glance might be misunderstood. We also do it as an instinctive defensive measure against allowing someone to 'read our minds'.

Eye contact has a language all of its own and it can be used to convey virtually every single emotion or thought we might wish to transmit. Too much of it with strangers could be interpreted as a threat or an insult while too little might be regarded as a sign of dishonesty, shyness, lack of interest or evasiveness.

Therefore, how we look at people, how long we hold their gaze, and how often we look away can make a vital difference to the success or failure of each encounter.

That was the difference between Jill and Lynn. One used eye contact to positive effect, the other avoided the use of it completely and the result was a negative effect.

A mouth can fool us with a smile but eyes rarely lie – which is why the person who becomes adept at interpreting and transmitting the subtle messages eyes communicate potentially has complete control and while the subject of eye contact and body language is too vast to cover here, even a little understanding of some of the more common cues and signals could be enough to provide you with an advantage.

The eyes have it

Although everything about our bodies – from the way we move, sit and walk to the kinds of gestures we use and our posture – says something about what we are thinking and feeling, experts say that no one part of the body should be interpreted in isolation and that if we want to get an accurate picture we have to read every gesture, position and expression together.

But of all the messages we transmit in this way, the signals we send with our eyes are the most important.

Novelists love to write phrases around eyes. They'll wax lyrical about hypnotic eyes, hooded eyes, burning eyes, wise eyes, malevolent eyes, glowing eyes, mocking eyes and even come-to-bed eyes. Can eyes really be all these things? They can, for the simple reason that we can use our eyes and facial expressions to communicate virtually every subtle nuance of emotion there is, despite the fact that experts say there are only six basic human emotions to express: fear, happiness, sadness, anger, disgust and surprise.

Staring and looking both say a great deal, but what they say is often determined by how long the eye contact lasts. When people's eyes lock, each is aware they have the other person's attention, and if they remain locked for any length of time, each knows they also have the other's interest, too. Without one word, messages can be broadcast and intentions clearly understood.

Although we're never taught exactly how long a look is too long, by the time we become teenagers most of us have acquired an instinctive knowledge of what is termed the 'moral looking time' and rarely overstep the boundaries – unless, of course, we consciously intend to provoke a response.

Prolonged eye contact, therefore, usually only ever occurs in two situations. The first is when two people wish to communicate intense interest, attraction or love and the second occurs when two people are openly confrontational, hostile and antagonistic. Some youngsters use the term 'eyeballing' to infer that a person is staring them down in such a way that means they're spoiling for a fight.

There is actually a third occasion when people will stare, which is when they consider the object of their eyes to be a non-person, but because the person they're staring at, in their minds, doesn't exist, this isn't normally counted. Non-persons are usually those of inferior status, such as waiters and shop assistants and those to whom we wish to show contempt. Women will often give this kind of stare to a man who's been presumptious and most people use it when they wish to put somebody down.

The quick look-and-look-away can cover embarrassment. This is what we do when we see someone unusual, someone who's handicapped or someone who's famous. It's a look that is supposed to say, 'I know you're there but I don't want to intrude or embarrass you.'

People who are forced into close proximity against their will, such as when they're in a lift, on a train or bus, or pushed together in a crowded room, will never use eye contact if they can avoid it. Because their personal space has been invaded, they have no other means of defence than their eyes. To look too long at someone at such close quarters means you can't help but acknowledge their presence and perhaps even invite communication, which is something most of us wouldn't welcome with a stranger.

According to the Spanish philosopher, Gasset, men and women who have 'come-to-bed' eyes possess 'a treasure'. 'Come-to-bed' eyes is the description given to the slightly veiled, half-closed, eyes narrowed, sleepy-but-nevertheless-acutely-aware look that some film stars have tried to perfect. Some famous people like Robert Mitchum, Mae West, Marlene Dietrich, Steve McQueen and Simone Signoret have – or had – it naturally, and there's no doubt it contributed to their sex appeal. However, some myopic people have it, too, though it usually stems more from squinting than any desire to seduce.

Most of us have heard that when people lie their pupils contract, while when they see something that interests them their pupils will dilate. One researcher studying this subject found that, not surprisingly, most men's pupils will enlarge when they see photos of attractive women or the real thing in the flesh but show no reaction at all to images of other men or babies.[23] Women's pupils, on the other hand, generally respond to both babies and men but not to other women.

Changes in the size of the pupils of blue-eyed people of both sexes are more easily discernible than those with brown eyes – which might explain why Paul Newman, whose famous blue eyes have been a useful trade mark, is said to have so much sex appeal. True blue eyes, such as Newman possesses, are quite rare, and their startling clarity and piercing gaze often marks those who have them as something special.

Enlarged pupils, however, don't necessarily indicate sexual attraction as many people suppose, but what they can do is make the person who's looking at them more receptive and responsive to the owner.

This was, in fact, borne out by one US study in which two identical sets of pictures of attractive ladies were presented to a number of men to rate. The only difference between the pictures was that in some, the subjects' pupils were artificially enlarged, while in others they were artificially reduced. Not surprisingly, the girls with the larger pupils were rated as the most attractive.

In another experiment, this time conducted at the Frances Hiatt School of Psychology, around 50 pairs of students who had never met each other before were asked to spend some time gazing into one another's eyes. A surprisingly large number of the group afterwards confessed that during the staring they had become strongly attracted to the person they were looking at.

Perhaps that means that when lovers do stare deeply into each other's eyes, they're not just behaving this way because they find their partner so fascinating, they're also subconsciously trying to make their lover become even more attracted to them!

Very few of us fully understand quite how significant eye language can be. Or, for that matter, how much power we can gain just by learning how to use it positively. For example, just by modifying the length of time you look into other people's eyes, you can control how long people look at you.

This is what politicians and film stars do when they 'make an entrance', in order to achieve maximum effect. These people are acutely aware of the need to control an audience's response; so, by walking confidently into a room and merely pausing in the entrance until all eyes turn their way, they can hold the attention of every person present simply by gazing slowly and deliberately about them until their eyes locate and hold those of the most important person in that room.

A trick like this isn't recommended for those who lack confidence or the status to carry it off, however, because it could just be taken for the kind of arrogance that most of us particularly resent.

A far better way of making a good impression on people and of ensuring a positive response, would be to catch someone's eye as soon as you walk through the door and then smile warmly before you proceed. This will be interpreted as a sign that you are friendly, confident and enjoy meeting new people and once they've formed this impression of you, people will feel more relaxed when they get to speak to you.

Interest and encouragement can be conveyed in a number of ways. For example, when holding a conversation with someone, it's likely that you'll look at them more often when you're listening than when you're talking (and you'll notice that they'll do the same) because this implicitly conveys your interest in what they have to say. But if you open your mouth while you're looking at them, they might cut short the conversation in a mistaken assumption that you've already made up your mind on the topic and wish to speak.

Public speakers are often taught the subtle techniques of establishing and maintaining control over their audience. These include looking directly at individual members when they wish to emphasize what they have to say and the deliberate widening of their eyes when they want you to believe they're sincere.

I once attended a series of demonstrations and lectures that I had helped organize about healthy food. When the first demonstration was over, someone asked me what it had been about, and the odd thing was that though I had enjoyed watching the practical part, I couldn't recall a single word the demonstrator had said when she'd given her talk.

During the next lecture I deliberately tuned out and concentrated my attention on observing the speaker and the audience's reaction to her. What I discovered was that though she might have learned some of the basic techniques of control, she certainly hadn't mastered the art of using them. For instead of allowing her eyes to sweep the audience with a constant progression of brief eye contacts from left to right along each row, her rapid swivelling head movements made her look more like a demented umpire trying to keep pace with a fast and furious game at Wimbledon than someone who desired to make contact with her audience.

Naturally, the poor lady was oblivious to what she was doing wrong, and the audience weren't consciously aware either, but their fidgety movements indicated that they did feel uncomfortable and this, in itself, was enough to prevent them from being able to concentrate on what she was trying to say.

Body language and eye-contact can be used to great effect to put people at their ease. For example, if you're having a one-to-one conversation with a person who is nervous, shy or reluctant to talk at great length for any reason, you can put them at ease and encourage them to continue by nodding at frequent intervals. Not only is nodding seen as a form of agreement, it's a useful way to draw someone out, to give them encouragement and to reassure them that you both understand what they're saying and have empathy for the way they feel.

Women, it has been found, look at other people (regardless of their sex) more than men. Some psychologists explain this by saying that women, generally, are more submissive than men, while others say that it's because women are more interested in people generally and in their reactions to them. Men tend to adopt a more dominant form of direct eye contact when they're with women, and people in superior positions do it with subordinates. We also tend to trust people more when they look at us directly than when they avoid our gaze.

The way people break eye contact can also tell us a great deal. For example, there is some evidence to suggest that people who look away to the left of us are likely to be more artistic or religious, while those who look away to the right usually tend to be more scientific in their approach.

One situation in which eye contact is used to great effect – and great eloquence, too – is when we're flirting. Flirting is a harmless little game we all enjoy playing. Not only can it be used to contrive the perfect opening, as when two strangers' eyes meet across a crowded room and the look exchanged signals their mutual interest, it can also be used verbally to deflect jokingly an unwelcome advance without causing too much offence, or even simply as an effective method of breaking down resistance in non-sexual situations where a person's insecurity leads them to become too defensive.

We're all susceptible to flirting because it boosts our egos and shows we're still attractive to the opposite sex, while adding a sparkle of good old-fashioned mischief to a relationship. Most flirtations are little flights of fancy that neither party would wish to become fact, some are mildly pleasant diversions indulged in to relieve a moment's boredom while, in a few cases, a flirtation may continue for years without ever developing into anything more.

Flirting can be a simple camouflage for expressing real interest when used by those too shy to declare themselves, or a disruptive force if taken too far. But the really important thing about flirting is knowing when, how and with whom it can safely be used – because if you choose the wrong person to flirt with it could be disastrous. Nowadays, it can be dangerous to flirt with strangers when you're alone, although still possible when you're at a party or dance surrounded by people you know.

In the days when nice girls didn't dare speak to a man unless they'd been introduced, silent flirting with the eyes was elevated to an art form, particularly when it was used in conjunction with ladies' fan when it had even more impact because the eyes were usually isolated by the fan from the rest of the face. One old magazine I came across in an antique shop even ran an article on the art of flirting and illustrated what different messages could be transmitted with the eyes and positioning of the fan itself.

I once carried on a whole conversation with a man I liked the look of, purely between our eyes.

I was at a dance with several friends. I saw him as soon as he came in but the minute his eyes met mine I looked quickly away. I thought he was attractive, so naturally I stole several discreet looks. Each time I could see he clearly had his eye on me.

Knowing he'd hardly cut in on my girlfriends, I decided to advance the situation myself by leaving the floor and sitting down on my own. I glanced at him to see if he had noticed, and this time I made sure I held his eyes for a few seconds longer. But before anything could happen, three of my friends joined me and another man asked me to dance. I started to refuse, but my friends kept urging me on and I felt bad about hurting his feelings.

We danced an excruciatingly slow dance and then I tried to leave. He kept pleading with me to dance more and I found it hard to refuse. I kept praying that the DJ would speed the music up so I could make a quick getaway, but as luck would have it, the slow dances went on and on. In the meantime, as we slowly twirled around the floor I kept peeking around my partner in order to spot the man I was really interested in who by then was nowhere in sight.

I was on the fifth dance when suddenly I spotted 'him', seated all alone at the edge of a table right next to the floor – and his eyes were following my every move. When they met mine, they clearly transmitted the message: 'What are you doing with *him*?' The next time I twirled past, I allowed my eyes to lock with his for several moments until the movements of the dance took me out of range.

Each time I passed him, I was careful to send him a long level look and to briefly raise my eyebrows in a question. And each time his eyes echoed mine. When it didn't appear as if my opportunity to break politely away was going to come, I finally sent him a hopeless look (with eyes raised to heaven) as if to say, 'Help me! I'm trapped.' Within thirty seconds he was tapping my partner's shoulder to cut in. We continued the dance, smiling, with no immediate need for any of the usual social small talk. We were smiling in recognition of the fact that we had been accomplices together. And we were together for four years!

If the face fits

After the eyes, the face is the next most important means of communication that we use. Faces express emotions, and although we've been told that there are only six principle human emotions, we use subtle alterations to indicate the degree of emotion we're expressing.

Faces also reveal a person's state of health. Tiredness, stress, anxiety and pain are all clearly seen in the face. Women smile and laugh more than men, but that's more likely due to discomfort than greater sociability.

The facial expressions we use are learnt rather than naturally acquired. Children, for example, don't employ them as much as adults, which is why they're so often asked by their parents whether they're listening to what they're being told. And cultural and social conditioning also affects what we allow our faces to show.

The Japanese are known for being 'inscrutable' and unemotional because they tend to blank their faces of all expression or else greet everything with a smile. In fact, Orientals are just as emotional as the rest of us, it's merely that their culture teaches them not to display certain negative emotions such as sadness and anger.

Smiles universally indicate pleasure, happiness, amusement or reassurance – although certain types of fixed smile, such as a grimace, can also indicate pain, derision, contempt and ridicule. However, when we smile ourselves, it really does make us feel better, while smiling at others has been found to have beneficial effects, too.

Research has shown that if people are asked to smile when doing something they dislike, they often find themselves feeling happier. When people are asked to smile and then shown photos of different events, they often report a greater liking for what they see. And when people have been told to frown during similar experiments, they've reported they actually feel angry and annoyed.

Of course, smiles can also deceive, as when they're used to mask real feelings, but the interesting thing about smiling at people you don't like is that it can often actually change their attitude towards you.

Body language

The interpretation of bodily gestures is known as the science of kinesics. As I said earlier, this fascinating subject is so immense it's really not possible to do it any kind of justice here, and not being an expert, I wouldn't even attempt to. However, it might be useful for you to know about a small number of typical gestures and what they're commonly held to convey.

When people are sexually interested (what the experts term

courtship readiness), their muscle tone changes, almost as if the body is gathering itself inwards and upwards in readiness. Preening behaviour occurs more openly, as when men straighten their ties, pull up their trousers, and women pat their hair and smooth down their skirts.

When someone's interested in you, or when you'd like to communicate that you're interested in them, synchronizing of gestures is an effective signal to watch for or to use. This indicates a similarity in attitude and, as we've already discussed in an earlier chapter, we warm more to people who we assume are similar to ourselves than to those who don't appear to be.

The folding of arms across the chest is assumed to be a defensive gesture, though some people use it when they're interested in what you have to say. If you're not sure how to interpret this one, watch for the slight cock of the head to one side which is something we all do when we're listening intently. Women are said to adopt open-arms positions with people they like, and are more likely to fold their arms when they're uncomfortable, unrelaxed or with someone they dislike.

Confidence is displayed by an erect posture and an upward tilt of the head, while insecurity, depression and shame can clearly be seen in a slouched posture, sagging body, drooping shoulders and a downward dropping of the chin.

Positioning is also very important. Where you stand or sit in relation to the person or people you are with can say a great deal about your status in that situation. For example, we all know that in a boardroom the Chairman will sit at the top of the table, while in the dining room it will be Dad and that in both instances this denotes the 'leader' of the group. In competitive situations people will usually stand or sit directly facing one another, while in a co-operative situation they'll choose to stand or sit side by side.

When entering an office, for example, people of low status will often hover by the door while those of high status will enter quite boldly and come right up close to a desk. Colleagues of equal status will often seat themselves beside a desk without being invited, while those who are friends or whose presence is regarded with warmth will usually meet or be met halfway across the room.

How we allow people to invade our own personal space also says a great deal about our relationships with them. Lovers are allowed extremely close proximity (and when this doesn't naturally occur, one partner will tend to think something is wrong), while strangers are kept at a safe distance. If a stranger, or someone we dislike or are wary of, attempts to come too close, we'll back away from them to maintain the distance we can cope with. Policemen use proximity as a trick to intimidate suspects in such a way that as they gradually move closer and closer the perceived threat to the suspect becomes greater.

I once attended a seminar in which the speaker gave a number of important and amusing tips on how to use body language. One in particular related to lying and I was so intrigued that the moment I got home I put it to the test with my children: 'Have you done your homework, Gemma?' I asked from a distance of about ten feet. Naturally, she said 'Yes'. I dropped the subject for several minutes and we went on to talk about other things. When enough time had elapsed for her to forget all about her homework, I casually walked up to where she was sitting at the kitchen table, draped my arm around her shoulder, leaned close till our faces were almost touching and, looking her straight in the eye, said in a casual voice, 'Er, did you tell me that you *had* finished your homework?' Immediately, she moved backwards slightly, lowered her eyes from my face, and started mumbling: 'Em, yes, I mean, no, I mean I've done some of it but it's not all finished.'

The technique worked. And it has continued to work to great effect ever since!

How to detect when someone is lying to you is probably one of the most common issues raised whenever people talk about body language. The problem, as has been mentioned before, is that one gesture or movement in isolation doesn't provide enough conclusive evidence one way or the other. However, there are some gestures that are more common when people are deliberately trying to deceive. These include scratching or touching the side of the nose, running a finger around the collar (in men), playing with a necklace (in women), touching or rubbing an eye, licking the lips, gripping the arms of a chair and drumming fingers on a table or counter-top. Research also shows that when people are lying they tend to speak less, speak more slowly when they do talk, and make more errors in their speech; they're also less likely to touch you or even approach you too closely.

As we've seen, body language can be used to draw attention to yourself and to control situations. But body language can also be used to attract members of the opposite sex. People who look at us are more attractive than people who avoid our gaze, so if you want to attract someone's interest you should look at them as openly and as often as you think they can cope with. People who smile often and have a warm, open, friendly manner are more attractive than those who don't, so if you want to arouse someone's interest, let your own interest show in your face and smile.

When talking to someone you find attractive, try not to adopt a defensive pose such as crossed legs or crossed arms. Use open gestures as often as you can without it looking false, angle the head slightly to one side when they speak and use small nods of the head to indicate understanding and encouragement. If you're sitting down, lean forwards towards them to show your interest.

When it comes to speaking, attractive people tend to talk more than unattractive people, but if you're trying to engage someone's interest, you should talk and listen an equal length of time, without talking too much or too fast. Your voice should be pitched at a pleasantly low, but clear level (the lower the pitch of the voice the harder people will listen to what you are saying), without being so quiet that the other person will have to strain so hard to hear you that they become irritated and turn off.

And finally, if you want to get to know someone better, they'll feel far more comfortable about opening up and revealing themselves to you if you encourage them by revealing one or two things about yourself first. However, don't be tempted to overwhelm the person with too much personal information too soon as this can only result in them backing off. Self-disclosure should be carefully timed, with each person taking it in turns to disclose a little bit more about themselves in turn.

Chapter 12

The Power of Touch and the Sound of a Voice

In the same way that there are universal rules governing body language and eye contact that we all subconsciously adhere to, so too, do these rules apply to voice and touch, both of which can exert incredible power and influence over how other people react to us and how we respond to them.

The personal touch

Touch is a very personal thing and we're exceedingly choosy about whom we touch and whom we allow to touch us, because not only does touch convey intimacy, it also conveys power.

Some forms of touch are, of course, impersonal but neverthe-less necessary in certain situations; these include touches given by doctors, dentists, hairdressers and dressmakers, while other touches might be accidental, or required according to custom, as when we shake hands when greeting people.

But few of us realize how and where we touch people can make all the difference to success or failure in a relationship. If we touch at the right time, in the right place on the appropriate occasion, people will, in the main, respond in a positive manner.

Some years ago an experiment was conducted with members of a library's staff in which they were each required to touch some members of the public 'accidentally' when they were checking books in or out.[24] Later, the people who had been touched were questioned about their attitudes towards the librarian who had touched them and, though none of them could remember being touched, each recorded a warmer and more positive attitude towards the librarian than those who had not been touched.

The rules that govern touch are quite rigid and, not surprisingly, most of them are concerned with sex. Studies concerning the areas of the body that are 'permissible' and 'no-go' have revealed distinct differences in relationships between people of opposite sex and people of the same sex.

When it comes to friends, men touch other men mostly on the hands, sometimes on the arms and shoulders and occasionally on the back of the head, thighs and legs, but hardly at all on the face or around the lower part of the trunk. Women touch each other mostly on the hands and lower arms, sometimes on the upper arms and the back of the head, occasionally on the shoulders and feet and hardly at all from the chest down to the ankles.

With friends of the opposite sex, however, it's different. Here the findings showed that women will often touch men anywhere on the upper body, including the face and head, but only sometimes will they touch the rest of the body below the waist. Men, on the other hand, feel quite free to touch women in the knee area, arms, shoulders, head and face, but will touch them rarely on the rest of the body with the exception of the entire pantie-zone which they only tend to touch very occasionally.

Even parents feel bound by certain restrictions when touching their grown-up sons and daughters. Mothers feel they can touch their daughters' hair and arms quite freely, with only small reservations being applied to the face and upper chest. They're less likely to touch daughters below the knees and seldom touch them on the areas of the body between the knees and breasts. With their sons, they feel they have unrestricted access to their hands, reasonable access to their arms, shoulders and heads, restricted access to their chests and lower legs and hardly any access at all from knees to waist.

Fathers have even less access to sons and daughters than mothers do. For them, the only safe place they can touch their daughters is on the hands, they feel relatively safe with arms, shoulders, heads and hair, but the rest of the body is definitely a no-go zone. While this is understandable, what's less so is the amount of restriction they feel is applied to permissible areas of touching with their sons. Here, they feel free to touch hands, fairly safe with arms, less safe but still reasonably okay are the shoulders and head while they seldom, if ever, touch their sons anywhere on their bodies below the chests.

Arms are generally considered to be safe (or neutral) areas to touch on friends and strangers alike, while the vulnerable areas of head, neck, shoulders, chests, hands, bottoms and legs are off-limits to anyone other than our most intimate acquaintances.

However, touching certain 'vulnerable' (though still relatively safe) areas has been shown to be beneficial. For example, experiments carried out with waitresses have revealed that when they touch a customer on the hand or shoulder they are far more likely to receive a larger tip.

Men are more inhibited about touching each other than women, presumably because of the risk of sexual inferences. When they do feel free to touch, however (on the football field, during sports and team games, etc.), they tend to do so in a more exaggerated fashion.

Women, on the other hand, will spontaneously and intentionally hug their female friends, kiss them on the cheek and put their arms around their shoulders without any embarrassment at all. Not surprisingly, women feel more uncomfortable touching and being touched by men than men feel about being touched by women!

Status also plays a role in touching. Superiors feel freer to touch their subordinates (both male and female) than vice versa and when people observe others touching, they tend to make the assumption that the person who is doing the touching is of higher status than the person who is being touched.

Touching and close physical contact is absolutely vital for babies who have actually been shown to suffer mental symptoms of apathy and withdrawal when they have been deprived or denied physical contact, and this deep physical need seems to resurface again when we're older and fall in love. This could have something to do with the fact that during both these periods humans are extremely vulnerable and need an abundance of reassurance.

Touch conveys warmth, sympathy, understanding and caring, provided it's done in the right way. People who like touching and being touched have been shown to be more talkative, more cheerful and more dominant than those who don't. Conversely, those who dislike touching and being touched seem to have lower intellectual levels, are often less emotionally stable and can be more reticent in social situations.

Touching, according to the experts, is a deep, subconscious primal need that all of us have. Adults who feel uncomfortable with touching are usually the ones who have received fewer physical demonstrations of affection during their childhood and have, therefore, become inhibited because of that. Touching ourselves can often reduce anxiety and tension and induce a feeling of comfort. Touching an area of pain, such as holding our faces when a tooth aches, doesn't actually do much to relieve the pain, but we all know that somehow it helps.

People who touch themselves a great deal are often thought to do so out of a sense of discomfort, and this particularly seems to apply when we're with people who induce negative reactions in us. One study involving simulated interviews revealed that when an interviewer touched himself a great deal in this situation he was more likely to report a negative attitude towards the person he was interviewing.

Touching, it seems, is more likely to be done in certain circumstances than others. For example, we're more likely to touch people when we're supplying them with information than when they're giving it to us; we're also more likely to touch people when we make a request, give an order or ask a favour than vice versa; and we're far more likely to touch other people when *we're* excited than when they are and when *we're* comforting them than when they're comforting us.

Children are far more spontaneous about expressing pleasure and warmth through touching than adults are, though they're also less likely to accept touching from someone they don't know.

Touching can be a way of getting through to someone who has erected barriers against us, provided it's done without being too intrusive or evasive, because touching people can actually cause them to like us more.

Making love could hardly take place without touching. Some people will have sex with a virtual stranger and allow themselves to be touched in the dark with a level of intimacy they would never normally allow with that same person in daylight.

Sonia fell deeply in love at first sight with a man whom she later discovered was uncomfortable with touching. Being a tactile, demonstrative person herself, she found her lover's unwillingness to touch or be touched outside of the bedroom immensely distressing:

'I fell for him at first sight. I don't know what it was, he wasn't particularly handsome, but there was just something about him that drew me instantly. Perhaps it was chemistry.

'On our first date I found it very curious that there was no body contact at all. I didn't expect him to get intimate, but I imagined that at some point in the evening we would touch, even if it was only an accidental brush.

'We got on well, though he seemed a little shy. In fact, the evening – apart from the lack of touching – went so well that I broke my golden rule and invited him back to my flat for a coffee.

'We sat there for hours talking about everything under the sun. I was seated on one side of the room, he on the other. He made no attempt to come near me, to touch me, or to bridge the gap in any way at all. And yet, I was aware of this incredible electricity in the air.

'Something was happening between us and it was so strong I could almost feel it. I started to perspire, so I got up and turned the fire out. It was ridiculous really, at one point I even began to shake with the intensity of it. That's when he turned to me, looked deeply into my eyes and said, "Something's happening and we both feel it, don't we?" I could only nod my head. "The strange thing is," he said, "we haven't even exchanged so much as a touch."

'At that point he finally got up out of the chair and came over to me. He pulled me up into his arms and began to kiss me and before I knew what was happening we were making love on my sofa. I couldn't believe it. I'd never ever done or felt anything like that before.

'From that moment on we started seeing each other a great deal. At first, we spent so much time in bed together – the sex was incredible! – that I didn't notice the absence of any touching out of it. When I did, I assumed it was because he was shy.

'However, after we'd been seeing each other for two years, I knew that shyness couldn't possibly be the cause. He just couldn't cope with touching. In the end, I decided that he was so repressed for some reason, that if I couldn't reach him after all that time, there wasn't much point in carrying on.'

Touching, as Sonia discovered, is vital to us all for many reasons. When people touch us it is a sign that we are accepted, liked and warmly regarded. To spend your whole life with a man who finds touching so distasteful must be hell. One can't help but wonder what sort of childhood this poor man had, and feel concern for his future relationships.

Stroking, caressing and tickling are all intimate touch gestures which in many cases are used as substitutes for intimacy itself.

Adolescent boys will tickle and play-fight with their friends, but otherwise never allow them any close body contact at all. Similarly, people who are attracted to each other may often use a pretend-game of tickling or fighting as a way of creating intimacy before they've gone through the process that would lead naturally to it in time.

Politicians know the value of touch and the term 'pressing the flesh' was coined to describe the way they will often touch constituents when they're canvassing for votes because: (a) they know touch will break through any barriers; (b) it will soften up the attitude of the person who is being touched, and (c) it can actually convince the person being touched of the toucher's sincerity.

Certain women, though ordinary in looks and personality, seem, for no discernible reason, to be enormously popular with members of both sexes. If you were to observe such a woman when in the company of people, you'd probably notice that she's a subtle but sympathetic 'toucher', who gets through to people simply by sensing how, when and where to touch to invoke the right response and to make them feel good about themselves.

Yet another experiment, this time conducted with salesmen, found that salesmen who touch the arms of prospective customers are three times more likely to achieve sales than their non-touching colleagues. This experiment was repeated in a number of different situations amongst a variety of professions and each time the conclusion was the same: people who touch are more likely to receive a positive response from others than those who don't. However, timing is absolutely critical, in that if you touch a person too soon, they'll see you as false and probably become wary or suspicious; touch them too late and you lose the effect.

When in doubt, apparently the best thing to do is to use the kind of touch that can be construed as accidental – brushing an arm briefly, an accidental nudge, or even a quick grasp to steady yourself are all acceptable ways to instigate a warmer, more relaxed relationship with someone.

Touch, as we all know, can be a healing experience, a comforting and relaxing experience and even an exciting experience. Faith healers have allegedly produced miracles just through the laying on of hands, while some people's touch can be like an electric current that sends a frisson of excitement throughout your entire body to awaken a strong sexual attraction that you never knew was there.

Body language, touch, eye contact and gestures can all be used to great effect to break through barriers that neither speech nor long acquaintanceship could ever remove. We all unconsciously erect barriers against intimacy, against sexual approaches and particularly to prevent ourselves from becoming vulnerable in some way. That's why each of these is such a vital component of sexual power. With them we can create opportunities to make people more receptive and responsive to us, without them we can accomplish very little at all.

The sound of a voice

The voice is another useful tool that most of us ignore. How we speak can be just as important as what we actually say.

If you watch politicians on TV during difficult, confrontational interviews, you'll probably notice how they rarely allow themselves to be provoked into raising their voice above a certain tone. Margaret Thatcher practises this art well and with great effect.

When people are angry their voices usually rise an octave or two as they lose control, but psychologists say that if you want to control an argument or to win your case, the moment you allow this to happen you've lost.

The speed at which we talk can also convey a great deal. If we speak too rapidly, we can irritate and sound as though we're trying too hard to convince, while if we speak too slowly we could sound indifferent, too thoughtful or even unintelligent.

Short, sharp words and phrases often imply dominance and anger, while a steady build-up in volume is often used to indicate power, as when parents admonish children or superiors lose their temper with their staff. Experiments conducted with voice contact alone have revealed that merely by softening the tone and lowering the register you can improve your chances of a successful encounter or negotiation. Women who make tele-phone complaints are usually more successful when they use a softer, sexier voice than when they allow their anger and annoyance to show through rising pitch or stridency.

Control in certain situations can also be effected by what you choose to say and the order in which you elect to present it. For example, an old, but very effective, trick that salesmen are taught in order to overcome objections is one that is called the 'last word'. This works in the following way. The salesman makes his pitch, the customer makes his objection. Looking thoughtful and repeating the very last word or two that the customer has used, in a tone of voice that implies consideration, is usually enough to ensure the customer feels compelled to enlarge on what he has said and in doing so attempt to explain his objection. This trick can be repeated several times throughout the conversation and each time the customer will respond by expanding and explaining his last sentence until eventually the salesman has taken him right back to the very root of the objection itself. That's when the salesman finally knows whether he is going to make a successful sale, because if he can overcome this basic objection, the customer has then run out of arguments to block the sale.

Experts say that how we speak, what we say and the order in which we say it, can be used as an effective tool to impress a prospective employer during an interview. For example, when responding to a question, the subjects you choose to present at the very end of your statement are very likely to be chosen as the basis of the next question. Therefore, if you wish to avoid the conversation taking a particular course, but need to provide essential information, phrasing the topic you least want to expand on at the beginning of your response will deflect the interviewer away from it and focus his attention on the subject matter you mention last.

The timbre and quality of a voice are very important, too. Everyone must have laughed at that famous scene in *Singing in the Rain* when the glamorous lady film star's voice is recorded for the first 'talking picture'. The moment she opens her mouth, the image of incredible beauty is totally shattered because it's at such odds with her high-pitched squeaky, nasal tones.

Nothing can turn a person on or off quicker than a voice. You could be the most visually attractive person in the world, but if your voice is wrong, forget it. You won't stand a chance.

Tom Jones believes that it's a man's voice that really turns women on. Well, he would, wouldn't he? After all, his voice has, apparently, been turning women on for decades. But support for his view comes from more expert quarters, as well. Andrew Stanway is a marital and sexual psychologist who published a book entitled *The Woman's Guide to Men and Sex* in which he maintains that a man's voice is crucial when it comes to sexual attraction and that his female patients always put voice towards the top of their list when they're describing their ideal man.

Accents are often considered sexy, particularly Italian, Spanish and French. German accents, however, rarely have the power to excite as they tend to sound harsh, guttural, and too clipped and controlled to Anglo-Saxon ears. But accents can sound sexy partly because of the mental associations we have. For example, we're all conditioned to believe that the French are sexy and Latins are passionate, so when we hear their accents, the reaction we have is a conditioned response.

People have been known to fall in love with a voice before they even see the face behind it. Radio presenters of both sexes get sacks full of mail from their listeners and people have been known to propose marriage to someone with whom their only contact has been via the telephone or a two-way radio.

I once had a business contact whose voice for some reason had the most incredible effect on me. I loved listening to it and would use every opportunity I could to talk to him and to prolong each conversation. I wove fantasies around that voice, constructed an image of what he looked like and even filled in all the details of the personality that I imagined him to have. Eventually, I just had to meet him.

You probably won't be surprised when I say that the actual physical reality was a huge disappointment. Nevertheless, the voice had worked its magic and despite the fact that there was no physical attraction between us at all, we developed a good working relationship and a mental rapport that was a joy to both of us. I've often wondered whether we would have achieved the same relationship if I had met him prior to experiencing the magic of his voice!

It's true that sexy voices can potentially be incredibly seductive, though few of us could pinpoint exactly what it is that makes a voice sound sexy. Timbre is a vital ingredient. Lowering the register of your voice, therefore, can add enormous impact not only to your delivery but also to the effect you have on people.

Loud voices are associated with stridency, threat, anger, fear, authority and even stress, and soft voices signify gentleness, intimacy, conspiracy and secrecy while deep voices are often perceived to be masculine, positive, sexy and sophisticated. If there's a gravelly quality to a man's voice, this, apparently, can give the added effect of wickedness. Which probably explains why Richard Burton's deep, gravelly tones, combined with his lilting Welsh accent proved to be such an attractive feature. According to recent reports, though, Burton's voice wasn't, in fact, natural but had been developed by spending a great deal of time shouting himself hoarse up in the Welsh hills! Said Burton's widow, Sally, 'His voice was slightly beaten-up, as if it were carrying a wealth of experience, humanity and understanding. It was a wonderful voice which women found incredibly sexy – I still get letters about it.' Unlike some perfectly modulated, British voices, Richard Burton's had a touch of imperfection and it was that, experts say, that gave it an added edge; because for women, a touch of imperfection can make a man sound that little bit vulnerable. And vulnerability itself is a great allure.

Marilyn Monroe's soft, breathy babyish tones made her sound vulnerable, and that, combined with her little-girl-lost look, provided a combination that most men couldn't help but find irresistible.

Voices, it has been said, are the essential person because they have the ability to express so much more about us than our looks. Attractive voices can be developed. Stars, actresses and TV presenters do it all the time. Many of us unconsciously moderate or adapt our voices on the telephone in order to sound more sophisticated, intelligent, capable, helpful or of higher status than we might actually be. It takes practice to develop a voice, and it's not considered a good idea to change your own voice totally, but learning to lower your register can help a great deal when it comes to self-presentation and the impact you make.

However, never forget that before you open your mouth to speak, your state of mind, your mood and your attitude towards the person to whom you are speaking can all exert a subtle influence on your tones. So it's just as important to rid your mind of negative thoughts and attitudes, so that when you do finally begin to talk, the words and the sounds that come out have the effect that you *intend* them to have.

Chapter 13

Neuro-Linguistic Programming – A Unique Key to Understanding

If we are ever to identify and understand what sexual power might be, it is imperative that, firstly, we attempt to achieve as deep a comprehension as possible of our own and other people's behaviour and then, secondly, to gain some understanding of how and why we all respond to certain behavioural patterns.

Most of the branches of psychology, psychotherapy and psychiatry are fundamentally concerned with past experiences and how our experiences shape the way we are likely to respond to future experiences. Recently, however, there has been much attention given to a relatively new (and only recently officially accepted in the UK) field of psychotherapy termed Neuro-Linguistic Programming (NLP) which appears to go far beyond merely identifying and coming to terms with past causes of present attitudes and actually offers a number of intriguing, systematic approaches to positively changing attitudes in order to help people achieve desired objectives.

The discovery and development of NLP began in America in the early '70s when two men, Richard Bandler and John Grindler, who both had a mutual interest in communication, met at Santa Cruz University. At the time of their meeting, John Grindler was mainly involved in studying psychology and linguistics while Richard Bandler's interests were psychology and computer mathematics. Both men were also interested in a concept called modelling and they applied their collective skills to the development of a therapeutic model of the English language and then created linguistic strategies which could be used in responding to any individual's verbal patterns of expression. They then went on to construct some useful techniques for changing attitudes, perceptions and beliefs which today form the basis of NLP therapy.

Together with Richard Bandler's then wife, Leslie Cameron-Bandler, they identified a number of components and patterns of behaviour which demonstrated how all of us deal with our own individual experiences of the world through *representational systems*. A representational system is the method in which each of us represents our own *subjective* experience of the world.

In her fascinating and excellent book, *Solutions*, Leslie Cameron-Bandler describes how we have five recognized senses through which we experience everything around us and everything that happens to us: we *see*, we *hear*, we *feel*, we *smell* and we *taste*. In addition to these sensory systems (visual, auditory, kinesthetic and gustatory) we also have a language system which we utilize to *represent* our own experience. Furthermore, we store our experiences in the representational system that we most closely associate with that sensory channel.

What this means is that, when recalling past experiences or conjuring up thoughts of experiences, some people may tend to create *visual images*, some may choose to create *kinesthetic representations* (sensations or feelings) such as actually feeling muscles tense in a moment of anger, stress or fear. Others might instinctively create *auditory* (sound) *representations*, such as hearing their own breath exhale a sigh of pure pleasure, while others still would re-create the same experience through a *gustatory representation* such as taste or smell. Whichever of the representational systems outlined above comes more closely to your own experience (i.e., whether you actually identify with the feeling, the sound, the taste, smell or the visual imagery conjured up by any of the examples given above) is the representational system that is most highly and strongly developed in yourself.

The mapping process

Because we operate primarily through our own experiences of the world we live in, we have to create maps of that world to guide our behaviour in it and to make sense of it. And it is the maps we create which so often limit us from doing, becoming or achieving what we might like to do, become or achieve. Thus, it's not that we make *wrong* choices, rather it is simply that we are not able to see that we have *enough* choices available to us at the time that we need them.

What NLP therapy seeks to teach people is that each of us have different expectations based on our own personal agendas which are in turn based on our own subjective perceptions of our experiences. Moreover, most of the problems we encounter in our relationships only arise because while we *think* we are communicating with everyone else (and particularly with those who are closest to us, such as lovers), the *way* in which we communicate may not actually have any real impact or relevance to them because: (a) what we are communicating may not fit into their own personal frame of reference or subjective map of perceived experience, or (b) because we just aren't communicating *enough*.

The following fictitious example may help to clarify this.

Jean falls in love with Tom. She confides her hopes and desires about a prospective partner to Tom as their relationship deepens in the belief that everything she is communicating to him about what she actually wants and needs in a man will be understood and acknowledged by him (if he truly loves her as much as he says he does) and that the degree to which Tom understands and acknowledges her needs, wants and desires will be expressed by the degree to which he actively demonstrates the behaviour she needs.

In Jean's mind, therefore, she has now given Tom possession of *all* the information he requires in order to fulfil every one of her hopes and desires. So, let's suppose that what Jean has told Tom is that she needs and wants to be loved with overwhelming passion and adoration. Her message is loud and clear. Isn't it? Well, if it is, how come within a year or so Jean and Tom are fighting like cat and dog and all the love that once appeared to exist between them is dwindling fast?

Jean *told* Tom what she wanted. Clearly, he's not giving it to her, because if he was she wouldn't now be feeling unloved and unwanted, would she?

This hypothetical problem arose because Jean has never stopped to consider that Tom's method of *displaying* overwhelming adoration for and passion towards her is simply not being expressed in a manner that she can recognize or, identify with. The result? Crossed wires, feelings of disappointment, failure, frustration, rejection and, ultimately, Jean comes to believe that Tom isn't capable of giving her what she wants, or worse, as she's explained it so fully (she believes), he doesn't *want* to give her what she wants and needs.

But what about poor old Tom? Actually, you (and Jean) might

be surprised to learn that Tom *believes* he *has* been giving Jean every sign that she's loved passionately, adored totally and desired endlessly and, naturally, he simply cannot understand why she's being such a bitch and constantly carping at him about all the things he's *not* doing.

So, why would a situation that had such a promising beginning result in such a debacle of mutual disappointment, disillusionment and unfulfilled expectations? For the simple reason that while Tom and Jean were (they thought) confiding all their hopes, dreams and desires to each other, both Tom and Jean *neglected to tell* each other precisely which specific actions or behavioural displays make them *feel* that they are *being* loved, admired, respected or adored!

Jean, you see, only feels loved when her man constantly verbalizes his admiration and passion for her while Tom, who's a shy chap at heart, firmly believes that actions speaks louder than words and has, therefore, been demonstrating his love and passion for Jean in the only way *he* knows how: through taking her dog to the vet, through lovingly washing her car each week, through decorating each room in her house and through a myriad other *silent* methods that *he* recognizes as declarations (albeit silent) of his love for, and commitment to, Jean.

It would have helped Tom and Jean to learn that relating *subjectively* to each other, can, in effect, be just the same as not relating to each other at all.

Jean's primary representational system for experiencing experiences is auditory, but Tom's is not. And when analysed from the NLP premise that all human experience is generated as a direct result of the interaction between the external world (what is happening around us) and what our own senses perceive of it, one can easily see how most people's relationship difficulties stem from the fact that there is often an incongruity between what people perceive on a personal level as opposed to what it is actually *intended* that they should perceive. And the reason the incongruity exists is because we don't communicate on the same wavelength.

In *Solutions*, Leslie Cameron-Bandler explains how by *listening* attentively to the words people choose to verbally express their thoughts rather than the content of what they are saying, it is perfectly possible to identify the actual processes by which they personally represent their own experience of their experiences. For example, people who use a visual representational system will tend to use phrases that include visually-oriented words, i.e., they'll say something like, 'I *see* what you mean', or, 'I can't quite *picture* that, somehow', or even, 'Yes, I can *imagine* how that might *appear* (or *look*) to you', whereas a person who represents through an auditory system would couch similar phrases in one of the following possible ways: 'I *hear* what you're *saying*', or, 'it just doesn't *sound* right to me', or even, 'Yes, well now that you mention it, it doesn't *sound* right, in fact, it doesn't come across *loud* and clear at all.' Listen more carefully to how people speak and you will notice how they tend to use one process far more than the others.

Accessing cues

But, as we have already learned in the chapter on body language, because none of us communicates solely on a verbal level, there is much also to be learnt from the way in which a person goes through the process of obtaining internal information, such as pictures, sounds, smells, feelings or tastes that make up memories or fantasies, from the unconscious mind.

In the same way that people favour one particular representational system – and this becomes evident through the words they use when they articulate their thoughts – so do we each favour one particular internal process for stimulating the accessing of that piece of information to our conscious minds. These non-verbal clues, which are to be found in a person's eye movements, are termed *accessing cues*.

To observe accessing cues, try watching a televised interview. Note how the person who is being asked a question usually takes their eyes off the interviewer and either looks upwards, downwards or away while they think about and construct their reply to a question. Moving the eyes upwards and to the left or right indicates that the person is a 'visual' type. If they move their eyes downwards to their left, the lead system they favour is that of listening to internal dialogue (auditory) whereas if they cast their eyes downwards to the right, they favour the kinesthetic lead system of feelings and emotions.

When you become adept at interpreting lead systems it becomes easier to understand *why* someone should have a particularly highly developed response mechanism that you personally might not have been able to relate to. Leslie Cameron-Bandler uses a delightfully graphic analogy to clarify this by offering as an example the suggestion that to a highly visual person, the experience of having to live in a constantly messy, untidy and visually unappealing house is directly comparable to the way in which a highly kinesthetic person would feel if they had to sleep in a bed full of uncomfortable biscuit crumbs! Which might possibly solve that long-forgotten childhood conundrum we could never quite fathom in the popular fairy tale of the Princess and the Pea!

Once you have grasped these amazing principles, you will discover just how simple it is to attract members of the opposite sex. Listen carefully to them, hear how they formulate their phrases, tune into their way of thinking and not only will you be able to understand their behaviour, you will be able to respond to them in such a way that they will find you irresistible! Once you have decided whether they are a 'visual', 'auditory' or 'feelings' person just respond to them accordingly. When you reply to them in 'their own language', so to speak, they will believe they have found their true soul-mate. This is a method that is used by salesmen, politicians, and TV chat show hosts to get people to open up and respond positively to them. You can use the technique as a wonderful way to get a new relationship off the ground. After that, however, you're on your own – but I suggest you read on for further hints on leading successful relationships . . .

The way in which you individually perceive the experience of being loved – whether it be in the form of verbal confirmation, the buying of gifts, through the feeling of being touched or whatever is appropriate for you – is perceived by you to have a *specific meaning*. And, in fact, so much do these forms of behaviour have an individual specific meaning for you, that the intent of the message that is actually being communicated by your loved one is never questioned; it is *assumed* by you to be true and is, therefore, responded to fully and automatically whenever any such behaviours occur. For example, if you like being touched when people talk to you, you will automatically and without question respond to 'touchers' with warmth, then form your own subjectively coloured opinions about that 'toucher', their behaviour, their manner and even their personality and character and respond to them accordingly. If, on the other hand, you harbour deep suspicions about or feel abhorrence for all 'touchers', you would respond to such people with a distinct lack of warmth, possibly a cool withdrawal or maybe even total dislike and distaste and then make generalizations about them according to your own *personal complex equivalences*. It's the same person, the same piece of behaviour, but two entirely different *subjective* interpretations!

Leslie Cameron-Bandler has evolved what she terms a map of the experiential journey that people typically take from attraction and falling in love to separation and falling out of love. This is called the threshold pattern and each of the following words charts the course from beginning to end:

ATTRACTION → APPRECIATION → HABITUATION → EXPECTATION → DISAPPOINTMENT/DISILLUSIONMENT → THRESHOLD REACHED/PERCEPTUAL REORIENTATION → VERIFICATION → RELATIONSHIP TERMINATED.

And it is during the first phase of ATTRACTION that behavioural complex equivalence have a special role to play. This is how it works.

Each of us has evolved for ourselves (consciously or unconsciously) certain criteria that represent for us what is attractive in another person. It might be a sense of humour, good looks, wealth, status, money, power, a good physique . . . and we have also established behavioural complex equivalences for each criterion which tell us which specific set of behaviours indicate that a certain person does indeed satisfy our own criteria and which do not. For example, if we rate a sense of humour the most attractive characteristic of all, clearly we would need to have a demonstration of a sense of humour before we would rate a person as attractive.

So, the initial ATTRACTION phase of a relationship commences when you encounter someone who meets your own criteria of important behavioural complex equivalences. For example, if you believe you can only love someone who is patient, kind, good-looking, etc., the moment you meet any person who appears to display all of those characteristics (according to your own interpretations of their behaviour) you will be attracted to them.

Then you move on to the second phase. APPRECIATION is attained when the attraction is maintained long enough for a steady relationship to form. Both parties are now experiencing a state in which they perceive and feel that the qualities they most desire and need to have fulfilled are, indeed, being filled by the other person.

However, this phase could either be based on illusion or varying degrees of real understanding of each other's wants and needs, but it is the extent to which it is actually based on *knowledgeable understanding* that will ultimate dictate whether the relationship endures.

This phase, then, is where it is most vital to ask yourself such honest questions as: How do I *know* I am in love? How do I express my love? How does my partner know that he or she *is* being loved by me? And, perhaps, the most important question of all – Am I sure? Or am I just *assuming*? You also need to question what significant aspects are most necessary for you to establish and maintain a fulfilling relationship; what gives you the experience of actually *being* loved; what is it that gives your partner the experience of being loved and does your partner set the same store by the same experiences as you?

For example, if you can't stand a person who is consistently late for dates and interpret such behaviour as a lack of respect and consideration, how accurate can your interpretation really be? Remember, your belief that unpunctuality represents disrespect and lack of courtesy doesn't necessarily make it so if your partner doesn't set the same store by punctuality as yourself. This is an illustration of an experience where one of your behavioural complex equivalences doesn't match your partner's.

And that's why it's vital to understand what is important to each other in each behavioural context. If you wish to achieve and maintain the APPRECIATION phase of your relationship, you *must* know what you want and need, what your partner wants and needs as well as knowing what specifically fulfils those wants and needs in order to elicit the kind of behaviour that you each personally find fulfilling and rewarding.

The third phase, HABITUATION, occurs when you become accustomed to each other. This is, if you like, the familiarity stage when things become accepted, taken for granted and comfortable. The danger here, of course, is that things can become too much taken for granted and one partner could become bored, because while the habituation phase might represent security, commitment and comfort to one of you, it could well represent dullness, habit and lack of excitement to the other. Again, this is yet another good reason for fully comprehending your partner's needs and wants because if you don't, the fourth phase of EXPECTATION could be the start of the downhill slide.

EXPECTATION occurs when certain behaviours that were once a source of delight and appreciation become expected (duty) and the way things *ought to be*. What was once meaningful and appreciated when it occurred is now only meaningful when it doesn't!

This then leads to the fifth stage of DISAPPOINTMENT/DIS-ILLUSIONMENT. You begin to ignore certain previously good things and concentrate only on what is now 'bad'. Now, you'll begin to notice behaviour that has always been present but you'll start attaching too much importance to it and be less willing to tolerate it.

At this stage the situation can be caught and possibly even reversed before things go too far, if the desire is there. And anyone who might recognize that they have reached this stage in their own relationship should easily be able to gauge whether the desire to save the relationship *is* still there if they can still recall the past as wonderful and wish that it could again be so. Those who have gone beyond this stage and are firmly on the irrevocable path to separation will certainly *not* feel any longing or desire to recapture the past!

In order to rescue a relationship that's in the EXPECTATION phase, both partners need to be re-motivated to recapture what once was and both need to make a firm commitment to being responsible for eliciting from their partner all the behaviours they want, need and desire. Each needs to re-experience all the previously fulfilling and rewarding behaviours before they're able to believe that such behaviours can be recaptured and sustained in the future.

If this cannot be achieved, perhaps because one partner has crossed the threshold before the other, then it's likely the relationship will fail. The THRESHOLD is reached the moment one or both partners *believes* that it is impossible for the other person ever to fulfil their needs or wants again and starts to disassociate themselves from all their past pleasurable experiences and only associate with the negative, unpleasant ones; the negative and unpleasant now has more meaning and is more real than the positive and pleasant.

To build and sustain relationships with a high level of love, appreciation and passion, it is important to:

● Know what you want and what your partner wants. Do not assume.

● Have the courage to express (in terms your partner can relate to) precisely what you need to see demonstrated to make you feel loved, as well as being flexible enough in your own behaviour to match what your partner needs from you.

● Learn how to read and take note of any cues that may alert you to the fact that your partner is no longer in any of the positive phases of ATTRACTION, APPRECIATION and HABITUATION.

- Have the skill and commitment to lead yourself and your partner back to the positive phases if necessary.

Anyone who can achieve all this will always have sexual power for their partner!

Chapter 14

Discovering Your Own Sexual Power

All that we have looked at so far in our search to discover the secret of sexual power – beauty, bodies, sex appeal, charisma, glamour, power, how we relate and respond to other people, even the very foundations of love itself – has shown us that each of these aspects is controlled (albeit subconsciously) by *ourselves*. How we then behave depends largely on our previous conditioning processes, our own set of behavioural complex equivalences, a response to our *perceptions* of what we are at that moment experiencing, or even whether we are modifying our behaviour in order to suit other people's expectations.

Thus, the statements we all make about ourselves through speech, attitude, image and appearance are, in effect, a compromise between how society expects us to conform, the level of confidence we have to project our individuality and our own set of individual perceptions of the experiences to which we are responding.

Now we know that beauty *is* in the eye of the beholder. Sex appeal and glamour *are* ideals as individual as the people who hold them. Power is something that exists only so long as people *allow* it to.

And sexual power – as a visible characteristic feature – does not exist – *except in the eye of the perceiver*. Sexual power is not something tangible like, for instance, brown hair or blue eyes. Neither is it a personal characteristic we might possess, such as a sense of humour, strength of character or sharp wit.

Sexual power is an abstraction in precisely the same way that charisma, sex appeal and glamour are also idealized concepts that others can bestow on *you*. However, like all concepts, it's something that can first be fostered by yourself and then be projected back on to you – *and other people's expectations are the ultimate key*. When people perceive that we possibly possess the ability to fulfil their expectations they're only too willing to endow us with the imagined reality. For instance, everyone around you has visual access to you and, depending upon their own particular preferences, they may – or may not – be attracted physically. A smaller number of those people have access to you personally, and though initially the same response-mechanisms will apply, you have more opportunity than you realize to influence their opinions through the presentation of your personality. Furthermore, because of the way we all interreact, the effect you have on those people who meet you influences *their* representation of you to the people *they* meet.

For example, take a look at the process of how sex symbols or cult figures are established. The subject (whether it be a person, programme or even a concept) is presented to a number of people, some of whom will be susceptible to the idea or the image of whatever is being conveyed because it *fulfils* certain needs or expectations within *them*.

Those people will then 'sell' the idea or image to others (who might not otherwise have been influenced) who, because of *their* own susceptibility, then become receptive to the notion purely on the basis that they should conform to certain commonly-held ideas. That's how the conversion process begins and it keeps on growing until it becomes a widely-held consensus. To illustrate this we can use the scene in an earlier chapter in which Lynn and Jill demonstrated how people respond to body language signals. We saw how, at the end of that evening, both girls went home with entirely different views of the people at the party, and of the time they had had there. And the other people at the party also based their assumptions about each girl upon her behaviour.

One meeting, one group of people, but – and here's the potential danger – each has several opportunities to pass their opinions on and influence what other people might think of both girls. In this case, neither Lynn's beauty nor her own knowledge about her character, personality and motivation for behaving as she did, could protect her from being stereotyped; which illustrates only too clearly that while good looks can be the key to the door, it's attitude that gets you invited in. As we now know, beauty on its own *can* make people more receptive, but if the beautiful person lacks certain other vital ingredients the door to opportunity will remain forever closed.

You don't need beauty to have sexual power. All you simply need is the ability to influence others' perceptions of *you*. Let me explain why. Whether we're young or old, rich or poor, successful in our careers or abject failures, the one thing we *each* possess is a need to interreact positively, for, as the saying goes, no man is an island. Human beings are incapable of functioning efficiently in isolation – and I doubt that any of us would ever want to.

We all need to form relationships, to bond and to share in order to sustain us throughout our entire lives. We all need people to love, to laugh with, to share our joys and our sorrows and to exchange opinions and ideas with. But most of all we need relationships to provide the mental, emotional, psychological and physical stimulation as well as the interreaction that is as fundamental to our survival as our need to eat and drink. Without such relationships we would have no means of establishing a sense of our own identity.

Psychologists and social workers have long been aware that when people are cut off from contact with others for any length of time, their health can fail, their minds can falter, they lose all ability to relate and, in some cases, they can even lose the will to live.

Relationships are something we rarely think about too deeply because few of us have ever been without. From the moment we're born we're part of a relationship and although as we grow we may at times lack the specific type of relationship to fulfil a particular need, we're rarely without access to a variety of others which can support us until the right one comes along. Good relationships are worth more than all the material benefits the world can provide because they alone can demonstrate that *we* are accepted, approved of and loved, which in turn increases our confidence and self-esteem.

However, if we accept this premise as fundamental to understanding all we need to know about ourselves, then we also have to acknowledge that it must *equally be true for everyone else*. Therefore, if we need people in order to achieve our needs – whether these are success at work, a helping hand from a neighbour, or the attention and love of someone we desire – understanding and meeting *their* needs can be crucial when it comes to fulfilling our own.

Sexual powerpoints

In understanding and responding to other people's needs, whether physically, verbally or even silently with body language, we are using our knowledge to exercise our *sexual powerpoints*, which are fundamental (though largely unrecognized) components of sexual power.

There's nothing remarkable about sexual powerpoints. All of us have access to them, though few of us understand the nature of how and why they work, and they might at first seem so obvious that you'll be tempted to ignore them. But that would be a big mistake, because having acquired the knowledge of *why* they work, you're already more than halfway towards making them *work for you*.

Our ability to project sexual power is very much dependent upon our ability to develop its component parts. For example, although good looks are unnecessary, if you happen to have them and learn how to use them to your advantage, it can be one powerpoint in your armoury. If you don't have them, it's unimportant because there are far more effective components that are within *everybody's* reach.

The first – and most important – ingredient of sexual power is *self-awareness*. With it you can rapidly absorb all you need to learn about projecting sexual power. Without it you cannot achieve anything.

The next most important ingredient is *confidence.*

And finally, all you need to learn are the simple techniques of *behaviour modification* that will lead you to an understanding of your own behavioural processes which, until now, may have prevented you from becoming who you wish to become and achieving all the success you have ever desired – whether professionally, personally or romantically.

And each of these three vital ingredients is an essential element of Neuro-Linguistic Programming.

Self-awareness

All of us recognize – and perhaps envy – beauty, attraction, confidence, self-assurance and sexual power in other people. Very few of us acknowledge or even dare to hope that we could have any of these vital qualities ourselves.

For many people, happiness seems to be a matter of luck;

something that happens *to* them, rather than being caused *by* them. How many times have you heard people say: If only I were *lucky* enough to be good-looking/slim/rich/successful, I know I could be happy.

Too many people blame their failings and their unhappiness on *luck* when in reality the responsibility for their own happiness lies only with *them*.

Happiness is an individual thing, we all have different criteria for what would make us happy; for some it's money or professional success, while for others it's looks or love. Some people will spend their entire lives pursuing a concept of happiness that they will never find because they truly don't know *what* would make them happy, while some believe that their happiness depends on what others bring into their lives.

The fact is, happiness is within *everyone's* grasp for the simple reason that happiness comes from *within*. And it starts with being satisfied with who and what you are. It's like the definition of the difference between being an optimist and a pessimist: the optimist is ecstatic because his bottle of booze is *half-full*, while the pessimist is miserable because his bottle is *half-empty*.

Happiness is the ability to be positive; to make the most of what you have and the things that happen to you in life, rather than dwelling on your dissatisfactions, worries, insecurities and setbacks. Happiness, as we are now also aware, comes from freeing ourselves of past behavioural restrictions in order to make the most use of all the choices that life offers us.

Psychological research has shown that habitually unhappy people adopt a negative view of life and reality, preferring to believe that they are helpless and have no control over what happens to them, while the people who adopt a more philosophical attitude towards negative life-events and take more control of their lives express greater satisfaction and happiness.

Furthermore, doctors predict that given a patient with an optimistic, positive attitude and a patient with a pessimistic, negative approach, the person who is positive and optimistic will enjoy better health, recover more rapidly from illness and have greater disease-prevention potential than the person who is self-centred, despondent, negative and pessimistic.

When things go wrong, when our hopes are dashed, all of us naturally feel disappointed and frustrated – but how we cope with disappointment and frustration when these are thrust upon us depends largely on whether we have a positive or negative attitude towards ourselves and life in general. But none of us should ever forget that, in the first instance, choices begin and end with *us*.

When things go wrong, either because of something you have or have not done, or even due to circumstances beyond your control, how you *choose* to respond could have potentially far-reaching consequences for the rest of your life. For example, if you have been disappointed in love you can *choose* to allow it to embitter you to the point where you develop an unreasonable, suspicious attitude to *all* members of the opposite sex, or you can simply *choose* to put it down to experience and keep trying. Similarly, if you've been passed over for promotion in favour of a less experienced colleague, you can *choose* to believe that 'fate' is against you and give up because trying is hopeless, or keep plugging away in the hope that your turn will come next.

Both these choices are fundamentally wrong because each of these potential reactions are essentially negative in that neither contains the required element of *control*. Far better, therefore, to respond *positively* by assuming control and examining the reasons for your failure in that particular instance and, more importantly, identifying and acknowledging whether the fault lies with *you* (perhaps because you have an unrealistic view about yourself, your capabilities, your expectations or even about other people) and then set about altering whatever it is within your power to alter or accepting what you truly do not possess the power to control.

Being in control of *your* life is an essential element of happiness. Because, as we have learnt, power can only ever be given *by you* to other people. Therefore, feeling powerless can only ever be controlled from within yourself.

Two of the biggest factors that prevent people from being happy are fear – fear of losing what they have, or not achieving what they want – and apathy; both can lead to procrastination, helplessness and hopelessness.

But fear, as a good friend of mine so often says, is only ever in the waiting room! We fear what *might* be going to happen long before it does, so we procrastinate. If we know our relationships aren't working, few of us have the courage to face up to the fact and respond positively in a way that will either resolve the situation or end it. Instead, we bury our heads in the sand and hope the situation will go away, or vainly pray for a magical solution to make all well – that's procrastination.

We all fear risk-taking for a variety of reasons. Some people are afraid to take risks because their self-esteem and belief in their own capabilities or worthiness is so low that they'd rather hide behind excuses such as, 'I don't have the time right now,' or, 'I'll *definitely* do it – tomorrow,' than have their worst fears about themselves confirmed. Others might fear success because they've spent so many years dreaming about the difference success would make to their lives that they can't face the prospect of having success within their grasp and then discovering that it doesn't make any difference at all.

Dreams and fantasies only ever have value when they're harnessed to positive, life-enhancing actions and thus used as a spur to motivate us towards achieving goals. Or when they're employed as an occasional and temporary means of escapism or support during the 'down' periods of life. Procrastination is one of our biggest enemies, not only because it allows us to spend too much dangerous time 'in the waiting room' but also because it blinds us to the real truth; that the biggest failure of all is our repeated failure to take risks.

To expect to be happy *all* the time is unwise and unrealistic. Likewise, when you experience unhappy times, experience alone should tell you that feeling unhappy now does *not* mean that you will *never* feel happy again. Moreover, there is much that you, personally, can do to protect yourself from self-inflicted unhappiness (no matter how subconscious the cause) and to create the right situations in which happiness can be found. This is where *self-awareness* comes in.

Analysing, coming to terms with, and, ultimately, accepting yourself is, then, the first vital step to acquiring sexual power.

If self-discovery highlights certain elements about yourself that you dislike, don't simply allow them to make you feel despondent and negative; try counter-balancing them with a list of your admirable or positive traits. Accepting yourself, warts and all, means acknowledging the things that are unalterable (and giving yourself permission to be less than perfect), and altering the things that are changeable *without* having to compromise either your integrity or your sense of 'self'.

For example, if (like me) you're short, stop wasting precious time wishing you were taller or blaming your lack of height for all that's wrong in your life. *Accept the way things are.* If you're not classically beautiful, *learn to make the most of what you do have.* If you're unhappy at work, *change your job*, make a positive commitment to furthering your education or acquire the necessary skills that will equip you for the job you'd really like to do. And if most of your dissatisfaction stems from your personal relationships, *identify how realistic or unrealistic your expectations and requirements might be and then do something about them*.

Someone once said, 'We feel before we think,' which is perfectly true. But that doesn't mean that what we feel should necessarily dictate how we respond. By all means feel, but always make sure that you *think* about what you feel and even *why* you feel it before you react. Then learn to rationalize your feelings and your thoughts so that you increase your ability to respond to negative comments, occurrences or events realistically rather than instinctively. For we must never forget the lessons to be learnt from NLP inasmuch as while people aren't always as kind or as thoughtful as we would like them to be, often *they* are only reacting to what they perceive is currently happening to *them* or what *has* happened to them in the past. And remember, what *we* perceive them to mean might have nothing whatsoever to do with *their* original intention.

You might believe that developing self-awareness requires a kind of courage that you don't think you possess. If this is how you feel, think about this: even the biggest self-confessed coward, when faced with a potentially life-threatening occurrence, would instinctively choose courage over annihilation, though he'd probably call it self-preservation. In changing the word 'courage' to 'self-preservation' (which is possibly the strongest instinct mankind possesses), self-awareness suddenly ceases to seem so difficult after all.

Change can only come about through knowledge and understanding and only *you* have the power to change *your* life. And while I won't deny that change will inevitably involve a certain amount of risk-taking, if you're unhappy and dissatisfied enough to seek change, it might help if you remind yourself that these feelings cannot disappear *without* change.

Intelligent and worthwhile risk-taking will inevitably lead to loss of some kind, but it's important to recognize any losses you sustain as positive, inasmuch as eradication of what makes you unhappy can only *increase* the odds of replacing that emotion with something more rewarding. If you allow yourself to accept that it's perfectly natural to be fearful and constantly remind yourself that all human beings fear change for the simple reason that change presages unfamiliarity, things won't seem so difficult. Besides, we all know that nothing remains unfamiliar for long.

Learn to recognize and acknowledge the potentially self-defeating, negative behaviour patterns and thoughts that have contributed to your present misery and frustration and try to discover whether your present situation was actually engineered by you in any way. For many of us, our destructive and self-defeating patterns of behaviour were first learnt and acquired in response to childhood cues and conditioning.

For example, you might secretly feel that no matter what you do you'll never be 'good enough', but it's unlikely that you know quite *why* you should feel like this. However, if you reflect – as objectively as you are able to – on the way your parents, teachers or even childhood friends may have made you feel (perhaps through criticisms, statements, or certain forms of behaviour) in the past, you might be able to pinpoint the cause.

Intellectually you may already recognize that you are not really inadequate or incapable, but still be unable to reconcile your intellectual thoughts with your emotional responses. Very often this is because how *we* see ourselves (and therefore how we react and respond) stems from how *other people* see – or saw – us. Hence, if you suffered ridicule as a child and were never taken seriously, it's possible you now have a deeply-buried, subconscious emotional resistance to proving your capabilities for fear of risking further ridicule.

If you can regularly put into practice the techniques NLP offers for discovering self-awareness, you cannot fail to become self-aware.

Confidence – how to increase it and make it work for you

'Confidence', as Maxwell Maltz so wisely pointed out, 'is built upon the *experience* of success', but if we don't take risks, not only will we *never* experience success, we will *never* increase our confidence. Confidence is essential because it is a commitment to ourselves.

Conversely, lack of confidence is not only socially and psychologically crippling, it's also the worst betrayal of the 'self'.

Everyone, even the most apparently self-confident people, will confess to being shy and insecure. So how come we don't know it? The reason is that some people are better at projecting aspects of their character (real or fantasy!) than others. But that doesn't mean that *you* can't. Confidence isn't about boasting of what you can do when you know you can't, or drawing attention to yourself because you can't bear being overlooked. And it isn't necessarily true that those who appear to possess it in abundance have any more than you or me.

Confidence is about self-assurance; it's about not being afraid to be wrong, because you accept that nobody's right all the time; it's about knowing what you want and not compromising when faced with what you don't. Above all, confidence is about having respect and regard for yourself and valuing what and who you are *in spite of* what and who you aren't. Having confidence is self-generating – while not having it is self-destructive. If we experience failure, our confidence falters but when we experience success it grows by leaps and bounds.

Sue had supreme confidence in herself and it showed. It wasn't false; she'd long ago come to terms with her limitations and what she couldn't change she refused to worry about; while what she could alter, she did. And every time Sue went out, the image she projected was specifically designed to achieve one thing: the confirmation and reinforcement of *her* own ego and sense of self-esteem.

Once you realize, like Sue, that what you are and what you have, though not perfect, *is* unique, and that you *do*, personally, have a great deal to offer, you'll have taken the first step on an ascending spiral that will repeatedly confirm and reaffirm your sense of self-confidence.

Confidence is an essential powerpoint – and once you possess it, you'll have the second vital weapon in your armoury of sexual power.

Confidence at work

When you are confident of your professional abilities, you can achieve anything you desire. When you aren't, work is just a treadmill that takes you nowhere and becomes harder with each passing day.

Not surprisingly, more men have confidence at work than women. Well, they ought to, they've been there longer, climbed that much higher and have considered it their own personal domain for so many years that it would be surprising if they didn't hold this view.

Women, on the other hand, despite their belief in equality, find it difficult to rid themselves of the notion that they still might possibly be inferior. Which isn't surprising, really, when one considers that most men still behave (and believe) as though they were! Consequently, women often feel ridiculously inhibited and duty-bound not to antagonize the men they work with or tread on too many toes. It's an understandable attitude, but if you know it's one you hold, you'll never get anywhere until you develop sufficient self-confidence to break the mould.

So what can you do to increase your self-confidence and to assert yourself more at work?

- Be realistic – but also optimistic – about your talents and your capabilities.

- Don't dwell too much on your failings (because everybody else has them, too) but *do* take advantage of every opportunity to highlight (and make others recognize) your strengths.

- Ask yourself, 'What am I good at?' 'What skills do I have?' 'Am I good at sympathizing with others?' 'Do people enjoy talking to me?' 'Do I like delegating?' 'Can I speak any foreign languages?' 'What can I personally do in order to change my life for the better?'

- Be friendly, relaxed and don't allow temporary setbacks to paralyse or affect your self-esteem. Remember, you're all you've got, so, if you can't bring yourself to treat yourself as a god, well, why not treat yourself as a demi-god?

- If you don't know something, don't be afraid to ask or to take advice from those who do know. Being deficient in knowledge is not a crime, but pretending that you're not could be fatal.

- Don't elevate your superiors to superstar status, they're simply human beings who either know a little more than you or who have been around longer.

- If you have knowledge your superiors don't, or if you can do something they can't, don't be tempted to hide your light under a bushel for fear of upsetting them or making them look small – be confident enough to promote yourself, but do it helpfully, tactfully and with consideration for *their* own insecurities and possible lack of self-confidence.

- Never make the mistake of *assuming* what other people want, think or do – particularly when it concerns you. It's all too easy to misread a situation and believe that someone is against *you* or dislikes *you* when, in fact, they might simply be in awe of you – or possibly even have the impression that *you* don't like *them*.

- Don't crawl or flatter in order to advance your career, but do be generous enough to give praise where it's due, both to people's faces and behind their backs. This applies just as much, if not more, to subordinates and office juniors (because you never know when you might need their support) as it does to superiors.

- Let people know, as subtly but as firmly as you can, that you have respect for yourself; that you have feelings, opinions and choices of your own. Don't allow people to put upon you, take you for granted or delegate more than you can safely and comfortably handle. And don't do it to them either!

- If someone should put you down or disagree with you in public, don't sneak away and hide. Take a deep breath, consider what you really feel and whether the criticism might have been justified or not. If you're itching to say something to someone who has been rude, should you go ahead and say it? What's the worst that could happen? Could you lose your job? Would it *really* matter if you did?

- Remember that everyone has different standards, different strengths and different paces at which they prefer to work – but don't be tempted to translate 'different from yours' into 'not as good or efficient'. Allow people to work at their own pace, and if you should experience difficulties don't criticize or blame.

- You can avoid antagonizing people and develop better working relationships if, instead of accusing (which can only put them on the defensive), you speak from what psychologists term the 'I' rather than the 'you' position. For example, if you're unhappy with somebody's work or performance, saying something along the lines of, 'I'm feeling disappointed because I expected . . .' rather than, 'You haven't . . .' or, 'You should have . . .' is far more co-operational and less likely to threaten their ego than an accusational approach. Threatening a person's ego will only result in their retaliation or defensiveness in order to protect themselves from your criticism. Both responses are negative and both are likely to result in heated arguments.

Confidence with personal relationships

Many people feel that falling in love and having relationships will give them confidence. It won't. In fact, falling in love and having relationships when you *don't* have confidence is more likely to lead to a loss of *all* self-confidence. That's because people with little self-confidence or low self-esteem are often so grateful to discover someone who appears to love them that they're likely to subjugate all sense of their 'self' and possibly do *anything* in order to keep their partner happy and thus retain both the person *and* the feeling.

Some women have been known to claim that their lovers put them down in dozens of subtle ways, or say and do 'outrageous' things when, in fact, we all know that no one can 'make' us do anything except ourselves. How many people do you know who say their partners treat them badly and they don't know why they stay (as in addictive, co-dependent relationships)?

If you want good relationships that sustain and benefit both of you, you must have the confidence to be self-assertive when required and not automatically anticipate that your lover will fulfil all your sexual and emotional needs, or be able to read your mind, or even share the same opinions and views as yourself.

- Self-confidence means being able to recognize arguments for what they are; merely disagreements or differences of opinion, rather than anticipating the holocaust.

- Self-confidence means being able to admit you're wrong when you are without seeing it as submission or abandoning your pride.

- Self-confidence means being able to stick to your principles and your own beliefs and opinions rather than automatically acknowledging them as ill-conceived or wrong just because they're *yours*.

- Self-confidence means having the courage to acknowledge your *own* needs and being able to *communicate* them to your partner – not waiting and hoping that he or she will suddenly develop ESP or accidentally stumble upon the right 'button' in bed.

- Self-confidence means being relaxed enough to allow your lover their personal space or freedom when required, and not being seized by irrational fear or paralysing jealousy each time they spend more than five minutes alone with a member of the opposite sex.

- Self-confidence doesn't mean surrendering your own (or demanding the surrender of your partner's) friends, life, hobbies, interests, ideals and even your innermost private thoughts.

● Self-confidence means having respect for, and loyalty to, the things that are important to *you* (regardless of how unimportant they are to *them*), as well as extending the same courtesy, consideration and respect to the people and things your partner holds dear.

● Self-confidence means having the courage to recognize and accept when a relationship is not right for you – and being able to walk away from it with dignity, self-respect and self-esteem – without the unnecessary or cruel infliction of pain.

● And finally, if you're not in a relationship, but would very much like to have one, remember this: If you want someone or something in your life, have the confidence to go out and start looking for it, or go to the places where it can find you. Because wishing and hoping on their own will never be enough. But if you mix wishing and hoping with determination, you're bound to end up with a winning combination!

We each have all the resources we need to make any changes we may need or desire to make in our lives. These resources lie in each of our personal histories. All of us have had an experience of being confident, courageous, assertive, bold, frank, positive or relaxed at some time or another. And each of these experiences is a positive resource just waiting to be tapped. The problem is, few of us have, until now, been aware of the potential within ourselves.

In the same way that certain external stimuli can become associated with past experiences (remember the example of the smell of chalk being associated with childhood schoolroom experiences?), you can learn to *deliberately associate* a stimulus to any specific experience and then trigger the experience whenever you need to. Recalling past experiences can actually bring them into your present experience. For example, if you recall the last time you felt dynamic, unbeatable and full of confidence, it's almost impossible *not* to re-create that feeling in yourself right at this very moment. Similarly, if you were to recall right now an occasion when you felt extremely angry and frustrated, the chances are you'll immediately re-experience a certain amount of that frustration and anger again.

Anchoring is the NLP term for making a deliberate association between a stimulus and a specific experience, and virtually any stimulus can be used as a positive anchor. For example, chalk is, if you like, the anchor for your schoolday experiences. Similarly, most couples have an 'our song' which becomes their anchor for recapturing their 'special' experiences. No matter what might happen to that couple in the future, their song (their *anchor* for certain shared experiences) will always be able to re-create romantic or poignant emotions within each of them.

You too can use your own positive past experience resources and make them become an anchor for triggering off certain positive experiences in the future. For example, try this little exercise for increasing your confidence, utilizing one or two techniques from NLP. Think about something you would like to do but feel you don't have the confidence to accomplish – it could be asking for a raise or promotion at work, or even asking that guy or girl you've fancied for ages for a date.

Now, when you contemplated this risky venture that you don't believe you have the confidence to pull off, what specifically were you feeling? Recall and observe your inner reactions and note whether you were instinctively listening to your thoughts, to the sound of that inner voice that might have been whispering, 'Hey, *you can't* do that' or were you actually visualizing a scene, image or picture of yourself being rejected and humiliated? Alternatively, were you actually *feeling* that acutely painful, crushing sense of disappointment and failure?

Next try and think hard about whether what you were hearing, seeing or feeling was an actual past experience of your own, or something that you *constructed* for yourself without ever actually experiencing such an experience? This step should help you ascertain whether your negative responses that prevent you from exercising the choice of taking the risk are based on a past reality, someone else's reality that you've witnessed or heard about, or something that you just *believe* would automatically happen to you.

Now, think about a time (an actual experience of your very own from your past) when you *actually were* so confident and flushed with success that you felt you were capable of conquering the world. Is there a smile on your face as you conjure up these thoughts, sounds, feelings or emotions? Are you already squaring your shoulder as that powerful, unstoppable surge of confidence is being re-experienced?

If you are – and I'm sure that you are – hold on to that feeling, keep that smile of triumph on your face, that positive and confident stance and *now* think *again* about the thing you would like to accomplish but didn't dare to imagine you could succeed at just a few months ago. Doesn't it all seem so much easier? So much more within your grasp? Not merely more *possible* but infinitely more *probable*?

Whenever you feel a lack of confidence, repeat this exercise as you contemplate whatever negative experience is sapping your confidence.

Another useful technique is that of looking at yourself through the eyes of someone who you know loves you – not someone who you merely *think* loves you, or even someone whom you desire to have love you; it must be someone who beyond a shadow of doubt really *does* love you.

What does that person love about you? What positive qualities do you have that makes that person hold you so dear and value you so highly? Try not to deprecate whatever it is about yourself that this other person values so highly and loves so much. Don't be tempted to denigrate or devalue yourself by saying such things as: 'Oh well, of course he/she would love me, they're my mother/ father/sister/brother/best friend', because, remember, self-deprecation is nothing more than *your own perception* of the experience of being loved by that person and your own perception of your *self*.

That is anchoring. By using any of your own positive personal resources that are – and always have been – available to you and associating them with something you'd like to do, you have had your first taste of reframing your experience and rebuilding your confidence. That was also your first taste of the possibility and the probability of experiencing success and your very first taste of your own sexual power!

If you regularly practise these techniques you *will* soon learn to associate positive, confident feelings and emotions with yourself and disassociate the negative response patterns that have been holding you back from achieving your true potential.

Chapter 15

How to Use It

Once you have mastered the two most important powerpoints, i.e., the art of self-awareness and the art of developing your own self-confidence, it's remarkably easy to assimilate and learn the lesser powerpoints which are nothing more than techniques which will help you project sexual power.

Understanding what motivates us all has taught us *why* people respond negatively or positively to each other, as well as *what* makes them respond in either way. Other people aren't, therefore, so very different from us inasmuch as we all need the rewards of approval, respect, interest and affirmative experiences. When these are forthcoming we can't help but warm to the people who consciously or unconsciously engender these positive feelings within us.

In the light of this knowledge, it would be tempting to believe that all we need to do to win friends and influence people is to be permanently pleasant and agreeable, smiling at everyone we meet, and heaping praise and approval on all and sundry in order to make ourselves popular and to be perceived as having sexual power.

Unfortunately, it doesn't work quite like that. In the first instance, you see, most people have access to a variety of potentially rewarding resources such as friends, lovers, families and congenial colleagues who may already provide them with all, or most of the positive experiences they currently need. If being pleasant, agreeable and positively responsive were all there was to sexual power, certainly Sue – alone out of all the many girls in that nightclub (many of whom were much younger and better looking, remember) – wouldn't have had the power to affect quite such a large number of men as she did.

But what Sue did have – and what you can have, too – is the ability to project sexual power in such a powerful way that no matter how well-served or well-satisfied people were, she was able to make them believe that she, alone, could provide them with *so much more*!

It didn't matter what age Sue was (I'll wager she'll still make the same impact when she's 70!), it didn't matter that her body was less than ideal, or her face no more than pleasant. What mattered was that Sue *instinctively understood* what men and women want and need and with her clever (and it *was* all the more remarkable because everything Sue did *was* unconscious) ability to use body language, eye contact, positive signals and cues, she projected an image that cut right through to the heart of people's insecurities, thereby setting up the perfect conditions that allowed them to *see* and to *believe* whatever they needed to see and believe in her. And having accomplished that, Sue aroused certain expectations that (again consciously or unconsciously) she was able to fulfil.

And *that* is the real essence of sexual power.

Making an impact

Because the art of stereotyping is learnt so young and absorbed so well into our subconscious minds, once people label you, it can be quite difficult to alter their opinions. Seeing them again in different environments and under different circumstances may make it a little easier to modify their perceptions but effecting a radical alteration in others' opinions can only be achieved through repeated encounters.

This can make life difficult if you meet someone you'd like to impress while wearing totally the wrong clothes to project the image you feel would best get you noticed, but there are a few little techniques that can be used to ensure that you make a lasting impression; because anyone can be made susceptible if you know how to *stimulate* a reaction that involves an emotion more complex than polite interest. This could be anything from mild tension (as in taking them off-guard by challenging them in some small way), humour or wit (which doesn't need explaining), anger (a little mild provocation or the very gentlest verbal attack), or even the smallest shiver of fear – though I hasten to add that we're not talking real fear here; more a little comment aimed at making them conscious of the impression *they're* having on *you*. For example, you could try telling them (with an enigmatic smile) that they're not quite what you expected, without revealing what you did expect, or even find some small discrepancy in *their* appearance to comment on, such as pointing out that they've got egg on their tie, a stain on their dress or even birdshit on their shoulder.

Attacking a person's confidence in this way is not as dangerous or even as cruel as it might seem, it's merely a useful technique for taking control of the situation in order to ensure that *they* feel compelled to rebuild their own self-confidence by making a good impression on *you*. After that, it's a simple matter for you to appear just impressed enough for them to want to see you again.

Another technique I've seen used to great effect is that of ignoring or appearing to dislike the person you want to notice you. You'd be surprised how often this works simply because none of us enjoys being disliked – particularly when we don't understand the reason for it, so when it happens to us we puzzle and ponder over it for hours, then often retaliate by appearing to dislike the person we think dislikes us.

The next step is to engineer another meeting but on this occasion you should greet them warmly and appear to find them fascinating and eminently likeable. Because you previously touched on an anxiety area, thereby creating a slight loss of self-esteem and self-confidence in their mind, your sudden apparent change of attitude will be guaranteed to make them feel ridiculously pleased; consequently they'll now be far more responsive to you than they would otherwise have been.

Self-confidence has an important role to play in relationships. When someone is temporarily lacking in it, that's the ideal time for you to step in. That's how rebound relationships work, and if you're smart and time your move carefully, even the seemingly most unapproachable person will be more susceptible to you when their self-confidence is at a low ebb. And if you can succeed in increasing their self-confidence, why, then you're on to a winner!

How to increase self-belief

Clothes are a great camouflage for projection. The moment we put them on, it's somehow easier to believe that we are what they represent. The same applies to labels. We're all adept at labelling each other (stereotyping) and we're even better qualified at labelling ourselves.

Each time we tell ourselves: 'I can't do that because I'm not clever/confident enough, etc.', we're hanging a 'failure' label on ourselves. Every time we say, 'I'm this', or, 'I'm not that', we're restricting our options and setting the scene for self-fulfilling prophecies to come into play.

It's well known that when people put on uniforms, they stand straighter, their attitude becomes more confident and their manner more officious. The woman who wears sexy clothes actually *does* feel sexier, so why can't she achieve the same effect simply by changing the label she hangs on herself? The answer is, she can. All she needs is a little objective re-evaluation to understand that what *she* perceives has nothing to do with what actually *is* – or could be – if she gave herself half a chance.

As I've said before, labelling yourself and then spelling out to others what's written on the label only results in reinforcing those labels. Once you believe your labels, your mind will be remarkably quick to provide further reinforcement by determining how you should behave. And how you behave can have enormous repercussions on how others respond to you. So the vicious circle begins – but, remember, it can only ever begin and end with *you*!

How to develop a positive mental attitude

Cultivating a positive mental attitude towards yourself can reap tremendous benefits in terms of self-image, self-esteem and self-confidence.

Sue could have elected to allow her age or her weight to restrict the highly individual way she chose to dress and the image she had of herself. Even today I wouldn't wear a Monroe-style dress like Sue's, not because I lack confidence in myself, but because, having experimented enough over the years I'm aware that it would look over the top on anyone who doesn't have Sue's build (or her nerve!). But Sue was smart enough to realize its effect on her and confident enough to adopt a slightly over-the-top image of herself.

The interesting point is that given what nature had endowed her with, Sue had been faced with a choice. She *could* have allowed herself to become a victim of the 'thin-is-beautiful' regime, but she didn't. Why? For the simple reason that she possessed enough self-confidence not to allow her self-image to be dictated or adversely affected by fashion. Moreover, Sue had taken control of her life by developing a positive mental attitude towards creating and projecting the image that she believed suited *her* – regardless of whether it actually did or not.

Sue got (and still gets, by all acounts) what she wanted, purely because she *wanted* what she got, and never doubted that she *would* get it.

And, of course, the lesson to be learnt here is that positive thought breed positive attitudes and positive attitudes are precursors to positive events.

Creative visualization

Use your imagination! Don't look at yourself in the mirror and home in on all your faults. Look at the good points, see only the things you like and imagine that you look just how you want to look. Imagine yourself in situations that fill you with fear. And imagine yourself conquering that fear. See the approval on other people's faces as you win and enjoy it. See yourself as sexy!

Developing self-awareness, confidence and a positive mental attitude can only enhance your life. When you've been through these stages, you'll then be ready (and armed) to tackle some serious experimentation with clothes and your appearance.

Don't dismiss certain styles as 'not being you' because they're outrageous, fun, colourful or even subdued. Fashion experts are always coming across people who are stuck in a time-warp with regard to their appearance and invariably they find that once a person has allowed themselves to be 'made over' by an expert, they're delighted with the result.

We've all heard the cute phrase 'Wannabees', which was coined to described people (usually girls) who desperately want to emulate their heroines and be 'something', or 'someone'. 'Wanting to be' is important, because if you don't have the hungry need or desire to 'want', you won't accomplish anything. But there's something more important still, and that's determination. So if you're a 'Wannabee', you've now got to push yourself that much harder and determine to transform yourself into a 'Gonnabee'.

How to be an accomplished flirt

When you have confidence and self-belief, flirting (in the right circumstances) can be a useful aid to the projection of sexual power. Everyone can flirt, but to elevate it to an art form it's essential to understand the golden rules that govern the how, the who and the when.

- Accomplished flirts never flirt when they're drunk; they're all too well aware that too much alcohol clouds the vision and the brain. And whilst it's true that a little alcohol can help you to shed inhibitions, too much could well result in shedding far more than you bargained for!

- Accomplished flirts never flirt with more than one man or woman in the same company – because it dilutes the effect. It's also risking the label, 'fake charmer' or 'tease'.

- Accomplished flirts are clever enough to know when to be selective. That's why they don't always pick on the most obvious person to flirt with. For example, handsome men and beautiful women are often accustomed to attention, so when accomplished flirts choose less spectacular targets for their apparent interest, they're being clever enough to ensure that they intrigue and pique their *real* target's interest to greater effect.

- Accomplished flirts are always bold and confident; they wouldn't be accomplished flirts if they weren't. They don't slither quietly into rooms and hide in corners; they're right there, centre-stage where the action is – in fact, they very often *are* the action.

- Accomplished flirts use body language and eye contact to devastating effect. They hold conversations with their eyes; lean in close to the person they're flirting with and adopt relaxed, open poses. They're also careful not to give too much away but always to leave a slight question mark about themselves behind to stimulate intrigue.

- Accomplished flirts know which foods to choose as an aid to flirting; soup, spaghetti, garlic, spicy foods, sloppy foods and noisy, crunchy foods are out, while little snacks, sensuous foods, finger foods and any food that can be eaten seductively are in!

- Accomplished flirts project mystery and intrigue. They listen a lot while revealing very little information about themselves.

- Accomplished flirts dress appropriately for flirting. They know they can't seriously flirt when dressed like a bag lady or a *hausfrau*. What they do wear doesn't have to be revealing, but it should be stylish and clean, worn with confidence and must definitely *fit well*.

● Accomplished flirts use their voices to good effect. They don't speak loudly, they're not raucous and they favour little amused twitches of the lips or enigmatic smiles with crinkled eyes rather than belly laughs when they hear a side-splitting joke.

● Accomplished flirts know how to use their eyes to convey interest and warmth. They don't have to be witty (though it can help if they are) or even have much to say. All they need to do is nod occasionally and softly murmur little phrases such as 'Really?', 'How fascinating!' and '*Do* tell me more.'

● Accomplished flirts know the difference between flattery, which sounds sincere, and sycophancy, which is not. They also know that an appreciative remark made about the obvious (such as beauty) is less likely to impress than a casual compliment paid to other less apparent qualities such as intellect, wit, humour, style, conversational ability or an individual physical feature.

● Accomplished flirts don't look over their target's back to see who's just come in or cast their eyes around prospecting for better targets. They *always* appear totally fascinated and enthralled!

● Accomplished flirts have a finely-developed sense of timing. The female flirt knows just when to lick her lips (so that he'll find it seductive); the right moment to dip a finger into her glass and then absent-mindedly, childishly and – *apparently unconsciously* – pop it into her mouth (so he'll read it as vulnerable); how and when to alternate between lowering the lashes (so that he'll perceive it as submission) and when to transfix him with a (seemingly helpless) direct eye-to-eye stare (so that he'll regard her as fascinating and irresistible)!

● And finally, the accomplished female flirt's sense of timing is so acute that she'll know exactly when he's hooked. Which is precisely the moment she'll choose to regretfully (but none-theless prettily and seductively) make her excuses and exit – leaving him devastated and desperate for more!

Now *that* is how to use female flirting powerpoints to maximum effect in order to project sexual power!

- If the accomplished flirt is male, he, too, will know precisely the correct moment to choose to stare deeper, longer and more frequently into his target's eyes (so that she'll read him as being authoritative, masterful and sexy); when to brush her arm, leg, hand or face (so she'll accurately gauge his interest); and the opportune moment to suggest the next slow dance – or a walk around the block (when she'll be intrigued enough to feel flattered by his apparent desire to isolate her from the competition).

- And, of course, the accomplished male flirt's impeccable sense of timing will enable him to gauge just when to take her home and when he should commence his Oscar-winning performance of a man who is wild with wanting her yet values his new relationship so much he won't *allow* himself to ruin things by taking her to bed – which of course, his sense of timing has already informed him he won't need to, because by then she'll be so turned on by the – apparent – effect *she's* having on *him*, that if there's any taking to be done, it will be done by her!

And *that* is how to use male flirting powerpoints to project sexual power!

One important point to bear in mind about flirting is that it's not advisable to use it overtly when you wish to be taken seriously in business. By all means use your femininity (or your masculinity), but the last thing any serious female executive needs is to be taken lightly or to be patronized; or, for that matter, to be accused of using her sex to achieve what she would not otherwise have been capable of!

How to shine at work

- Firstly, dress to impress. If you wish to be perceived as management material, adopt the kind of clothes that you feel best reflect the fact that you *are* management material. Even if your salary is low and you can only afford to buy one really good outfit a year, the investment will be worth while. Styling experts say that it's always more cost-effective in the long run to buy clothes that will mix well so that when money permits you can build up an entire wardrobe around one basic outfit – and do remember that smart doesn't have to mean dull.

● Develop a trade-mark, whether it be belts, brooches, hats, flamboyant ties, pocket handkerchiefs – anything that enhances both your outfits and appearance, because that will make you identifiable and distinctive.

● Make sure your hair and nails are always clean and neat. And don't forget that shoes are important, too. It's amazing how often I've seen both men and women who do all the right things with their appearance and then spoil the whole effect by wearing scuffed, dirty or down-at-heel shoes.

● Observe carefully the people who are regarded highly in your company. Watch how they operate, what they do and how they do it.

● Be enthusiastic, helpful, sharp and confident without appearing arrogant, pushy or too clever by half. And take every opportunity to prove your reliability – it's a very positive asset!

● Get involved with what the company is marketing, familiarize yourself with its products, clients, hierarchy and competitors.

● Develop a high profile and make sure that the people who count know *you*.

● Use your initiative. When you hear about problems think about them, even if the problem's not yours. Try to use a lateral approach and then test your theories out if you can. When you're sure they're sound, approach the right person and offer your help – but do it sensitively.

● Don't be afraid of drawing attention to yourself or putting your viewpoint across in meetings, even if you think what you have to say may conflict with what someone else has said.

● Seat yourself close to, or directly opposite the person who's chairing the meeting. Look directly at the chairman (or woman) as often as possible, smile when it's appropriate, sit forwards into the table and be interested and alert. People who lean back in their chairs, fold their arms above their heads, doodle or don't get involved in the discussion are usually considered to be insignificant, bored, arrogant or so professionally superior to every member of staff that they have no need to impress.

● If you want promotion or a salary increase, be careful about timing. There's no point asking for a rise or promotion when the company's going through upheaval or a difficult patch financially. The best time to ask is when your profile is high following the successful completion of a difficult task, when you've won new business or when your performance has just been praised, perhaps after an annual appraisal.

- Learn the art of negotiation. Don't be unrealistic in your demands, you'll only make them easier to refuse. Be clear about what you want, state your case firmly but pleasantly (having first decided what you want to say and how you want to say it), and always leave the other person room to manoeuvre. The worst thing you can do is to be so adamant and fixed in your demands that you force someone into a corner. Because if you do, you'll only have yourself to blame if they behave just like a cornered rat and attack! Be flexible, be charming and practise the art of effective compromise.

- If questions or issues are raised that are designed to distract you, keep a cool head and say something like, 'That's an interesting point and I will respond to it in a moment, but first I'd like to say . . .'. People who allow their attention to be diverted lose control of the situation.

- Don't tell your colleagues what you intend to do, and if you know that others have not received a recent rise, don't be tempted to boast about yours, when you get it.

- Don't put your boss in a defensive situation and don't begin by complaining. It's far better to say, 'I feel that I deserve a rise because . . .' and then outline all the positive reasons why than to say, 'I want *x* and if I don't get it I'm off.'

- Don't ignore the value of networking. If your industry has its own organization and offers opportunities to attend meetings where individuals from different companies can socialize, use these occasions to make contact with other people. You never know what they might have to offer in the future. Networking is the name of the game of getting on and you should use it to the best of your ability.

How to have a successful first date

- First dates can be nerve-wracking and exciting. So, although it's often difficult, try to remain calm and not let your nerves show.

- If you're shy or find it difficult to hold conversations, try not to concentrate on your own feelings and the impression you're making, but on the fact that your date may well be feeling just as nervous or shy as you.

- Don't talk too much about yourself, give your date a fair chance to speak, but don't be reticent about speaking, either.

- If you don't know what to say, ask your date questions about what they do, what their interests are, where they went or are planning to go for their holidays. A good trick is to ask whether they've seen such and such a film/concert/play/show or read a particular book. Questions that require 'yes' or 'no' answers can be conversation-stoppers, so always try to phrase your question in such a way that your date has to respond with a fairly lengthy answer.

- If their opinions differ with yours on specific topics such as those above, don't get too argumentative or be overly critical. Opinions are subjective and we all have our own personal viewpoints.

- Don't get drunk, and don't be too *risqué* and do avoid potentially contentious or emotive subjects such as religion, sex or politics.

- Don't dump all your problems on your date, he or she is not there to be depressed or to act as your own personal agony aunt – and do be wary of someone who immediately dumps all theirs on you! Needy people are desperate people and the relationship's too new to withstand pressures like these.

- Don't assume too much and don't try to find hidden meanings in everything they say or do. If you enjoy yourself and want to see the person again, don't be afraid to tell them so or to suggest that you give them a call.

- And finally, don't embark on each first date with the attitude that your date will be Mr or Miss Right. Try to see each new person you meet as a potential new friend, not as a potential new partner. That, alone, will help you feel more relaxed and in control.

How to be successful in love

- Be clear in your own mind about what you need as opposed

to what you want. The two aren't the same thing and many people who spurn potential relationships because the other person doesn't fit into their concept of what they *want* could be cutting off something that might be wonderful. For example, if the new man or woman is kind, sensitive, warm and funny but lacks a quality such as dynamism, ask yourself how important dynamism really is in a partner and try to project forward in time to anticipate what problems might later arise out of having someone who's dynamic, but lacking in other essential qualities.

- Don't let your emotions be ruled by sex. If your first sexual encounter with a potential partner is less than perfect, give the relationship time to develop before you discard it out of hand. Remember, most people, no matter how sexually experienced, are usually nervous and shy the first time in bed.

- If the sex is fabulous, but outside the bedroom things aren't so good – they won't necessarily get better, particularly if the reasons they aren't so good are fundamentals like disparate personalities, or serious character flaws. If it's just a fling, fine, but you can't build a successful long-term relationship based purely on good sex.

- Be aware of your behaviour in past relationships and be realistic about whether it went wrong because of you.

- Be firm with yourself about accepting or 'putting up with' things in a relationship or a person that you know are wrong.

- Have the courage to be honest with yourself and about yourself. It's no good trying to feign interest in something that you secretly loathe or pretending to be someone that you are not. Sooner or later the truth will come out and if the relationship does survive, at the very least an element of trust will be lost. If it doesn't, you'll have no one to blame but yourself.

- Don't sleep with someone until *you* are ready. You'll only feel resentment and guilt if you do.

- Don't be influenced by what other people think of your partner – it's what *you* think that matters.

- *Don't* look for perfection, it simply does not exist. If you've got 90 per cent of what you want, need and value in a person, that's more than enough to build a solid foundation on.

- Don't expect that the path of true love will always be smooth; every couple has ups and downs and compromise is important.

- And, finally, when things get boring or routine and it seems as if some of the old magic and sparkle have gone, try to think of love as being like a river: sometimes it will eddy and whirl with a wild and raging force, at others it will flow smoothly and calmly. Sometimes it will tumble down a hill in full view, at others it disappears out of sight beneath the ground. But the vital thing to remember is: despite the fact that it cannot be seen, the river is *always* there.

And just like the river that cannot always be seen, sexual power is there within us all just waiting to be acknowledged and used.

So there we have it. We began by observing that for no apparent reason certain people are able to weave a special kind of magic that makes others remarkably reponsive to, and fascinated by, them. Now that we know what that magic is, there's no longer any reason to *wish* you could be more like them – you *already are* like them, it's just that you weren't aware of it.

We've seen what sexual power is and now we've examined all of its various elements it's no longer a mystery. All you need to use it is simply the *will* to make your life richer. Because, it *is* possible to improve your relationships with your friends, acquaintances, families, colleagues and potential lovers. And it *is* possible to have for yourself all the admiration and envy that until now you've only ever envied and admired from afar.

No one person is better than you or me, though we *are* all unique. And yet, strip away the glamour, the facade, the image behind which we all hide and you will find that beneath the skin we all have the same fundamental needs. The only difference that now exists between you and the people that you once thought *had it all* is that you haven't yet put what you have learnt into practice. But take it from me, when you do, the world had better watch out!

Since researching this book, I've learned a great deal about what sexual power is and how it can be used. I've personally put it to the test and used what I've discovered in a variety of situations with a variety of different people and found that *it really does work*.

Moreover, I've also used what I've learnt to show others how to handle situations and people more positively and in every case I've only ever had reports of success.

The important thing to remember is that *you can be anything you want to be*. Self-awareness takes courage, courage breeds confidence and confidence increases self-esteem. When you believe in yourself and value yourself it's *impossible* for others *not* to share that belief. Nothing can stop you now except ignorance, fear and *you*.

If you *want* success *it can be yours*. If you want better relationships *you now know how to get them*. If you want love *you have the powerpoints – use them*!

You don't need beauty, you don't need wealth. Because what you've now got is the most influential power of all. You've got belief in yourself – and that's all it takes to have and use sexual power!

Notes

1. Lake, Dr Tony, *Relationships*, Roxby Press, 1981.
2. Brenner, M., 'Caring, Love and Selective Memory', *79th Annual Conference of the American Psychology Association*, 6, 275-6.
3. Morris, D., *Bodywatching*, Cape, 1985. Morris, D., *Manwatching*, Cape, 1977.
4. McKeachie, W.J. 'Lipstick as a Determiner of First Impressions of Personality', *Journal of Social Psychology*, 36, 241-4.
5. Efran, M.G., 'The Effect of Physical Appearance on the Judgement of Guilt, Interpersonal Attraction, and Severity of Recommended Punishment in a Simulated Jury Task', *Journal of Res. Personality*, 1974.
6. Sigall, H., and Ostrove, N., 'Beautiful But Dangerous: Effects of Offender Attractiveness and Nature of the Crime and Juridic Judgement', *Journal of Personal Social Psychology*, 31, 410-14.
7. Cook, Mark, and McHenry, Robert, *Sexual Attraction*, Pergamon Press, 1978.
8. Huchstedt, B., 'Experimentelle Untersuchungen zun "Kindenschema" ', *2. Exp. Angew. Psychol.*, 12, 421-50.
9. *The Economist*, May 5th, 1989.
10. *What Diet and Lifestyle*, 1989.
11. Jourard, S.M., and Secord, P.F., 'Body Cathexis and the Ideal Female Figure', *Journal of Abnormal Social Psychology*, 50, 243-6.
12. Buchanan, Caroline, and Sedgbeer, Sandra, *The Sensuous Slimmer*, New English Library, 1984.
13. Feldman, S.D., 'The Presentation of Shortness in Everyday

Life – Height and heightism in American Society: Towards a Sociology of Stature', Paper read to the American Sociology Association.

14. Donnenmaier, W.D., and Thumin, F.J., 'Authority Status as a Factor in Perceptual Distortion of Size', *Journal of Social Psychology*, 63, 361-5.

15. Wilson, P.R., 'Perceptual Distortion of Height as a Function of Ascribed Academic Status', *Journal of Social Psychology*, 74, 97-102.

16. Lee, J.A., ' A Typology of Styles of Loving', *Personality and Social Psychology Bulletin*, 3, 173-82. Lee, J.A., *Colours of Love*, Toronto: New Press, 1973.

17. Kirk-Smith, Michael D., *Possible Pheromonal Components in Social Attitudes, Mood and Behaviour*, Doctoral thesis, Department of Psychology, University of Birmingham, 1978.

18. Lewis, Dr David, *Loving and Loathing – the Enigma of Personal Attraction*, Constable, 1985.

19. Liebowitz, Michael R., *The Chemistry of Love*, New York: Little Brown, 1983.

20. Liebowitz, Michael R., and Klein, Donald F., *Hysteroid Dysphoria, Affective Disorders, Special Clinical Forms*, paper read to the Department of Psychiatry, University of Tennessee.

21. Mathews, A.M., et al, 'The Principal Components of Sexual Preference', *British Journal of Social Clinical Psychology*, 11, 35-43.

22. Moir, Anne and Jessel, David, *Brainsex*, Michael Joseph, 1989.

23. Hess, E.H., 'Attitude and Pupil Size', *American Scientist*, 22, 1965, 46-54; *The Tell-Tale Eye*, Van Nostrand Reinhold, 1975.

24. Knapp, M.L. *Nonverbal Communication in Human Interaction*, Holt, Rinehart and Winston (2nd ext. edition, 1972).

Useful further reading

There is a great deal more information and many techniques available to improve your ability to attract, handle and influence other people, and if you're really interested in becoming adept at using sexual power, I would strongly recommend that you read many of the excellent books available on body language, psychology, interpersonal relationships, self-improvement and human nature in general, some of which are given below.

de Angelis, Barbara, *Secrets About Men Every Woman Should Know*, Thorsons, 1990.
Argyle, M., *The Psychology of Interpersonal Behaviour*, Penguin, 1972.
Cameron-Bandler, Leslie, *Solutions – Practical and Effective Antidotes for Sexual and Relationship Problems*, Future Pace, Inc., 1985.
Cook, Mark, and McHenry, Robert, *Sexual Attraction*, Pergamon Press, 1978.
Fast, Julius and Bernstein, Meredith, *Sexual Chemistry – And How To Use It*, Arrow Books, 1984.
Lake, Max, *Scents and Sensuality*, John Murray, 1989.
Lake, Tony, *Relationships*, Roxby Press, 1981.
Lewis, David, *Loving and Loathing*, Constable, 1985.
Marsh, Peter, *Eye To Eye – Your Relationships and How They Work*, Andromeda Oxford (Sidgwick and Jackson), 1988.
Moir, Anne and Jessel, David, *Brainsex*, Michael Joseph, 1989.

Nierenberg, G.I., and Calero, H.H., *How to Read a Person Like a Book*, Thorsons, 1984.

Penney, Alexander, *How to Keep Your Man Monogamous*, Bantam Books, 1989.

Wainwright, Gordon R., *Body Language*, Hodder and Stoughton, 1985.

Winter, Ruth, *The Smell Book – Scents, Sex and Society*, J.B. Lippincott Co., 1976.

Of further interest . . .

The Dance of Intimacy

A Woman's Guide to Courageous Acts of Change in Key Relationships

Harriet Goldhor Lerner

All intimate relationships can be terribly damaged by too much distance, too much intensity or simply too much pain.

In clear, direct and dramatic terms psychotherapist Harriet Goldhor Lerner illustrates how we can move differently in these key relationships — be they with a distant or unfaithful spouse, a depressed sister, a difficult mother, an uncommitted lover or a family member that we have written off.

This compassionate book uses poignant examples from case studies, and stories from the author's own life, to illuminate the steps that women can take towards a more solid self and a more intimate connectedness with others.

Whatever your own definition of intimacy, this book will challenge and enlarge it, as the author provides a sound framework for understanding how we get in — and out — of trouble with the most important people in our lives.

Secrets About MEN Every Woman Should Know

Barbara De Angelis

The No.1 US Bestseller

If you have ever wished that men came with instruction booklets, you need despair no longer. Barbara de Angelis' best-selling *Secrets About Men Every Woman Should Know* is the book you've been waiting for since your first date!

Revealed in this book:

- Secrets about men and sex that men will never tell you
- The six biggest mistakes women make with men
- What men say ... and what they really mean
- Men's top twenty turnoffs
- The five biggest mysteries about men
- How to spot — and avoid — the men who will give you the most trouble
- How to get the man you love to open up
- Techniques for becoming a more powerful woman

Barbara De Angelis is America's foremost relationships expert. This book will give you the tools you need to create the relationships with men that you always dreamed were possible.

Men, Love & Sex

A couple's guide to sexual fulfilment

Joseph Nowinski

- What drives male desire?
- How can it be restored once it has waned?
- Where does it fit into men's own ideas of love and intimacy?
- How can a man and woman overcome the effects of male sexual problems, and rebuild their relationship?

Myths about male sexuality deny the existence of such problems as low sexual desire, inability to relax during sex, difficulty in maintaining erection or reaching orgasm, and premature ejaculation. The embarrassment and taboo surrounding these issues force many men — and couples — to suffer in silence.

Highly respected psychologist and sex therapist Joseph Nowinski uses proven sex therapy techniques, made accessible through case histories and easy-to-follow programmes — including special sections on sexual communication, building intimacy, and the use of fantasy — which will help women and heterosexual couples to gain a better understanding of the male view of intimacy, love and sexuality.

An invaluable tool for professional counsellors as well as couples seeking to enhance sexual desire, MEN, LOVE and SEX is a unique guide to a better sex life.